IMPROV AND THE ACTOR'S IMAGINATION

For my parents.

For Bill Esper, my beloved teacher and mentor,
who helped me develop the true craft of acting
and welcomed me into his Studio to share my gifts.

For Richard Powell who empowered me through his
example to live a full, creative life.

For Kenneth Axen who showed that improv is for everyone,
and wide-eyed wonder is forever.

For Carol Burnett and the cast and creative team
of "The Carol Burnett Show" who ignited the spark,
right from my own living room.

And, thanks to Julia Cameron. "The Artist's Way" is
perhaps the sole reason this book was completed.

IMPROV
AND THE ACTOR'S
IMAGINATION

Robert Z Grant

CONTENTS

INTRODUCTION — iii

1. Offers & Agreement — 1
2. Spacework & Environments — 45
3. Story Building & The Shakeup — 77
4. Energy Expansion & The Power of Pace — 107
5. Now You're Speaking My Language — 133
6. Give & Take — 149
7. What's This Scene About? — 165
8. Making Sense of It All — 185
9. A Few Things I Learned Along the Way — 201
10. Improv in the 'Real World' — 215
11. More Fun Things to Try — 223
12. For Starters — 235

ABOUT THE AUTHOR — 247

REFERENCES — 249

INTRODUCTION

I am an actor. And I love working with actors (and everyone) to discover improvisation.

I first started improvising decades ago. Since the beginning, it has been a passion of mine. I feel like I am always improvising. I have performed and studied and taught (and talked about) improvisation and the craft of acting every chance I've gotten—on stage, on screen, and in the classroom. And now, in a book I've written.

At one point after I had been improvising for a number of years, I started going on auditions again. I wasn't getting called back and I wasn't booking. I was intimidated. I sat on the benches outside the audition rooms watching person after person go in and come out, often smiling or laughing as they did. I felt clueless about what they knew that I didn't—why one of THEM was booking the job and I wasn't.

All those years of improv experience were relegated to the 'special skills' part of my resume. And, what casting directors interested in improvisers were really looking for, it seemed, was a comedian. Improv was inextricably linked with improv COMEDY. And there was a lot of it out there. And a lot of it was BAD. I always disliked improvised work that DEPENDED on the idea that 'we're just making it up'. It was an excuse to be careless and self-indulgent in the name of 'spontaneity'.

I believe that improvised work should be so good that, after the fact, people would INSIST that it was scripted. I have performed in shows that were like that. I take great pride in having someone challenge me after a performance about how we MUST have written it, or parts of it. That, to me, is one of the highest compliments to receive as an improviser.

Because I did not feel like a 'legitimate' actor, JUST an improviser, I chose to go to an acting conservatory and get the REAL goods.

I found a studio in midtown Manhattan that taught the Meisner technique. One of the primary reasons I chose the William Esper Studio was because of an article that was provided for us to read while we waited for our interviews. In it, the Studio's founder, Bill Esper, himself mentored by Sanford Meisner, discussed the role of improvisation in the work. That word, improvisation, appeared several times in those few pages. I was sold. I felt good about studying at a place that understood and acknowledged and applied my skills.

I spent two years at the Studio working to build my craft as an actor. And, yes, there was indeed a lot of improvised work. In fact, from the very first moment until nearly the end of the first year of study, there was not a script in sight. We worked moment-to-moment using ourselves and our impulses to craft character and story. We spoke what needed to be said. We behaved. Truthfully. Under imaginary circumstances.

This is one of the basic tenets of the Meisner work: "Living truthfully under imaginary circumstances." And it was from this place that new connections started to form for me. I saw that my experiences as an improviser aided my work as an actor. I thought how lucky I was that, in those first few months of the work, I was already ahead of the curve in many ways. I already knew what it was like to just play a version of myself—to not be able to hide behind a character. To let words and thoughts come out of my mouth that were not scripted for me. To know that what I said and how I reacted WAS me—or a version of me in those circumstances. If I reacted irrationally, angrily, or in an ugly way, did that make me those things? If I said something offensive or inappropriate, was I a bad person doomed to be rejected by my peers for letting them see the 'real' me? No. I knew the truth of the moment had little to do with who I was in the 'real world' even though the words and the actions were my own. Because I had built those skills, I did not have to struggle through many of those early vulnerabilities once I started my acting training.

This led me to believe to me that actors and improvisers are one and the same. That the skills needed to be a successful improviser were the SAME as those required to be an actor with solid craft.

I spent two years in class drawing parallels between what I was learning and experiencing through Meisner with what I had already been taught or knew to be true as an improviser. I kept thinking: other actors would benefit from this, too. When I finished the work at the Studio, I proposed offering improvisation as a specific class to supplement the Meisner acting training. Not a different technique—and certainly not different skills, as I had discovered.

So I teach improvisation specifically for actors who trained in the way I did. I saw link after link between the skills of improvisation and the Meisner training. And much like the first steps of the Meisner approach, I will repeat myself a lot throughout this book. There are many key improv principles that inform the work, and they will come up again and again.

Which brings me back to the notion that improvisation is actually 'improv comedy.' In most schools, it is. Which is to say: they are teaching you games and tricks that are intended to produce laughs. The setups are designed to put people 'on the spot'—to challenge them in the hope they will trip up, or embarrass themselves when forced to take a 'wacky' suggestion like 'bathroom' or 'proctologist.'

I performed this type of improvisation for several years, and it was ultimately unfulfilling. I felt like a hack. I was scoring laughs, but it felt devoid of substance. Of truth. Instead everything felt designed solely to get a chuckle, and spontaneity was scarce. This may explain why so many sit-coms ("The Office", "30ROCK", "Schitt's Creek", to name a few) make improvisation the butt of some nerdy inside joke—flashing a badge of honor as if to say 'we know improv comedy is crap because we, ourselves, have previously added to the pile.' My feeling is that a lot of improv is unwatchable because improvisers are chasing the comedy train at the expense of something more truthful.

So I tell my students plainly on day one: I am NOT there to teach improv comedy. To many, if not most of them, this comes as a relief. There is a terrible pressure to be funny that actually kills truth and spontaneity. Everything can become just about chasing a laugh, and as a result, feels inorganic. It too often creates work that is concocted in the head instead of borne from the gut. The 'comedy' feels manipulative and transparent, rather than honest and unexpected.

I actively discourage the actors I teach from trying to be funny. (And, my own acting coach heartily agreed with that approach when inviting me to teach at his Studio.) This can take time, but students begin to see how those who think they are clever and funny often appear disconnected from the reality of the scenes. Their 'joke' may get a giggle, but it is quickly followed by the death of the scene.

This is not to say that humor doesn't come aplenty. I just contend it comes from a different place than most people think. I think it comes from our delight when we watch someone solve a 'problem' in an unexpected way. Our personal experiences and frames of reference are so different. We go into a scene ASSUMING others share our same perspective, only to be thrown something unforeseen. These moments are often what we call the 'gifts' of the scene. And we laugh because we can't believe what we just saw—likely because there is an element of truth to it. We look at someone's behavior and say 'I never would have thought to do that. But OF COURSE that is what this person would (or could) do in that moment.'

I refer to comedy as a style, just like Shakespeare or American Westerns, or Film Noir are styles. We understand the tropes and the styling, and then we always play it for truth. Often what makes comedy comedy, in my opinion, is that the circumstances and characters are very real, and then behavior is exaggerated beyond what we allow ourselves to do in 'real' life. A character wants the same thing as any of us do (love, respect, money, etc.), they just behave in a way that is often extreme.

I like to think of improvisation as the place where we get to explore in real time what would happen IF. I think acting students often get too hung up on the IDEA of truth. Instead, the key is to use the actor's imagination to explore TRUTHFULLY what would happen in ANY circumstance. We don't have to have killed something, for instance, in order to be able to convincingly play a killer. We use our actor's faith. We say "What if...?"

It may be useful to draw the distinction this way: It is not 'acting' versus 'improvisation'. It is merely 'scripted' and 'unscripted' work. The essential skills are the same. If you are handed a script and have weeks or months to rehearse and prepare, the skill of the actor is then to let a rehearsed and prepared performance unfold, unanticipated moment by unanticipated moment, as though the actor has no idea what is coming next.

NOT working for a result is a difficult skill to master. We actors try to create a performance, and we want people to think we are 'good' actors, so we try to control everything. But the truth is: the NOT knowing is the best part. The rehearsal is to get the words and the technical elements into our bones so that we can live ON TOP of it. In improvisation, by the very nature of the work, we don't know what's coming. Thus, it demands that we stay locked into the present moment, and not to try to drive a certain outcome.

Even in scripted work, particularly live theatre, surprises happen all the time. By using our improvisational skills, we can keep the reality of the written scene alive when things do not go as rehearsed. Lines get dropped. Lights go out. Props fail. Costumes tear. Accidents happen. And if we are fully present, these are opportunities for unforgettable organic moments.

One such moment happened to me when performing in a short play with The Collective, a theatre and film production company I started with some fellow Esper Studio graduates. "Cafe d'Automatique" written by Dave Hanson, directed by Susan Aston. It was a three-person scene set in a fancy French restaurant. I played the waiter, and my two colleagues were on a date. As I was waiting backstage for one of my many entrances in this short scene, I heard a wine glass topple on the table. I heard the audience react. I think the collective (pun intended) response was to try to dismiss it as an unfortunate mishap of live theatre and move on as though it didn't happen.

My improviser's gut said differently. When I entered on cue, shortly after the spill, instead of forging ahead with my scripted line, I stopped dead and focused solely on the white tablecloth now soaked with red wine, as my very particular and unforgiving character would. The mess could not be ignored. I took in the sight of it, and it landed in me as if I had been shot. Without saying a word, I spent the next few minutes sopping up the spill and wringing it back into the empty wine glass. The audience could surely read my every thought, and they were delighted to see what was going to happen next as I seethed.

INTRODUCTION

Once I had pulled the mess together, we moved on with the written dialogue, which took on new meaning, given what we had just experienced. I also got to do a bit of improv spacework (see Chapter 2) in this part of the play. Some stage business was written where I smoked a spacework cigarette while I addressed the audience from a bright pinspot. I added a detail where I picked a piece of tobacco off my tongue between puffs while giving my address. I had many people mention this detail to me later.

Then, as I moved to make my final exit, given all that happened with the spill, I grabbed the wine glass and guzzled down the dregs on my way out, determined to prevent the lovers from doing any further damage. Now we KNEW what was going to happen because we had witnessed it, and it brought a huge reaction from the audience. Afterward, Dave, who was listening backstage, asked me what had happened. Clearly the play sounded different from past performances. And my colleague Kevin Kane, fellow founding member of the company who HAD witnessed the scene, said to me afterward, "You just gave a master class in improvisation."

That ONE performance of that ONE short play in that tiny Off Off Broadway theater in New York's East Village more than a decade ago stands out to me, to this day, as one of my most cherished theatrical experiences. Fortunately, I have been lucky enough to have lots of those magical moments in fully-improvised shows, as well—many of them are now those legendary 'you had to be there' stories.

When something happens, scripted or unscripted, we cannot ignore the truth. It happened. I tell my students that the work of improvisation will sharpen your 'bullshit meter' like no other. When something inorganic occurs (which is usually a 'funny' idea someone has been cooking up in their head), it immediately feels like a big cow pie has dropped in the scene. Someone was trying to control the moment by injecting their own idea instead of simply responding to the ideas already in place.

I often use the example that creating an improvised scene is like writing each offer on a piece of paper and dropping it onto the floor. By the end of the scene, we want to have collected and addressed all of the ideas that were introduced. Which is to say: keep it simple. Over-invention is a symptom of trying to control, and of NOT listening. We tend to get bored with our ideas before we have really even explored them.

You create reality in your work by embracing the details—by fully engaging, and using your imagination to explore possibilities, even when they initially seem unimportant. To give you an example, I once appeared in an improv comedy show as a literal piece of trash floating in a swimming pool. I was not the focus of the story (nowhere close!), yet I had an opportunity as a supporting player to help create a reality. My piece of trash didn't need a backstory or a name, but it could be affected by the ripples in the pool, and bring the reality of water and the environment to life. It mattered. I had someone tell me after the show how that unexpected detail delighted them.

Truthful, organic behavior is riveting. To see an actor's imagination come to life is thrilling. In yet another supporting turn in yet another Off Off Broadway play at The Kraine theater in the New York Fringe Festival many moons ago, I played a busboy (there seems to be a restaurant through-line to my career) in Joseph Langham's "Out to Lunch". The Biggest Busboy in the World, according to the script. I stood stoically on stage and did not speak for the entirety of the play (and even BEFORE, since I was already posted on my mark as the audience filed in). And, yet one of the reviews (one of my first in New York) described my work as "fascinating". My point is not to stroke my ego, but to underscore that there is no 'nothing'. Even the nothing can be something, if we treat it as such.

What I teach and what we will discuss in this book are the skills of improvisation and how they help us work truthfully in imaginary circumstances. When we improvise, It doesn't get more imaginary than to step onto an empty black box stage—no script, no props, no costumes, no designed set or lights—to create a story and characters and a world from NOTHING. And even when we have a wonderfully-written script and a fully-staged production we can approach the work improvisationally.

So, what about those auditions that were making me doubt myself? All those people coming in and out of the room with all kinds of secrets that I didn't have? Now that I had technique and training, I must have started booking everything I auditioned for, right? Nope. But now I understood that booking every job (or even most of the jobs) is not the point. And not even probable.

INTRODUCTION

Statistically, an actor is not going to book the job. But that does not equate to being a failed, talent-less hack. My mentor and acting teacher, Bill Esper, would say, "There is no compelling reason to be an actor, except that you can't NOT do it." What you have is your integrity and your craft. The job is just to do the work. To prepare as best you can, and go into the room and be present. Be yourself. And then walk out of the room knowing that you did what you wanted to do, what your instincts guided you to do, confident that you showed them your authentic self.

Too often, acting becomes about wanting others to think we are good actors. So, we hide the parts of ourselves we don't think they will understand, or like. Or hire. Our work becomes about trying to give others what we think they want instead of showing them who we really are. The skills of improvisation reveal your uniqueness, and help you understand that what you have is enough.

We are, after all, a collection of our individual experiences. We explore all that we can, and fill our tool chest with the knowledge we gather. Not every tool or every technique works for every person. Or works in the same way. No approach to improvisation or acting is universal. So, gather everything you can, and use what works for you.

What I have written in this volume is a culmination of my own experience, and what I know at this moment in time. I did not take one class and learn everything there is to know about improvisation and acting. It is a fluid, continuing process. And I have learned from so many people. Many are mentioned in this book, though there are many more who are not. Yet every scene partner I've worked with, every teacher, every student is reflected in these pages.

Although I wrote this book for actors, improvisation is for everyone. The skills of this work have far-reaching applications. It is possible to create a world of 'yes' whether your world is an office job, parenting, politics, medicine, sales, the stage... anything.

Improvising is human. We all do it all the time. So, although I refer to 'actors' and 'acting,' behavior is universal. Though you may have no interest in being an actor, you can benefit from this work. Every time I say 'actor,' just substitute the word 'human,' or find a word that resonates with you and your sphere.

So much of what you'll discover here is about stepping outside your comfort zone. And, really, stepping outside yourself—daring to attempt something that feels unfamiliar. Even silly, or embarrassing. Yet, if we can imagine all the terrible things that can happen, all the ways we will surely fail, and all the reasons why we shouldn't bother even trying, I argue we have an equal or greater capacity to imagine all the wonderful things that can happen. And we can embrace NOT knowing with hope and excitement for what's possible. **Give yourself permission to try.**

—Robert

1
Offers & Agreement

I suppose the best place to start is with some of the improv 'basics.' Do not rush over these skills. Keep in mind that you must hold yourself to a high standard throughout, if you truly want to build your craft. You have to, all at once, be honest with yourself about what you are TRULY doing in any moment while also extending yourself kindness. Acting is a living, breathing thing that happens differently for everyone—and differently for everyone in every moment. What I am asking is that you accept that there is always more to do, instead of diminishing the importance of seemingly simple games and exercises from the start. Acknowledge your resistance, and choose to dive in completely, in spite of it. This may prove to be a fundamental discovery for you: how it feels to RISK being vulnerable and uncertain. THIS is why improvisation is scary to most people: too much uncertainty.

As actors, though, we are trying to bring this uncertainty to life, not to run from it in favor of the illusion of control. We must get to a place where we welcome the lack of control and the opportunity to explore it—the place where we are all moving in the same direction, but no one is steering. It will feel wrong. It will feel uncomfortable. Yet most of our work will spring from this place. So we need to find a way to access and harness our abilities in some key areas: **agreement, listening and observation.**

Each of these areas requires the same fundamental approach: taking the attention OFF of yourself, and putting it onto your scene partner. It is very easy to get caught up in our own needs and insecurities. What do I look like? What do I sound like? What if I forget the next action, or the next word I'm supposed to say? What if I'm terrible and no one wants to hire me? What if I'm not funny? (Hopefully, we can agree the last one can be let go right now. Go back and read the Introduction if you don't understand why.)

And this is why I ask you to be honest with yourself. How focused on your partner are you REALLY? Or are you stuck in your head thinking about the next thing you are going to do or say? In our acting classes, there was a very clear way I knew when I had checked out, even for a moment: my teacher would gently snap his fingers. He saw something happening that I failed to pick up on. He could tell that I was stuck in my head, trying to work out how I was feeling or what I needed to do. He could tell I was THINKING.

Thinking is disastrous for actors, and especially disastrous for improvising actors. It is an equally slippery slope to focus too heavily on your emotional life. Just like logical thinking, it puts you in a place where you are looking inward for the answers. Everything we do as actors needs to be focused outward, toward our partners.

What I do and what I say in any moment will ideally come organically from a responsive place. I don't need to THINK about it or to decide. In the time it takes to reason out how I feel or what to say, the moment is gone. Snap. So, the practice of TRULY listening, TRULY observing, TRULY finding agreement is essential to the craft.

AGREEMENT

Let's talk about agreement. In the improv vernacular, this is "Yes...And."

So, what is the "Yes?" That word, in itself, is a word of agreement. When we respond "Yes" we're literally saying that we agree, and part of that yes is that we have heard what has been said, or witnessed what has been done, and accept it as true. Meaning: the truth of the scene.

"Yes" can trip people up. I am essentially asking you to say "Yes" to everything that happens. But what if something happens that you DON'T agree with? What happens if someone offers an opinion you don't share? Or one that makes you uncomfortable?

In order for the scene to move forward, the agreement MUST happen—the agreement that whatever was said was said, and that whatever was done was done. There is no requirement that you have to LIKE it. How you react is completely up to you. But you must 'agree' first.

If someone tells you they love you, that does not necessarily mean that they do, or that you love them back. But the truth of the moment, the thing you are agreeing to, is that it was said. It happened. ONLY once it is acknowledged and accepted can the next thing happen.

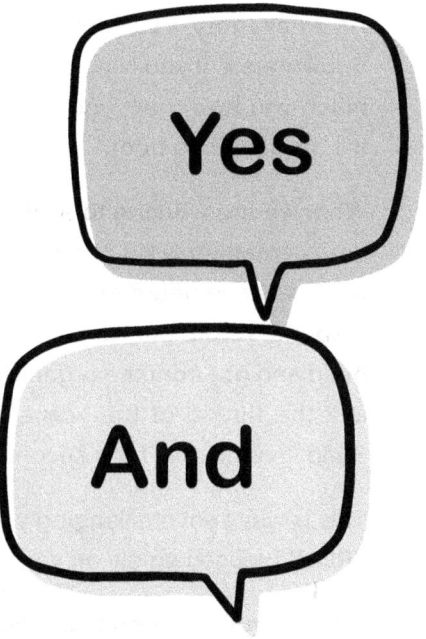

Which brings us to the "And" part. "And" builds on what was just said or done. It is an action (spoken or unspoken) that creates the NEXT moment.

In improvisation, we refer to these moments as offers. Any behavior, spoken or unspoken, is an offer. It is something that we observe, accept as the truth of the moment and then respond to. An offer is made ("I love you."). We say "yes" by observing that it happened, and we add to it by "and"-ing with the next offer...Which leads to agreement...Which elicits a response...Which leads to agreement...Which elicits a response... You get the picture.

In order to move forward, we must first receive the offer, accept it and THEN respond. And NONE of those steps are intellectual. They are purely observational and responsive. We move organically from unanticipated moment to unanticipated moment in this way.

Negation—denying an offer or literally saying "no"—stops the interaction dead. Negating words and actions signal we are not listening and are plotting and planning our next move instead. Words like "but" tell us plainly that 'whatever you just said or did, here is MY idea about what should happen next.' Rather than building on the offer our partner made by agreeing and "And"-ing, we choose to advance our own ideas, others be damned.

As an allegory, I sometimes reference John Steinbeck's "Of Mice and Men." Spoiler alert: if you cling too tightly to your own precious ideas, no matter how much you love them you may just end up throttling the life out of them. And kill the scene, to boot.

What we are working to achieve in improvisation is an effect whereby our focus is completely on our partner. We simply cannot move ahead in the scene until we have heard or seen what our partner has offered. Only then can we respond. And if our response is pulled from some 'clever' idea we had in our head and not from the organic response to what just happened, then we have lost the thread of the scene, and we have disconnected from our partner. Snap. Even if only for a second.

This is why I am challenging you to ask yourself if you are TRULY present, and TRULY focused solely on your partner.

New improvisers don't see the gift in this. They want to hold on to their own ideas and control the scene. That doesn't make you a better actor, it makes you a bully. Do yourself a favor NOW, and reject this bad habit. See that it makes it SO much easier when you give over to your partner and the scene. You don't have to invent ANYTHING because your partner's offer is the only moment that matters. Your response is the only offer that matters to your partner. And this volley continues.

LISTENING

Here is one of the first obvious parallels to the Meisner work. Those with a loose awareness of Meisner usually think of 'repetition.' One person makes an observation. The next REPEATS exactly what was said. The first repeats. The second repeats. Etc. This 'simple' exercise encompasses all of the basic skills we must build.

If we are to repeat accurately, we must first LISTEN. We must take the attention off ourselves and put it squarely on our partners. We have to be open to take someone in completely. The proof of our listening is that we can repeat EXACTLY what was said to us.

Just as quickly as we think how stupid and silly the repetition feels, we are ready to abandon it. DON'T. Don't allow yourself to indulge feeling silly or strange. Don't allow yourself to start THINKING. Challenge yourself to stay present. Just DO the task. REPEAT. **Funny thing how easily bored we become with simple tasks. And how grossly unprepared we are to be still, focus and listen.** We have BARELY begun a repetition exercise and already we feel strong urges to change it. To make it 'better.' To make ourselves look better.

This is what I mean about being honest with yourself. Fight the urge to think you've mastered something so quickly, when you have barely begun to experience it. And this all has to do with, again, taking attention off ourselves and putting it on our partner.

One of the most important things a former therapist ever said to me was 'people don't think about you the way YOU think about you. They are too busy thinking about themselves.' My point: whatever insecurities are pushing you to want to move on to the next thing need to be acknowledged. And often, that critical insecurity is coming from our perception of scrutiny and judgment from others. 'They know I don't have any good ideas.' 'They think I'm not funny.' 'They don't want to work with someone who's not clever.' **By taking our attention off of ourselves, we, in fact, silence the critic who is preventing us from being fully present.** If our attention is completely focused on our partner and the offer she makes, we leave no space for thinking to creep in. Our mind (i.e. energy and attention) is never idle. It is laser-focused on what is happening in front of us.

The repetition exercise starts just like any improvised scene will: with an observation. An offer. What was just said or done that I heard or witnessed? And what do I DO? Yes...And. And you are off and running.

In improvised scenes, and particularly performances, interactions often begin with a suggestion. Suggestions are just that: a starting point. The germ of an idea. The best way to take a suggestion is the way you would an observation. You SEE it, and you respond.

Suggestions, in my opinion, should be honored but never taken literally. Especially when they are given intentionally to shock or embarrass the players. "Bathroom!" someone shouts out when asked for a place you go on a date. Or, "Proctologist's office!" when asked where you may have lost your wedding ring.

This is a symptom of the improv 'comedy' trap. Don't play to manipulate or shock or provoke. We have this expression in improv that encourages us to 'play to the height of your intelligence.' This is not to say you should be THINKing. But you should elevate your work above 'humor' that is only there to get a stupid laugh from shock value. Don't try to be funny... Be truthful.

A scene can begin with ANYTHING. Or NOTHING. Don't feel beholden to come up with something clever. Whatever you see, or whatever sensation or impulse appears is a perfectly good place to start. Don't try to game out where it could go or what could happen. Make an offer and listen for the response.

We as actors are somehow hard-wired to look for the drama. We assume simple ideas and offers are TOO simple. Or more specifically, too boring. We want to create 'interesting' scenes, so we look for the drama. Someone is fatally ill. Someone is held at gunpoint. Someone is breaking up with you.

Or we rely on the 'wackiness' of improv to spice things up. What is your occupation? "A chef." Where would a scene about a chef take place? "On the moon!" I would argue that you already have enough to deal with creating a scene from NOTHING that you don't need the extra challenge of spending your entire scene trying to make sense of why you are currently doing your job on the moon. Keep it simple. The surprises will come. I guarantee you that there is no need to invent problems.

Our primary interest is the truth of the scene. Because we are constantly finding agreement from moment to moment, we are piece-by-piece building the truth of the scene. Yes! This is how people behave in this world. Yes! This is what people sound like in this world. Yes! This is how people walk in this world.

We don't want to fall into the trap that EVERY thing we witness is 'weird' or unusual. When you feel the impulse to call out something that strikes you as odd, try instead to say "yes" to that behavior. Accept it as true, and perhaps even ordinary, in the world you are creating.

A good philosophy for the work of putting your attention on your partner and off of yourself is to think of your sole task being to "make your partner look good." You do this in each moment you say 'yes.' You honor their offers, their  ideas, by accepting them and then building on them. You negate when you call out something as 'weird,' usually in an attempt to embarrass someone else, make yourself look clever, and all too often to get a laugh. Stop it! Risk to JOIN your partner, and see what happens.

 I will be constantly encouraging you, as I do my students, to 'get yourself into trouble.' Not to concoct some ridiculous circumstance, no. To take action (to respond) before you know whether or not it's a 'good' idea. See what happens, instead of killing the moment plotting out the scene, or worse, trying to manage how you might look to others as it does. Fear and insecurity will steal your abandon. Don't think. DO.

We also negate one another when we undermine the truth. Someone makes an offer or offers in a scene that build a reality. THIS is how things work in this world. THIS is the way people mow the lawn in this world. Whatever. Then we come along and say that it was all a dream, or magic. We explain away everything we were uncomfortable about or didn't understand by denying it was real. This is a shitty thing to do to your scene partners. Be brave enough to engage with what is being offered. Observe it for what it is and then build on it. Don't tear it down as a way to control your own discomfort. RISK to be surprised.

I have always said that when the day arrives that my scene partners don't surprise me or I don't surprise myself, that is the day I will quit improvising. Those unexpected moments are EVERYTHING. You should welcome the things that surprise you—and even confuse you—as gifts of opportunity. Engage. Don't deny.

Give yourself permission

I'll point out again here how important it is to give yourself permission to have an experience. To give yourself permission to look or feel silly. To give yourself permission to indulge in something that feels simplistic or beneath your talent. What we are trying to build here is the simplest, most truthful approach to the work. And often the biggest barrier to that is our own ego. We do not allow ourselves to experience uncertainty or to feel vulnerable when out of our element. But I assure you these basic skills will serve you well. So, don't shortcut them. I have been improvising for decades and STILL discover things all the time.

Many an improv and theatre class begins with warm-ups. Childish games, to some. If you choose to engage, however, there are many lessons to be gleaned from a 'silly' game. Warm-ups get us into a state of play. They get us out of our heads and into our bodies. This is where behavior originates, not in the mind. So, we do what we can to be able to engage physically. To leave the outside world, well, outside and become present.

Improvisation is a team sport. I can't make a move unless there is something offered to which I am able to respond. I can create a solo improv, but it is not unlike a monologue in which I am creating and responding to the impulses I have crafted. In a speech, I am not just going line to line. Rather, each subsequent thing I say or do is connected to an action. And that action is a response to what I observe. Even when there is no other person physically there.

Monologues aside, we NEED our partners. We need their offers. We are only there to make them look good, and to build on what they say and do. Our offers are not our own. They are merely responses and continuations ("And"s) of what came before.

Stand-up comedy always scared me for that very reason. It doesn't feel collaborative to me. It feels adversarial. It feels like me against an audience DARING me to try to make them laugh. DARING me to tell a story they don't hate. WANTING me to fail. A room full of people who are CERTAIN they are funnier and more clever than I am.

There is no place for that in improvisation. Every response lifts up the thing that came before. Everything that happens, ideally, is an organic and even NECESSARY response. So, we have to be present. We have to be tuned in.

And this, too, is an essential skill: to be able to focus. I am a very physical performer, especially when improvising. What exhausts me is not the intense physicality. It's the intense focus. You have to see and hear EVERYTHING. Not that we are doing this for an audience, but an audience doesn't miss anything. There is a balance to be struck between being an external observer, and being very much present IN the scene. So, in the unique circumstances of not having any physical props or sets or costumes or script, you can't miss any offer. One simple offer could be the essential nugget of the whole relationship. Of the whole scene.

I have a little ritual at the start of each class: First, I have my students make eye contact with one another. I ask them to look around the room at the others gathered. To remind them that THESE are the people who need their time and talent and attention for as long as we are working. I ask them to commit to being there for OTHERS. Put yourself in that same frame of mind.

In that spirit, I encourage them to be generous improvisers and actors. THOSE are the kinds of actors that get rehired. THOSE are the kinds of actors people WANT to work with. And all it takes is to consciously choose to take the attention off of yourself and to put it on your partners. And every time you pick up on someone's offer, they trust you more, because they know that you are truly in it for them and not just yourself. Make others look good, and you look good.

Lastly, I ask that my students give themselves permission. I remind them that there are no cameras recording the work. No playback or internet scrutiny. No one is sitting in the corner waiting to be entertained. Or to judge. The ol' "What happens in improv stays in improv" rule is in full effect.

In our work together, my focus is not to TEACH you anything. Rather, what I HOPE to do is to create experiences that allow you to trust yourself enough to give yourself permission to follow your own instincts. I think you already have everything you need. You are unique. Your voice is valid and deserves to be heard. You have committed to working on your craft. But, too many of us suffer from a lack of experiences where our instincts are rewarded. Particularly in learning situations. We feel an intense pressure to have all the answers right out of the box.

This is why I shift the power away from myself. It is not up to me to 'allow' anyone to do anything. It is up to the individual to risk making a move. To risk saying or doing something in the moment that perhaps doesn't land. Or doesn't make sense. That GIFT instantly transforms into the next offer. And, if we are all coming from a place of honoring one another's work, then that 'mistake' will likely become the hero of the next moment.

So, we warm up. We start with games. We try to get focused and be present, and to put our attention on others from the very start. They have many gifts to give us, and we don't want to miss anything.

I like to introduce a game called Whoosh Whoa first. It is a way for us to discover what offers are, in the most basic sense. And to start to see how the energy moves between us, and will ultimately move though a scene.

We start by standing in a circle. I turn to my right and make a physical gesture, a bit like I am tossing a box to my partner. And while I make that gesture I say "whoosh." Then my partner turns to her right and makes the same gesture and says "whoosh" to pass the energy to her partner. These offers and "whoosh"es continue around the circle.

Now, it is possible that the whoosh offer could go in the other direction. So we give it a try to see what it feels like to receive an offer from the other side.

Some of you may already be thinking this sounds stupid. If we were standing in the circle together, I would probably call out a condition I refer to as "stinky face." Stinky face afflicts people who not-so-secretly judge what's happening.

Who are so desperate to protect themselves from being embarrassed that they don't REALLY try. They are too cool to play a childish game. So that look of disgust or boredom or eye rolling annoyance shows up. Avoid stinky face.

After a round or two of passing an offer and saying a simple word, we are already beginning to see sprouts of what's important—some of the basic ideas that will serve us as actors in everything we do (and all too often THINK we are already doing). Be honest with how much more there is to do to be focused and present, and to give over to the moment.

Importantly, we want offers to be clear. I rhetorically ask my students 'if an offer falls in the forest and no one is there to observe it, did it really happen?' So we have to do everything we can to be certain that each offer is clearly made, and clearly received. This is not to say that offers won't be misinterpreted and that 'mistakes' won't be made, but the offer HAS to be clear as possible.

Sometimes that simply means slowing down. I only asked you to do a simple task: Pass a gesture and say "whoosh" while you do. This is not your Broadway debut. *The Times* is not going to write about your performance. So, take the time you need to be clear. Clarity comes from your physicality. Clarity comes from sharing your voice. Clarity comes from your energy and intention. Clarity comes from making sure your partner is with you and ready to receive the offer. Be generous—give fully.

As the receiver, you have an important role in being READY to accept an offer. Every game and scene you do is going to require you to show up ready to play. You have to be focused. Your partners need you. And there is great satisfaction in having your offer received. So do that for others.

Eye contact is key. We know that we can have 'contact' with our acting partners without having to stare them down. Behavior and words tell us a lot, regardless of whether people are looking at one another. However, because we are creating worlds and characters and scenes out of nothing when we improvise, what we SEE becomes more important. (Later, we will talk about seeing more as 'visualizing' and imagining, but for now I am literally talking about using your eyesight.) For now, simply notice in the passing of the whoosh the important role eye contact plays in being clear—both as the person who makes the offer and as the person who receives it.

The receiver also has another challenge: **Don't anticipate.** Right now the offer is moving person-to-person around the circle. But in scenes and in organic behavior, the offers do not move so predictably. Do not assume that an offer is coming to you. You can only be ready to receive it, if and when it happens. And ONLY once it does, can you respond.

I like to draw a distinction between 'readiness' and 'anticipation'. You can usually see the difference in the physicality. If someone is anticipating, you can see tension. Perhaps their shoulders are up, or their arms are crossed, or behind their back. They may be looking away, trying to hide from what's coming—the dreaded whoosh. Another telltale sign of anticipation is that we hold our breath. When the room gets too quiet I worry because it usually means that the group has stopped breathing. Don't make me worry. Breathe.

We never want to block our instrument. We want to be present, and that means we need to **let the energy flow.**

Readiness looks relaxed, if not eager. Someone is clearly engaged. Eyes wide, probably scanning the room and the players. Playfully excited to participate. Breathing. Nimble. This tells your partners you are there for them. And, just like being a generous actor, people want to work with people who want to work with them. If you send the signal that you are engaged and ready, I guarantee offers will come your way.

You can also help offers to be clearly received by matching your partner's energy. This is not intellectual. It is what actors usually do instinctively. Energy comes to you and you accept it and let it impact you. In this way, you are "and"-ing the offer energetically.

Depending how many people are in the circle, there may also be a tendency to lose focus or check out when the offer is passing on the other side of the circle. Any time you step into the circle (i.e. a scene) you have to focus, engage and be ready. The offers do not come predictably, as we will start to see.

Probably also worth noting here that we are all built differently. Learn differently. Have different strengths and weaknesses. In the spirit of making one another look good and sending and receiving clear offers, we need to allow for differences. Someone may not physically be able to swing their arms. Or turn their head. They may speak another language than our own. Despite whatever difference, it is still possible to communicate offers clearly—something I identify as "intention". If we are tuned into our partners, we will pick up the cues (auditory, physical, behavioral, energetic) that indicate an offer is being made. We can receive the offer and then respond.

Resist the temptation to judge others for doing it 'wrong.' **This is an important lesson of improv: what you expect to happen rarely does.** And nine times out of ten, it is a simple variation in interpretation or response that causes the shift. In the rarer case, a shift will come from someone INTENTIONALLY changing the offer. I discourage that sort of playing outright. Like I said before, there is so much to do creating something out of nothing that there is no need to further complicate it. A forced change usually happens just because someone is bored, or doesn't think things are 'interesting' enough. It is a form of control, and actors who try to work from the place of control will have a very difficult time, generally. You want to have solid craft and the skills to be able to deal with the surprises which happen... All. The. Time.

So, we've been passing this whoosh around the circle. You did it! You are now an improviser! But before you sign with an agent, let's see if there's something more. Let's add another option to the game. Based on the name of the game, you may guess what's coming next.

Whoa! Put your hands up over your head and say "whoa!" We know the whoosh can move in either direction, but we never set a rule for HOW it changes direction. Now we know. When the whoosh is coming around the circle, once my partner whooshes me, I can put my hands up and say "whoa!" That is my offer. And in response, my partner who just whooshed me sends the whoosh back in the other direction. It continues that direction until someone reverses it with another "whoa!"

A couple of things tend to happen with this second rule. Usually, questioning hands go up immediately and people ask "Can you whoa a whoa?" My answer is always the same: "Let's find out." **It is very common that we want to 'get it right.' I say, let's DISCOVER it together.** Rules often don't matter in improvisation, just as they often don't apply in human behavior. Play the game, certainly. TRY. But, in the end, all we can do is respond. So, WHEN someone whoas a whoa, based on their partner's response, we will have the answer.

The next thing that begins to happen when we add the second rule, is that we get LOTS of whoas. It's new. It's novel. And we have a tendency to get bored easily, so we TRY to change it. Which is to say: the offer could be on the other side of the circle several people away and someone has already determined that when it comes to them, no matter what they observe, their response will be "Whoa!" **You have to fight the urge to pre-plan.** It may not seem important in a 'silly' game, but we are laying the foundation for good habits. You simply cannot hold onto your 'clever' ideas. By the time you get your shot, the moment may need something completely different. Snap.

We also start to see people trying to mess with one another. Again, as a way to control the game. We see the 'whoa sandwich' pop up. A player makes a whoosh offer, and the response is 'Whoa!" The player then responds by sending the whoosh in the opposite direction, only to be met with another "Whoa!" on the other side. The player is stuck. The other two players seem to have ganged up on the whoosh-er.

Although the look on the whoosh-er's face says differently, the Whoa bullies have actually given the player a real gift. As always, all you have to do is respond, just like the Meisner repetition we discussed earlier. Listen and respond. Yes...And. It doesn't get any clearer than when you're in a whoa sandwich. Yet, the player in the middle often responds with frustration. They experience a lack of control. And instead of seeing the gift of clarity and the ease of simply responding, the player tenses up and wants a way out.

One of the Whoa bullies may sense this and relent. (Or not.) I think what's important here is to witness how we respond—to see what our go-to responses are and to find ways to relax and simplify in the face of frustration or tension. To recognize when the moment has changed, and respond accordingly.

In repetition, we refer to this as the 'pile up.' **We don't force a change… A change happens when it must. There can be no planning ahead.** Snap.

What do we do if someone makes a mixed offer? What if their hands go up in the air suggesting a Whoa reversal, but they say "Whoosh"? Or they make a whoosh gesture but they say "Whoa"? This gets back to intention. It is up to the receiver to respond, regardless. And their response will once again give us the answer. If the whoosh reverses, then we know the intention seemed to be a "Whoa!" The important thing, as always, is making one another look good. And in those moments of 'confusion' (which happen… All. The. Time.), it is up to us to keep the energy flowing and to respond.

Too often, players want to stop the game, fix the problem and start again. To ask questions to 'figure out' the answer. To disconnect from the feeling of uncertainty, and make sure the others know it was not their fault.

Mistakes—ours or others'—are often only seen as mistakes when we call them out. Find a way to squash the impulse to point out what you think others have done wrong. Instead, if we follow the intention, even if we are 'wrong', we keep the energy and the scene moving, and do not draw attention to the hiccup. We simply and neatly solve the problem by responding organically.

Our game continues, and we add a few more 'rules.' Next we introduce "Zap!" When the offer comes to you, simply point at any other player and say "Zap!" A zap can break free from the perimeter of the circle and jump to anyone the sender intends. The addition of this rule underscores that one cannot check out at any time. It more realistically shows how offers can come from anywhere, and how focused and ready you need to be at all times.

Zap is also one way to break free from the whoa sandwich we talked about earlier. When it feels like your offer is not being welcomed, or the offer is immediately returned to you, that is not a failure, or a problem. In those moments we simply acknowledge we need to try a different tack—usually in the hopes of making a clearer offer. And, it is always more fun to shoot an offer to someone who wants it than to someone who seems only to want to control the game and protect himself. Don't think, DO.

I like to add a few more rules. Let's introduce "Boing!" When an offer comes to you, you can respond with a Boing by making a fist, placing it atop your head and bouncing like a spring while making your unique "Boing!" sound. All the other players then mirror your offer and everyone does the Boing together with you, after which you, as the originating player, send the energy on via whoosh, zap, etc. Everyone gets a little "me" time, and then you send the energy on its way.

The key with the Boing, again, is that you cannot check out. You don't know what is going to happen, so you have to be in a constant state of readiness, with your attention focused outward. We want to mirror the originator of the Boing as closely as possible. Their timing. Their style. Their voice. We will discuss the power and importance of mirroring in the upcoming chapter, yet once again this simple game is bringing forward so many crucial skills.

Be aware that we often UNKNOWINGLY change someone else's ideas to suit us—to better fit into our comfort zone. Make an effort to build the habit of really listening, and really mirroring as closely as possible. Differences will occur by nature. The point is to TRY to be precise, which requires a great deal of observational skill. Eventually we will reach the point where we are so attuned to one another and our focus is so heightened that we almost act simultaneously. That is the goal, while being sure not to assume or anticipate what your partner is going to do. Observe, THEN respond.

Whoosh. Whoa. Zap. Boing. Next, we add "Groovalicious!" (a lovely combination of groovy and delicious) which is a little dance break. When an offer comes to you, put your disco fingers in the air and call "Groovalicious!" Everyone does a little dance in place, complete with their own soundtrack which they vocalize. We all have our idiosyncratic offers, and somehow my Groovalicious dance is always accompanied by something akin to a 1970's porn soundtrack. You do you.

The point here is to be bold. To be free. To feel what it feels like to have everyone jumping in with the same task at the same time. It is very empowering to see others going for it, and it often makes us feel like we have permission to go for it, too. So, go for it!

Unlike Boing, when Groovalicious is called, everyone does their own thing all at the same time. Once the caller feels everyone has had their dance break she send the energy on with a whoosh, zap, etc. The game keeps going, even with the growing number of possibilities (er, 'rules').

As the possibilities pile up, however, often so does the pressure. Our fellow players start to tense up. They worry about what they're going to do when the offer comes to them. They start to fret about whether they are doing it right. They are SURE that their choices are the most boring of the bunch. They start to plan, again, what offer they will make when it next comes their way. 'Let's see… I've done Whoosh and Whoa… I hate Boing…. Next time it comes to me I am going to call Groovalicious.' This is classic checking out. Thinking. Trying to control the game. It is important to recognize when you fall into this pattern, and gently bring yourself back to the present.

Worth noting here, as well, that nowhere in our rules did we say that you HAD to do something different each time. We are planting the seeds for a selfless approach to improvisation and to acting, more broadly. That means that if you simply responded with a Whoosh each time an offer came to you, and kept the energy moving by passing it on, you are giving the game and your partners exactly what they need. Each time an offer comes to you, you are not being asked to manipulate it. It is not your star-making moment to shine. You are simply being asked to respond—purely and without thinking.

Out of insecurity, players start to embellish. Instead of working simply and clearly, some players begin to add their own flair. (Perhaps encouraged by Boing and Groovalicious!) This bad habit, again, springs from boredom and the need to be 'interesting', or 'clever', or to stand out. It is not my goal to wring all the fun and personality out of the work. Not at all. But it IS critical from the start that we hold fast to the important underpinnings of the work. Remind yourself again and again that you are here in service of your fellow players. They need your offers and your focus and attention just as much as you need theirs.

Focusing is exhausting. But it is essential for actors, and especially for improvisers. When you book that movie role, and you're on set, you don't know how long your day may be. There are so many moving parts, of which you are only one. When lighting and sound and camera are ready to go, you have to be ready, too. Even with a tightly scheduled production, there is a great deal of uncertainty. So, use these basic skills of improvisation to feel relaxed and ready, on a moment's notice.

For fun, let's throw one more rule into our game: "Freak out!" When a player calls "Freak out!" everyone does just that. You shout ("Aaaaaaaagggghhhhh!") and scramble to find a new place on the perimeter of the circle. Once you arrive at a new spot, you must be sure that you are not standing next to either of the two people who were next to you before. Sometimes this leads to a long Freak Out while players try to find the solution that satisfies everyone. Once it seems like everyone has found their new neighbors, the originating caller of the Freak Out sends the energy on with a whoosh, zap, etc., as before.

It looks chaotic. It probably feels chaotic (and fun). Again, this helps us understand what it feels like to try to find control in an environment we don't actually control. To know what it feels like to TRUST yourself and your fellow players that you will all find the next beat TOGETHER.

When we add the rules that are kind of self-indulgent, like Boing and even Groovalicious, it is fun to watch a player's delight after they call it for the first time, do their dance or their springy bounce and then look to their fellow players for what's next. However, as the originator of the call, the job is not over. You have to make another offer in order for the game to continue. Sometimes we feel such relief and even joy that we got through something unscathed that we think we MUST be done.

When acting, and especially improvising, you don't get the luxury of being 'done'. **As long as your partners need you, you must be available and present and engaged.** The olden days of one whoosh making its way methodically and predictably around the perimeter of the circle are but a memory. Even in a scripted scene where you know everything that is going to happen, you don't just say your lines and check out until the lights black out.

In this short, simple exercise, we begin to see just how attentive we need to be. Dogs have this kind of alertness. They are so observant and aware. Everything seems so immediate. Their reactions are not intellectual. They are instinctive. Responsive. Unrehearsed. Be the dog.

Let's try something else. We already talked about agreement, generally, and the basic tenet of improvisation: "Yes…And." Sadly we do not live in a world where agreement is prized. In the "real" world, we spend most of our energy defending our position, fighting for our piece of the pie and trying to 'win'—for our ego, for our pride. Out of fear.

This is one reason I am completely hooked on improvisation. In the world of improv, I KNOW that my partners are there to say 'yes!' To find agreement so that we can ALL move forward. And because the agreement is reciprocal, we have no fear that what we give away will not be returned to us. My partners need my offers. I need my partners' offers. It doesn't work any other way. **What a joy to live in a world of 'yes.'**

I like to get this into our bones early in the process by playing a game called Point Yes. In this game, we make an offer and then look for agreement in order to move ahead, by pointing to another player across the circle. The partner who you point to confirms that the offer has been acknowledged and received

Offers & Agreement

by saying "Yes!" loudly and clearly. Once you have that verbal agreement, and ONLY then, leave your place in the circle and walk toward your partner. The goal is that your partner will point to someone new, get verbal agreement and leave their original spot in the circle before you arrive. This requires that other players are paying attention and are available to receive the offer of someone pointing to them.

Offers in improvisation scenes are rarely as clear cut as someone pointing at you looking for your agreement, but the process is EXACTLY the same. Offers are made. Players observe them, find agreement and then respond. The response becomes the next offer. Which needs agreement. Which creates a response. And on and on. The energy keeps flowing as we continually advance one another's behavior.

Inevitably, one thing comes up almost instantly when doing this Point Yes exercise. Someone asks, "Can you say 'no'?" (Or they just say 'no', and then I address it.) If we are to build the good habits of improvisation that will better us as actors, we've got to set aside this impulse of trying to block others. Some would argue that it is simply being playful. I mean, 'It's just a game', right?

I say, rather, that it is a symptom of the same insecurity that tells us that everything we give comes solely at our own expense and no one else's. And if we don't hoard what's ours, or worse, HELP someone else move ahead, we will be left behind, depleted. It's just not true. Generosity breeds generosity. Work begets work. Kindness is rewarded with kindness. Giving someone a 'gift' exponentially increases the likelihood that a gift will be returned to you in kind. For the purposes of this work, especially at this critical early stage, do your best to remove the word 'no' from your vocabulary. Instead, take every opportunity to say 'yes', to find agreement, and to collaborate. By giving you an offer, someone has given you the gift of something to respond to. That is the best gift an actor can receive, and one you should never refuse.

In our more advanced work down the road, we can discuss the 'higher form of no' which allows us to truthfully resist or reject the content of an offer while still finding agreement. For now, always say 'yes!' until it is second-nature.

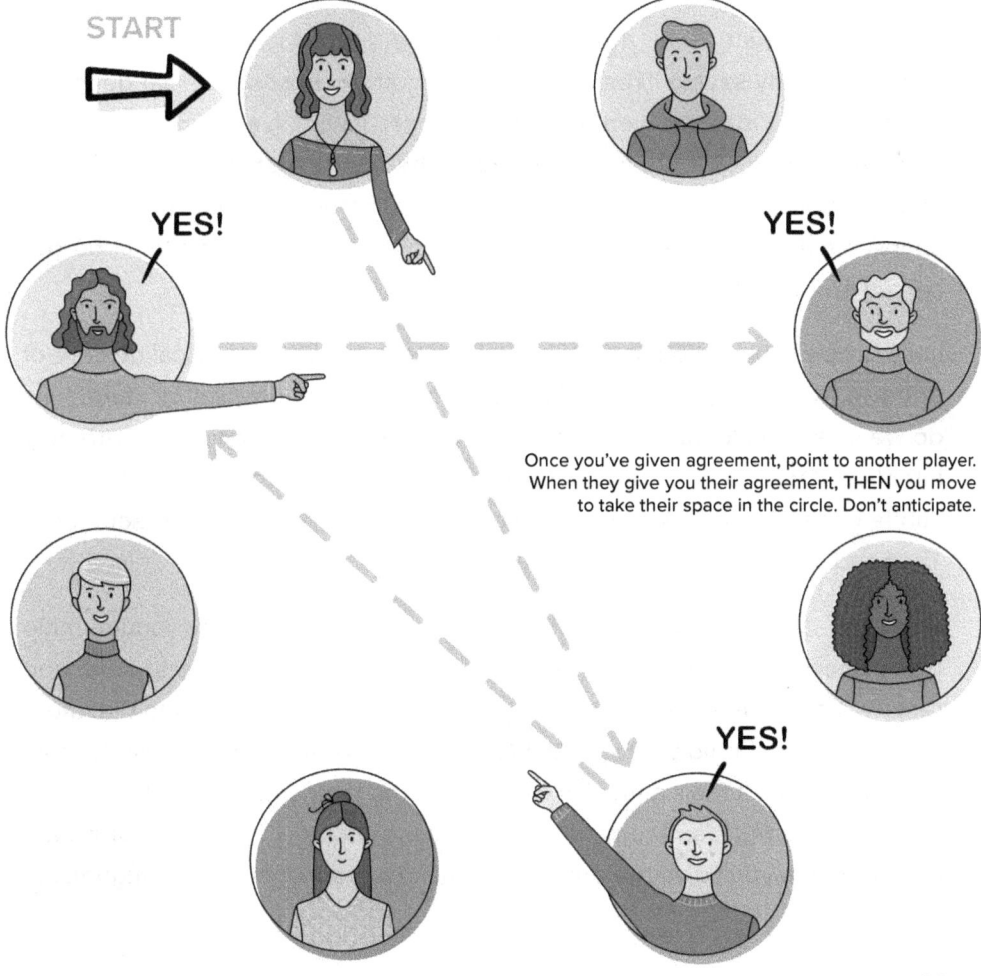

Once you've given agreement, point to another player. When they give you their agreement, THEN you move to take their space in the circle. Don't anticipate.

It takes a few rounds of Point Yes before players begin to feel the flow of it. The pattern of how offers lead to acceptance, lead to offers, etc. And the biggest challenge in the early going is usually to WAIT for the agreement BEFORE making a move toward your partner. **We always need to be sure the offer was received before we can (literally) move ahead.** We cannot assume that our offer will be observed, and we certainly can't be sure it will be interpreted the way we may intend. Yet none of that matters if the offer itself is not seen and accepted. So, be patient. Have 'sticky feet' as I tell my students. Stay put. Don't jump the gun. Don't anticipate.

After a few rounds of pointing and giving verbal agreement, I like to add a new challenge. We start to pare away elements of the game to see how little we actually need to be able to make and accept offers.

We start by taking away the verbal response. How do we give acceptance without actually saying "Yes?" What are the other cues? What role does eye contact play? Does the verbal agreement get instinctively replaced with a physical gesture of agreement? A nod of the head? A smile? Any and all of these options may occur. The point is to realize how varied offers and responses may be, and to test how subtle an offer might be and still be observed and accepted.

Let's keep pushing the challenge. Next we take away the physical gesture of pointing. What happens then? If the offer is not a bold physical gesture, how do we clearly make an offer? Can an offer be made energetically? With only intention? Or is the bold physical gesture merely replaced with smaller, more subtle ones? A wink? A smile? A small turn of the head? Eye contact alone? Try it and see.

Point Yes is our chance to PARE AWAY, and see not only the innumerable types of offers, but also how little we need in order to be able to send and receive a clear offer. This requires focus and intensity, and anything that muddies the water should be avoided. We peel away as much as we possibly can, to the point that it feels almost like ESP is driving the game. It does tend to get quiet, at this stage, so I remind my students to breathe. Holding your breath does not help you solve the problem. In fact, I'd argue it makes it tougher. Let it flow.

At some point, the group tends to get SO in tune with one another that leaving your spot and moving toward your partner almost BECOMES the offer AND the acceptance simultaneously. This is part of the beauty of improvising, of living in a world of "yes." If you KNOW that your partners are there for you, to make you look good, and that your offer WILL be accepted, you can begin to move forward with confidence, and any delay between offer and acceptance begins to disappear. Some refer to this as "group mind." We seem to 'think' and move and behave as one.

OBSERVATION

There's a game I like to play around the concept of observation. As we have already seen, much of the effectiveness of offers depends on the person receiving the offer. Or, being OPEN to receiving the offer. Being ready to say 'yes!' Not racing ahead with your own agenda and clever ideas. Giving space and attention and even time to your partners so you don't miss a thing.

The game is simple. I ask my students to pair off. And then to do one of the most difficult things: observe. Simply stand facing one another. No need to DO anything. Stand in a neutral position, feet planted, arms at your side, and observe.

We're literally looking for something deeper than the casual ignoring we do in most of our day-to-day personal interactions. The asking 'How are you?' with no real interest in the answer. We are often simply using our niceties to create opportunity for US to report on our own day, or to share something of concern to us. This is why bringing a sense of selflessness and generously giving our attention to others in our improv work can prove so challenging. It is completely opposite to how we usually move through the world.

That said, we can build this essential skill. So, we start by practicing. Observe. Take in your partner. We usually notice the obvious stuff first. Their height. What they are wearing. Their hair style and color. The color of their eyes.

Don't allow nervous tension to get your gums flapping. As soon as people start actively observing one another, they want to start giggling nervously and TALK about things—to start the small talk and the commenting. 'I like your ring.' 'This is stupid.' Whatever. Stop that urge. Feel what it feels like to truly put your attention on someone else in this easy way. To become incredibly curious. To investigate, like a detective, to notice EVERYthing you can about the person standing in front of you.

Like the start of a repetition exercise, or an improvised scene, let the observations be simple. As actors, we are hard-wired to take things personally and we want to FEEL everything. At this stage, it is not emotional. It is not subjective. We merely want to notice everything we can. Log it, like we are taking inventory. See how long a list we can assemble, and know there is STILL more that we have missed.

No need to form opinions about what you see. It is part of our nature to do this, of course, but we want to build the pure habit of being good observers first. There will be a time for your opinion, just not now. An observation follows the same guiding principle as agreement: we MUST accept that the offer was made and that it is true in the moment, while there is no requirement as to how we must FEEL about it—whether we like it or not. **What we're trying to do is make sure that we instinctively ACCEPT FIRST,** instead of negating or denying or rejecting an offer simply because we've judged that we don't like it. Or think that it makes us look bad. Or we have a 'better' idea already planned.

Try to find stillness as you observe someone. Notice everything you can. Yes, they are also observing you, but it should be without fear of judgment, or raise any insecurities. What we bring to improv is US. It takes actors a while to just get comfortable that they are who they are. Unique. Unusual. Individual. And always changing. Let someone see ALL of that, and know that it won't always land you the job. But you MUST be authentically yourself in each moment. Particularly when we're improvising, we start with our own self. We will get to building characters, but what you already possess is more than enough.

Pep talk aside, after a bit of time observing one another, I will ask one of the people in each pair to close their eyes. While their eyes are closed, I ask their partner to change three things about themselves. A flurry of activity begins as people swap their shoes onto different feet. Or roll up one sleeve. Or take off a sock. Or unbutton one button. Brush their hair differently. Take off their glasses. Turn their ring around. Whatever you want. Just change three things.

TRY IT. Observe these four people. Notice everything you can.

Then your partner is allowed to open their eyes, and their only task, based on comparing what they see now versus what they observed before they closed their eyes, is to tell you what has changed.

In this first round, many people get them right away. The changes are usually pretty obvious. If someone struggles, it's not that they are a bad observer, per se, it just illuminates how many things we take for granted. Or how little detail we actually take in even when we are TRYING to notice things. Or perhaps the things we tend to prioritize are not the things that are obvious to someone else.

So, with little surprise, once everyone has a had a go at guessing the three changes, we switch. I give everyone a minute to reset. Get still. Observe. And then the second person of the pair closes their eyes.

Once again the flurry of changes begin. Except this time, since the guessers KNOW what the challenge is like, I ask the changers to try something more subtle. My original direction was to change three 'things' about yourself. But there was no guideline that those things had to be big physical changes. Isn't it possible that an emotional shift could also be observed? Or what if someone merely shifted their weight from one hip to the other? What if someone was breathing more heavily? Or smiling? Or seemed more eager?

Some of those changes can also be easily spotted. But often they are not. And this is an important point. Because we are wired to look for the drama, and feel pressure to make things 'interesting,' we often only look for and only accept the MAJOR changes we observe. However, a subtle offer, a subtle change can be just as powerful. Someone casually tosses their hair and that in itself could be the thing that drives an entire scene.

I use the 'meteor' example: We don't need to have a major, dramatically catastrophic event occur in order to have something 'happen.' We don't need a meteor to crash through the ceiling in order for something to change. Someone inadvertently looking away from you is an offer. Someone flipping their hair. Smiling. Coughing. Shifting their weight. Sighing. Any one of these changes, if OBSERVED, could be the start of an entire interaction.

Likewise, even when we think we are standing perfectly still, I guarantee you things are happening. Small, perhaps, compared to the meteor, but useful nonetheless. IF observed. You see the key here? **You have to be tuned in enough to witness something. And that can only happen if your attention is more on your partners than on yourself.**

Sometimes, all that is required is a simple shift in HOW your observe something or someone. Imagine, for example, you have a piece of art in front of you.

IMPROV AND THE ACTOR'S IMAGINATION

What has changed from what you observed on page 25?

A sculpture. It appears solid and still. And yet, if you look at it from a different angle, you may see something new. Some detail you overlooked before. I think of the work of Alexander Calder, one of my favorite artists. Many of his pieces have thin, flat panels and surfaces. From one perspective they seem large and structurally dominant. When viewed from the side, however, the same panel will seem to disappear, giving the piece an entirely new appearance. And all we did was change our own perspective.

Of course, Calder took it a step further. He is widely credited with originating mobile sculpture. He did not wait for the observer to change her perspective. Calder went ahead and put the static pieces in motion. Or, more accurately, allowed them to balance and move on their own. Again, creating observable change without any effort from the viewer whatsoever. We merely have to give it our attention and witness the change.

When we're playing this observation game, often your partner will identify something that they observe has changed. They're right. There was a change. But it was not one of the three things you intentionally altered. So, is their observation true? The improviser would say "yes!" We have to be open, as actors and improvisers, in particular, to our intended offers being missed or misinterpreted. And for our unintended offers to be observed and accepted. No one in improv has the luxury of holding onto their own ideas. The only offer that matters is the one that is observed and accepted. Once someone makes an offer in a scene, it is true, in that it now exists in the world of the scene. Again, no one says you have to like it, but you MUST agree that it happened. Yes, they just said that. Yes, they just did that. Yes, that just happened. Yes. Yes. Yes.

And none of it needs to be invented or concocted, out of some need for cleverness, or to be funny, or because we keep returning to the nagging insecurity of being the most boring and uninteresting person on Earth. Your partners' sole job is to make you look good. If you offer it, and it is organic to the scene, your partner WILL accept it and respond. GENUINE offers are a joy to receive and the response usually seems effortless. However, inventions that rattle around in your head, those you can't wait to 'hilariously' inject into the scene, usually end up killing the momentum of the scene. We waste the rest of the scene trying to make sense of the odd offer out of left field.

It takes time. Be generous with your partners. Understand that it is harder for some than it may be for you to let go of control. But they need you, nonetheless, to be ready and open to receive whatever they put forth. Try to resist your OWN need to drag the scene back into YOUR comfort zone.

"Get yourself into trouble" is one of my improv mantras. Don't waste your time trying to plan something out because you want it go a certain way. Screw it! Try to TRULY say 'yes' and see where the next offer takes you. BUILD on what's there, and abandon the need to KNOW. Even in scripted work, this is our acting challenge: to let the moments unfold in an UNanticipated way. Even if you've rehearsed a play for weeks, each time, you live it anew. You stay true to the story, but you make discoveries each time. You NOTICE something new. Something HAPPENS to you in a way you did not expect. Once there is no longer any surprise in the work, it's time to get out. Luckily, surprise is

TRY IT! Observe.

SELFIE SWITCH
Take a selfie.
Wait one minute, and take another selfie,
attempting to match the original.
Compare them to see what's changed.

FRAME-TO-FRAME FLIP-FLOPS
Filmed content is often edited from multiple takes.
The shots are intended to match, but sometimes details
are missed, leading to hiccups in shot continuity.
While watching one of your favorite shows or movies,
see if you can spot any of those mismatches.

STILL NOT STILL
Sit still. Close your eyes. Do a body scan from your
head to your toes, noticing every detail you can.
Without judging or trying to 'fix' anything,
what sensations do you observe? And how much is happening,
despite trying to sit perfectly still?

Offers & Agreement

ALWAYS there, as long as you are tuned in enough to notice it. It can be small. But that doesn't mean is has less value or is any less important.

Remember, we are creating something out of NOTHING when we improvise, so use what you have. And there is an abundance, I promise. We just need to turn off our censor who is telling us it's not interesting enough, or big enough, or important enough to be observed, let alone offered. If you SAW it, it's enough. If you HEARD it, it's enough. If you FELT it, it's enough. Make the offer based on what you observe, and let your partner accept it and respond. Then you take THAT offer (the response) and accept it and respond... aaaaaand we're off! Whoosh!

MIRRORING

This leads us to an exploration of mirroring. It is such a powerful and significant tool which leads to all sorts of discoveries. Mirroring work will reveal where we are as listeners and observers, and highlight how much we feel the need to control a situation. Remember, there is no control. It is only an illusion that someone is puppeteering the proceedings. What is actually happening is that **moments are unfolding, offer after offer, and our energy should be focused on observing and responding, not playwriting.**

So, let's explore! I'll ask pairs to once again face off. Get into a neutral posture. Don't try to DO anything. Just be. And put your attention on your partner, and let them put their attention on you. Observe.

As you sleuth all the details you can, begin the task of mirroring what you observe, as though you were truly a reflective glass and your partner is staring into their own reflection. Of course, as I said before, we are all built differently. I am very tall, and yet I am tasked with reflecting someone shorter than I am (which is pretty much everyone). When faced with these inconsistencies, the guiding principle in improv is to 'solve the problem.' We said this journey is about the connection to the actor's imagination. Let's apply our imagination in this way to this task. Let's respond in such a way that we honor the offer(s) in front of us.

Remember when we were whooshing away and we considered the idea of intention. That applies here, too. You may not be able to EXACTLY mirror someone, merely because of physical differences. Your task is to TRY. Solve the problem to capture the essence, the intent, of each offer. Even physical ones.

Now, once you and your partner feel like you are one another's reflection, I ask one of the partners to begin to move. Raise an arm. Change facial expressions. Crouch. Walk. Practice Tai Chi. Whatever. The person who initiates the movement is the leader for this part of the exchange, which means the role of follower falls to the other partner, by default. The task is simple: the leader creates movement, and the follower mirrors it as EXACTLY as she can, in real time. **We want to become so well synchronized that if someone happened upon the two of you, they would not be able to tell who was initiating.**

This process is a good exploration of control and lack of control. As a leader, you have responsibility for your partner. They are depending on you to take care of them. If they are having difficulty following you, then you need to 'solve the problem' and adapt your movement until you find that you are perfectly in sync. You may be a master yogi and easily fall into a downward dog, whereas your partner may have mobility restrictions, or is not nearly as flexible. So, even when you are in 'control' of the scene, you have an obligation to be equally present for your partners. You are observing and taking them in at the same time. Trust that your partner is doing their best to follow you, and any disparity between the two of you should not be coming from a place of resistance or lack of trying. You are there to make one another look good.

Once you find the two of you are in a flow, and seem to be well synchronized, then challenge yourselves to see what else is possible. If you have only been doing slow, smooth movements, see if you can do something quickly or percussively and still stay connected. Do some trial and error.

If you have been standing the whole time, try mirroring while laying down. Or squatting. If you have been stuck in one place, trying moving about the room. If you have been silent, try making sounds. TOGETHER. At the same time. See what's possible.

This is not to say that you should feel any pressure to get 'creative.' Meaning: What happens organically is enough, and if you start to think you, as a leader, are being boring, try to reconnect with how well you and your partner are in sync, and know that THAT is the task. No need to make any recognizable movements, either. Don't try to tell a story in pantomime. I have some students who start to lead their partner through full dance routines. As soon as the exercise moves into the territory of cleverness and 'ideas,' we need to acknowledge that we have shifted into our heads, despite moving our bodies, and reconnect ourselves with the task and our responsibility for one another.

Who knows? Maybe your dance routine is one that your partner also knows, and the two of you seem more connected during that part of the exercise than when you were moving organically. That's a fun discovery, and we would all love to see the full performance later. But, there is a trap here: patterns.

Patterns, when they emerge in scenes can help us navigate the scene and the narrative. In fact much of improv 'comedy' depends on this idea of patterns, also often referred to broadly as 'the game' of the scene. We look for repetition of behavior and ideas as a way to explore and heighten them. 'If that's true, what else?' We push the boundaries by hooking into an anchoring pattern.

That actually sounds useful, right? It can be, as I said. But when patterns appear in this mirroring work, they can create a trap. We stop listening fully and we begin to anticipate. You are leading me and I start to recognize that you are doing the sequence of moves from the Macarena (a song and dance craze from the 1990's...look it up). I start to follow, and then get excited that I recognize it and I start to really get into it. Lots of attitude and sass. Then, all of a sudden, you stop and move onto something else. Anyone watching would see a big glitch in that moment. Because I started to ASSUME I knew what was coming next, I relaxed my attention. I am supposed to be following you, and you initiated the idea, but I was actually doing my own thing.

I'll admit my references can be a bit outdated (see also: Macarena, 1990's)... But everyone should know "I Love Lucy." If you don't, A) how dare you! And B) get on YouTube, stat! There is an episode of the show where Harpo Marx is a guest. (Again, if your response is 'Harpo who?', do your homework. You'll thank me.) Lucy and Harpo were literally doing a mirroring bit in the show, from opposite sides of an open doorway. They were walking, hiding, peering out, and in perfect sync. Then came the clapping. Harpo began a clap pattern and Lucy mirrored:

Clap-clap-clap. Pause.
Clap-clap-clap. Pause.
Clap-clap. Pause.

What do you think happened (assuming you didn't already put down the book to watch the episode)? Lucy clapped a third time, and Harpo didn't. The mirroring spell was broken because one person assumed they knew what was coming next. It was a delightful surprise and the studio audience laughed heartily on cue. The point being, the dependence on the pattern actually led to the break.

The Lucy bit was done for comedy, of course. Comedy relies on the Rule of Three. Simply stated: three is the smallest number of beats necessary to set up a pattern and break it, as Lucy and Harpo showed us. Clap-clap-clap. Clap-clap-clap. Clap-clap. It is the change, the surprise, that makes us laugh. We didn't see it coming.

When we are improvising, without chasing the joke or the laugh, just purely improvising, we don't need to look for surprises, or make any effort to break patterns. Unexpected things happen ALL THE TIME. So, you can relieve yourself of any obligation to DRIVE the story or the scene. It will unfold automatically from the focused, moment-to-moment work, and our attention placed outside of ourselves. All we need to do is release control and follow.

With that, it bears mentioning that **there is a concept in improvisation known as 'follow the follower.'** This is another way of saying what I described before:

The idea that if some outside observer happened upon your scene, it would be impossible for them to tell which of the players was leading the scene. Or that any particular idea or behavior originated with any specific player. It is seamlessly shared, this offer-response, Yes…And rhythm, to the point that it APPEARS as though what is happening was planned—that the players got together before the scene and mapped it all out. All they are doing, in truth, is putting their attention squarely on their partners, focused on observing, agreeing with the offers and then organically responding. That's it! Although I often refer to improv as 'magic,' there is no trick. Tried and true trickery may elicit a laugh, but it is a hack move. It is one player selfishly trotting out something they've done before because it makes them more comfortable than staying present and allowing for WHATEVER may happen.

I say: let's be generous improvisers and put our partners' needs before our own. We do not lose anything by giving space to someone else. In fact, without them, we cannot move forward. Until there is an offer to which we can respond, we are stuck. And the same for our partners. This give-and-take underpins all improvised work.

Let's check in with the mirroring exercise. The first person has been leading for a bit. We've tried some more challenging movements to see what's possible. Now, I want the leadership responsibility to shift to the partner who was following. A transition of leadership does not mean we stop cold and start over with new ideas. The newly assigned leader should simply pick up seamlessly from where the other leader left off.

How does the power transition feel? If you were the leader and are now following, do you feel relieved that you no longer have the responsibility to come up with movements for the two of you? Or do you instantly miss the 'control?' Likewise, if you were the follower and are now the leader, do you feel pressure to invent? Are you excited that now you get to do your own 'better' moves, instead of the stupid things your partner was coming up with? Do you abandon the movements your partner was leading and come up with movements that you prefer, and that are more comfortable and familiar to you? How much of the 'vocabulary' of the movement from the first leader has remained?

This switch often highlights how much we are really giving over to our partners (or not). You may be surprised, as you follow uncompromisingly, that your partner has introduced you to a way of moving that is unfamiliar. You may be surprised that you are even CAPABLE of moving in a certain way. Often that 'permission' comes from the exercise. **When we are TASKED with following as precisely as we are able, we get a taste of the freedom that comes with putting our attention outside ourselves and simply following**—giving over to each moment as it happens, and leaving no space for judgment and rationalizing. We get to a point where we are not CHOOSING to act, we just are.

Athletes refer to this as the 'zone.' There is no mental activity driving what's happening. It is simply happening. Energetically, we just respond to each moment as it comes. It feels effortless, because it does not require any cogitation. No reasoning, or planning. We simply act. And when asked after the fact what was happening, it may be impossible to describe. 'Things were just clicking,' some may say. Or, 'we were on a roll.' What they mean is that they let go of control and stopped trying to FORCE something to happen. They simply embraced what WAS happening.

Mirroring, believe it or not, is moving us closer to our own ability to relinquish control. It shows us there is value in simply honoring what someone else gives us and accepting it as though it is our own.

To further explore this generous 'follow the follower' philosophy in our mirroring exercise, I call a "switch!" That puts the leadership for the movement back onto the first partner, and the second partner returns to following. I ask again the same questions. I want you to check in with how you feel when you take leadership and give leadership. Whether you feel more comfortable in one role or the other. And, whether you even notice any difference at all. Maybe you are beginning to discover that 'leading' is no more or less responsibility than following, as long as we are BOTH committed to one another.

How has the 'vocabulary' evolved? When we returned to the original leader, did we revert back to THEIR movements? Or have we built something together? How is your focus? Do you find yourself checking in and out? Where do you place your attention when you are leading? When you are following? Do you 'look through' the other person so you can take in everything at once?

Have you both found the limits yet of what's possible? Have you tried mirroring one another with your backs turned? Have you gone high and low? Have you tried speaking and making sounds simultaneously? Have you tried moving around the room?

And "Switch!" Back to the second partner leading. Are you able to make the switches continuous? Or is there still a stop/start hiccup? Almost like finishing one another's sentences, let the movement pick up right where the previous leader left off.

And "Switch!" Leadership is back with the first player.

From this point forward, and for the rest of the exercise, I want you to keep switching leadership back and forth, but I am not going to call it. I want you and your partner to AGREE who is leading, and I want the leadership to swap back and forth between the players as many times as possible before the exercise ends.

How do we know who's leading? Is there a difference? Does it matter? Are you actually following the follower? It should get to a point where you and your partner are seemingly BOTH initiating at the same time. We will discuss this moment much more when we get into actual scenes, but one of the things about an offer is that it needs to be bold and specific enough to be observed. And yet, in the same instant that you put an offer into the scene, you have to be ready to give it up if another offer comes. There is no room to hold onto your idea, no matter how fantastic you believe it to be. You have to be willing and ABLE to not be precious about your work, and know that the real gift is that you get to respond to an offer—not that you get to have your way. **Let go. Everything you need is in your partner. Everything they need is in you.**

After a period of letting the pairs switch on their own, I ask them to find the ending. How do you come back to your starting position? How do you agree how to do that TOGETHER? And how do you know when it is finally over? Even when we are being 'still' there is a lot to observe. A cough. A smile. A sigh. A blink. A shift of weight. A fidget. By the end of the exercise, we are SO connected, it may be difficult NOT to notice (and reflect) every tiny change.

After the introduction to the mirroring work, pairs of partners are usually excited to share how they got into a flow and didn't really know at certain points who was leading. That's it! Try to remember that feeling, and let it be the thing that underpins all of your improvising. That's a taste of that selfless place where you are outwardly focused and ready for whatever comes.

We've been doing this work in pairs, but often our scenes involve three or four or more people. We should be able to apply this same mirroring work to larger groups. So, let's try.

Again, in a large circle, everyone is standing in a neutral position. Find the common position as a group. And then be still. One person in the circle will begin to lead the movement, just as we did in pairs. The task of everyone else in the circle is to follow in real time. Mirror the person who's leading.

One of the challenges of this larger group is that you may not be directly facing the person who is leading, like you were in your pairs. Don't get caught up in whether you are an EXACT mirror of the person. They may be raising their right arm, and because you are standing beside them, you are using your right arm, too. Whereas, the person across the circle from the leader may be using her left arm, as though she were an actual reflective mirror. In this circle version of the exercise, it's fine either way. Simply put your attention on the leader and FOLLOW.

Similarly, you may find it challenging to know where to focus. It is difficult to mirror someone standing beside you, as many of you explored in your pairs. Well, if everyone in the circle is mirroring the leader at the same time, try looking across at someone who you can see more easily. Try following THEM as they follow the leader and see if you can still stay with the leader.

To the person leading the group, you have more responsibility to make sure that there is agreement from the group. There will be a larger variety of skills, and the difficult choreographic moves you and your previous partner were able to do may not be possible for other members of this larger group. Be aware, and adapt your movements accordingly.

Once you all seem to be in a flow, then you can challenge the group a bit. See what's possible. Can a group of ten or twelve people all clap at the same time? If we can all stay together when we move slowly, what happens when we move faster? Because others in the circle don't need to look directly at you in order to be able to follow you, is it possible to turn your back to the group and still have them be able to follow? Try it. See what's possible, all the while checking in for agreement.

At some point, we'll shift the leadership role to someone else in the circle. And just like in our pairs work, we don't stop and start over with each new leader. The new leader should pick up right where the group left off from the last leader. It should be seamless, as though you were leading all along. As though the movements were your own.

Once everyone has had a chance to experience what it's like to lead the larger group, I'll start to call "Switch!" But I am not going to assign the leader at the switches, now. The group needs to AGREE each time who is taking leadership. Explore how this change occurs. Does someone have to make a bold move or a loud sound to get the attention of the group for them to follow? Or does the leadership somehow pass to someone CLOSE to the leader who is already in most people's line of sight? Can a small shift in movement be enough to make people follow? Be willing to take the leadership, and also be willing to follow, if another leader emerges. **Simultaneous offers happen all the time in scenes, so get a feeling for how adaptable you can be. Be bold, while equally willing to give focus.**

At some point, I will not call the switches at all. I want you to find agreement with your partners and switch leadership as many times as you can for the final minute of the exercise. Be sure to make space for everyone. Some people tend to be more bold, but we don't want to inadvertently shut down shier players. It's easy to be a bully and a stagehog when everyone is working on following. So, be sure to make it possible for someone to lead you, as well.

And then, find an ending together. How do we agree, as a group, how to come back to our neutral starting position? Does someone have to LEAD the return? Or have we become so in sync (*NSYNC, anyone? Look it up.) that we all do it the same without a leader? Group mind is an amazing thing. Always approach your work with a goal of tapping into the shared awareness.

I usually like to add a little challenge with this group mirroring, just to see if we are truly working together. I'll have one person come into the center of the circle and close their eyes. Everyone on the outside of the circle is standing in their neutral position. Once the volunteer has their eyes closed, I will walk the perimeter of the circle and point to a person who will be our leader for the game. Once that person is identified, hopefully unknown to the guesser in the center of the circle, they should begin to lead the group in a movement, just as we have done. Once I feel like the group is in a flow, I will step out of the circle and ask the volunteer to open their eyes. Their challenge is to tell us WHO is leading the movement. The guesser can move anywhere in the circle they like, but cannot step outside the circle.

Sometimes the guesser gets it right away. Other times, it may take four or five guesses. Much of it depends on looking in the right place at the right time. If the group is doing an especially good job fooling the guesser, I will encourage the leader to take more risks—to see if they can make a change to the movement right in front of the guesser's eyes and get away with it.

When I ask the guesser how they guessed correctly, the answer usually has to do with where people's eyes were focusing. Or a sudden, unplanned shift in the movement. This is good practice for what's to come. We need to get good at following the energetic focus of a scene. We need to find agreement in each moment, and that requires giving our focus to others. To observe where the energy is, and to focus our attention there, as though following the leader.

Last thing I'll say about mirroring at this point is that we will rely heavily on it as we move forward. Mirroring can help us find our connection to an activity, to our partners, and to the scene.

Let's try a game called "What Are You Doing?" which highlights this. Standing once again in a circle, a player starts a repeatable gesture. Maybe they are raising their hands one at a time, cupping their fingers and then pulling their hand down. They keep repeating the pattern of movement, and everyone in the circle mirrors the movement at the same time. After a few moments of doing the movement together, the originating player then tells the group what they are doing. "I'm climbing a ladder." And while continuing the motion, the player then asks their partner to the right, "What are YOU doing?"

Maintaining the same repeatable gesture throughout, each subsequent player identifies for the group what they are doing. "I'm picking apples. What are YOU doing?" "I'm washing a window. What are YOU doing?" "I'm organizing my Matchbox cars (Look it up.). What are YOU doing?" ...until every player has identified what THEY see when doing the movement.

Say whatever YOU see. If the movement is very clear to you, you may see the same thing that others see. That's fine. In fact, it's often desirable to have a gesture that is so clear that it can be easily identified. But, as always, the work is not about getting it 'right', it's about allowing your imagination to make the connections to the doing, whatever those impulses may be.

When the question makes its way around the circle and returns to the originator of the movement, that initiating player has a second chance to say what they are doing. It's possible that this time around, you see something new. Or you connected to something that someone else in the circle said, and it made you see the gesture differently. Whether it stayed the same for you, or evolved into something else, just connect to the physicality and say what you see in this moment. "I'm climbing a ladder."

The next player then begins a new, repeatable movement which everyone follows. They identify what they are doing, and ask their partner "What are YOU doing?" And so on. The game continues until every player has had a chance to initiate a movement.

There is no pressure in this game to come up with something new. (Or clever. Or funny.) I watch as players struggle with trying to say something no one else in the circle has said. Or show their disappointment when someone else 'takes their idea' before they have a chance. That approach misses the point.

We are LOOKING for agreement. We WANT our partners to see what we see, and do what we do, so that we can ground ourselves together in the scene. All the while keeping in mind that others may see something different than we do. Remember, each of those moments of dissonance is a chance to say "yes". And mirroring gets you to "yes".

If you start a scene, and you are observing your partner and you have no idea what they are doing… Instead of standing on the sidelines and waiting until you feel like you KNOW enough to enter the scene, try MIRRORING. Simply do what they are doing, just like the game, even if it seems like they are doing nothing. (Which as I've said before is never the case… Even when we THINK we are standing perfectly still, there is ALWAYS SOME behavior happening. We just need to be tuned in enough to observe it.)

Instantly, somehow, just by doing what your partner is doing, we FIND the scene. We connect to the same activity and we begin to explore it. We find agreement and build, agreement and build, agreement and build… And, all of a sudden, a scene that started with 'nothing' has revealed itself to be two people waiting to make confession at their church. Or two people auditioning to be birthday clowns. Or a couple who has chosen their friend's wedding as the place to break up.

When in doubt, mirror. You will never find the answer by THINKING about it. The answer is never found in trying to 'figure it out.' **The answer comes by giving over to the NOT-knowing, CHOOSING to engage, and then getting yourself connected to your partner.** And mirroring is the best way I know how to do that. Do, and discover.

MIRRORING

DOUBLE VISION:
Mirror your favorite character while watching a show or a movie. Do what they do, as they do it. Solve the problems of NOT being able to mirror them exactly. TRY. See if you can at least capture the intention of what they do.

SINCEREST FORM OF FLATTERY:
Imitate someone you admire. See how closely you can match their physicality, their voice, their talent or skill. Try to capture every detail.

PHOTO REDUX:
Recreate, as closely as possible, a famous photo or painting, or maybe a picture from your childhood. See if you can capture the essence, even if you can't mirror it exactly. Post the original and the new pic side by side. Let your friends tell you how you did.

2
Spacework & Environments

One of the aspects of improvisation that makes it different from a lot of scripted work is that we do not have props or sets or costumes, let alone a script. We are literally creating all elements of the story from nothing. And it has to be specific and fully realized, or we will have difficulty moving forward in our scenes. We will spend our entire interaction trying to solve all the problems we unwittingly created because we didn't anchor ourselves in activity and environment first.

In my opinion, one of the reasons why there is so much 'bad' improv in the world is that players choose to talk at one another instead of DOING. "Talking head scenes", as I call them. Just two people standing there, usually trying to outwit one another with their cleverness. Or embarrass one another by pointing out the mistakes, the anachronistic offers, the problems. It will probably get a laugh. But it will also kill the scene. Once you destroy the reality in a world created from nothing, once you start to say 'that's weird' or 'that doesn't belong here' or 'you're not who you say you are' or 'it's magic!' or 'it was all a dream', you undercut the investment your partners have made. Such a move is called 'commenting.' Instead of engaging and working together to accept and build on the offers, a player tries to control the interaction and protect himself by pointing out what OTHERS did 'wrong.' **Stay present. Get yourself in trouble, and SEE what's possible. Don't let your brain tell you to stop what's happening.**

Let's build, then, on the mirroring work we've been doing to be certain that we have the skills to be able to stay out of our heads and engaged in the physical world we are building together. It means that we need to advance beyond creating just ANY movement to creating movements that are SPECIFIC. Movements that are intended to represent specific objects or places or activities. We use our movement in improv to define the world. To define our activity. To define ourselves.

This is powerful stuff, so we ease into it with another game, one I play in my classes a lot. It's a great warm-up. It gets the energy flowing in the room. It gets us into our bodies, physically engaged. And it builds on the work we've done so far. That game is: Sound Ball.

We stand again in a circle, and I 'hold' in front of me a 'basketball.' (NOTE: This will get very trippy, since this whole section will refer to objects and other elements that we 'see' which are not really there. We are creating these objects through our spacework.)

So, hold a basketball. It has a size. Weight. Texture. Color. Markings. REALLY SEE the ball. Really FEEL it in your hands. Does it have a smell, too? Is it warm or cool? Just like our observation work has taught us, there are SO many details to be observed. Be curious. See what YOU can see.

And when I say 'see,' we are talking about what we can imagine. The imagination plays a HUGE role in improvisation. And it requires a great deal of focus, particularly until spacework becomes more habitual.

For those actors who have always worked with physical props and on fully-realized sets, spacework can feel extremely strange. It can even feel 'untruthful,' and may seem to go against everything we are taught in acting classes.

But what acting also demands of us is our "actor's faith." We know (and our audience knows) that what we are creating is not actually 'real.' We are not the people we play. These are not our words. The events are not really happening. Yet, we embrace our actor's faith, our BELIEF in the reality of what we're doing and saying, so that it becomes real to us and to the audience—as though they are a fly on the wall witnessing it all.

Spacework is actor's faith in overdrive. It requires us to engage our imagination on such a deep level that we can BELIEVE that an object we are creating out of the air is real. That it exists in the space. And just like in the real world, if a kitchen table is there, it doesn't simply disappear or cease to exist when you want to walk from one side of the room to the other. You walk around it. If you are sitting at the table, it doesn't magically raise itself up and down depending on what you're doing. It has a fixed height.

So SEE it. Whatever it is you're offering through your spacework, make it real to yourself. Don't shortcut the details. Specificity is EVERYTHING. And use your own experience as reference. Why not? If you had a basketball when you were a kid that was colored red, white and blue and had a big gold star on it, or was signed by your favorite player, use THAT one. SEE all those details. (Of course, then comes the challenge to communicate those unique personal details to your fellow players, but let's not get ahead of ourselves.)

The only REAL props we allow in purely improvised work are 'sittables.' A block or a chair. It is nearly impossible to believably pretend to sit in a space-chair for any length of time. So, we solve that problem by actually sitting on something so that we can focus on the object work of the task at hand. If you need to sit, and choose not to sit on the floor, keep the prop simple and something nondescript. It will be harder to believe you are sitting on a gilded throne if the actual chair is a beaten up recliner

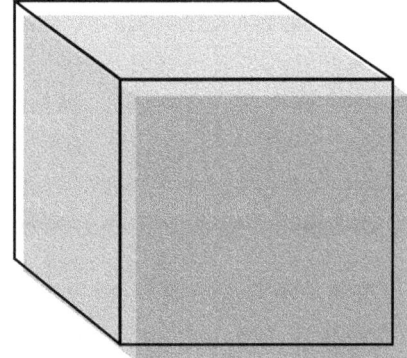

or a bean bag chair. A simple wooden box or sturdy stool or armless chair should do.

With objects and environments alike, keep it simple. I mean: don't intentionally invent unusual characteristics for the objects and places. In the case of the basketball, let's consider what the low common denominators are and start from there—the characteristics of the most recognizable version of that object. So, our basketball is regulation size. It has an orange and nubby surface. It has black grooves circling the ball. It is properly and fully inflated. Now, let's play.

We'll start with ONE ball. Whoever starts will pass the ball to someone else in the circle. And when they pass the ball, they will make a sound. ('Sound' ball, remember?) I don't want you to use words, no matter what language you speak. Just make a sound. A squeak. A heavy exhale. A grumble. A scream. Don't think about what sound you want to make, just pass the ball and let a sound go with it.

Now, because we want to keep ourselves in the place of being attentive observers and not anticipating any offer, if we are the receiver of the ball that was just passed with its accompanying sound, our task is to catch the ball and REPEAT or mimic the sound our partner uttered. Just like in the mirroring work we started, TRY to match the sound exactly. You may not like the sound that accompanied the ball, or you may not physically be able to reach that high or low pitch. TRY. As though you were capable of doing it perfectly. Don't judge it (or PRE-judge it). Don't comment with your stinky face about how you feel about the sound. Your only job is to accept the offer, and to say 'yes' by repeating what was given to you.

Similarly, pay attention to how you mirror the receipt of the ball. It doesn't magically change size when it gets to you. The object you received is the exact same one that your partner sent to you. Don't alter objects to suit your own likes or experience. 'Well, when I was a kid, we had a mini basketball that was made of foam.' Great! That is not THIS basketball. Let go of trying to make yourself comfortable, and simply respond to the offer made.

Once you have received the ball and parroted the sound, you can pass the ball to someone else in the circle. And, although the object remains the same (size, shape, color, etc.) you will send it with whatever sound YOU happen to make. Again, do not allow yourself to fall into the trap of trying to be 'interesting' or funny or clever. Don't THINK about what sound you're going to make. Believe it or not, this is actually difficult for many players. They receive the ball and sound that was sent to them, and before they can pass it along with a new sound, they pause to think about what sound they should make. It is not necessary. Whatever sound you make is great.

Many who are new to improv suffer what I call the "Goldilocks principle." They keep abandoning perfectly good offers in search of something that makes them more comfortable. They think that with enough time and effort, they can come up with the BEST idea. What sound to make. What name to have. What occupation to have. What day of the week it is. I say otherwise. I say your first impulse is the one to go with. I have never, in my years of improvising, found an offer that came after much delay and consideration to be any better than the first idea.

And, in this case, I am not asking you to even make sense, or communicate ANYthing. **I think the answer is always to DO something, and everything follows from that. And when we get into scenework, I will advise you similarly: DO FIRST, speak if you must.** Acting is behavior, not dialogue. (All due respect to the brilliant playwrights and screenwriters whose words we are thrilled to speak!) So, throw the ball and let whatever sound that happens happen. In doing so, you create an offer to which one of your partners will be happy to respond.

So, they receive the ball and repeat your sound, and then pass that same ball to someone new with a sound of their own making. And the energy continues to move around the room.

What if my sound is the same as the sound someone else made? Who cares?! Let 'er rip. Your partner will take whatever you give, and no one is going to stop the game because they don't approve of you recycling a sound. (At least, they better not!)

I guess we should mention that, just as a basketball has specific physical characteristics we want to maintain with integrity as long as that object exists in the space, it also moves in a specific way. You bounce it, or dribble it, or you pass it, or you shoot it, or you spin it on top of your finger. These are all clues that can help us, in addition to physical size, to recognize the object as a basketball—those quintessential characteristics that distinguish the object. And then FOLLOW the object as it moves through space. Do you pass it with a high arc, like shooting a free-throw? Do you dribble it once or twice and then pass it forcefully? Do you bounce it hard on the ground and watch it fly into the air before coming down? Agree with your partners where the ball is at any moment.

And don't look for problems. 'Uh oh! The ball is flat.' 'The ball got stuck in a tree.' 'I don't know how to play basketball.' There is ZERO need to invent things in this way. As you will see as we move forward, the 'problems' will happen all the time. We don't need to go looking for them. Focus on your partners and on their behavior. Do your best not to miss ANYthing, and in doing so, you keep the incongruence to a minimum.

When we get the flow of the ball moving from person to person, I like to up the ante. We add a second ball. And probably a third and a fourth. At this point in the game, we are passing only basketballs, identical in size and shape and in the way they move. Having multiple balls in play increases the need for our readiness, and more closely reflects the energy of a real scene. Offers will come fast and furious, and from all directions, just as they do in scenes.

Inevitably, someone will ask what happens if two people throw the ball to you at the same time. I say, FIND OUT. How do you solve that problem? Do you catch both and then put one down so you can throw them one at a time? Do you put one under each arm? Spin one on your finger while you dribble the next? The answer is not an intellectual one. Nor is it about right or wrong. You simply have to engage your imagination and respond in whatever manner feels truthful. Both of the basketballs continue to exist in space, so if you can SEE them, I guarantee you cannot only keep track of them both, but handle them with integrity and send each of them to your partners with a clear offer.

Can you get it wrong? I don't think so. The only way we know there is a problem is if you telegraph it to us with your behavior. If you stop the game. If you suddenly look around for answers. If you literally say "Oops!" Give your partners the chance to make you look good by sending them an offer to which they can respond. No apologies or oops-es required. TRY. Get yourself in trouble and see what happens.

Now that we have the makings of a pro team, let's challenge ourselves again. We're going to continue to pass a ball with a sound, as we have been, and we'll start with one of the basketballs we've been using so far. Then, I want to introduce additional balls, but these will not be basketballs. They will be different sizes and shapes and types of balls.

So, how do we communicate, through our spacework, the difference between a basketball and a baseball, for instance? Well, just like the basketball, each ball has unique, defining characteristics that are broadly accepted. A baseball is usually white with colored stitching. It is physically smaller than a basketball. It is more easily held and thrown with one hand. You pitch a baseball. You hit a baseball with a bat.

So each time you have an object to pass, take a moment to establish it clearly for your partner. If you are to throw a baseball, show your partner how you can toss it in the air with one hand. Assume a pitcher's stance and throw a fastball. Or toss the ball in the air and bat it to your partner.

If you are receiving the baseball, find agreement with your partner to confirm you see what they see. If they are pitching you the ball, crouch in a catcher's stance to receive it. If they hit a high fly ball, watch it move through the air until you catch it with your glove. Any accessory object you need (a bat, a baseball cap, a glove) is as available to you as the ball itself. SEE it. Give it space and weight in your hands. Use it in the quintessential way the object is used. If it helps you make a clearer offer (e.g. 'this is a baseball not a basketball'), do it. Just use each object with integrity.

I also find that the sound I make along with the pass can add clarity to the object. We never have the need to create sound effects for our spacework. (No need to vocalize the whir of a blender, or the sssssshhhhhhh from the water running in the shower, or the banging of a hammer.) Just create the object and use it with integrity in the way it is most commonly used. Though, in the game of Sound Ball I find that I begin to organically alter my sounds to reflect the ball I am passing. A shot of a small marble might get a high-pitched "Pyewwww-www." Whereas a large yoga ball may be accompanied by a deeper sounding "Boyeeeoyeeoy." Again, the task is not to be a master Foley artist creating SFX for each ball, but the tone and timbre and pitch DOES send a clue which may help your partner identify the object more clearly.

"Give it space in your hand" is a phrase I utter often for those new to spacework. When we hold 'space objects' our tendency is to clench our fists. But if I were actually holding the handle of a pitcher of water, or a bucket, or a hammer or a sword, I couldn't hold it with a closed fist. It would take up space in my hand. Likewise, objects don't appear out of thin air for your convenience. Break this habit early. Pick them up, and put them down. Be aware of this reality as you work.

So, we now have a basketball and a baseball moving through the room from person to person with an accompanying sound. Let's add a golf ball. What makes IT different? It is more rigid than the other two balls. Smaller. You don't toss a golf ball, you hit it with a club. There is a stance golfers take to putt shorter distances. You may be at the tee, preparing for a drive. Use supporting objects (a putter, a tee, pull up a tuft of grass to test the wind direction) to help your partner understand the object you are sending their way. And then follow its path as it moves through space to your partner. Agree, together, where the ball is at any moment.

If you are the receiver and you believe a golf ball is coming your way, pull up the flag from the hole on the green. Crouch to view whether the green is level. Be extremely quiet and still so as not to interrupt the shot. Anything that engages you and helps your partner know that you are in agreement about what is there in the space and what activity is happening.

Try adding a beach ball. A yoga ball. A marble. A volleyball. A soccer ball. What are the aspects of each of these different balls that would allow you to clearly make the offer of one or another? Their size. How they move. How you interact with them. What other objects are commonly used with the ball. Really SEE the object and really use it. If you make it real for yourself, your partner will likely see it, too.

And, be sure, just like our Point Yes exercise, that you have agreement before you jump ahead. With several objects moving around the room, your partners' attention is divided. Once you have found someone to receive your offer, take a moment to re-establish the object for them. It is highly likely that they did not see you catch a baseball. So if you throw it to them with one hand, just as you caught it, they may not get the necessary details. For clarity's sake, build the object for them.

What if you have never played volleyball? Or previously handled any object that is being offered to you? What if you know how to play a particular sport, but in actuality you weren't very good at it? It doesn't matter. USE your mirroring and engage with confidence. Your partner is not going to let you down. They will adapt with you. TRY to see what your partner sees, and then respond in kind.

It happens all the time with spacework that even though we think we are defining objects SO clearly, and working with specificity toward agreement with our partners, they may still interpret our offer differently than we intended. This should never be happening intentionally, but it DOES happen. A lot.

The guiding principle is that you must say 'yes.' So if things change as your partner responds to your offer (say that volleyball becomes a beach ball because of the way your partner received and interacted with it, for example), when the object comes back to you, it is whatever the current offer tells you it is. There is no holding on to past offers and it is not your job to FIX the 'mistake.' Take each offer as though it is the first. Respond to it without preconceptions.

At this point we have several different balls passing around the circle. After it seems like every player has had a chance to handle each at least once, I ask the group to freeze. Whoever currently has a ball should raise their hand. A couple of things start to become obvious. First, we usually lose one of the objects. We may have introduced four or five or six, and now we are reduced by one. What happened? Offers get missed. We don't actually get agreement from our partner and we go ahead and pass it to them anyway. We literally forget there was another object there. We get two balls at the same time and only successfully pass one back. It further underscores how important a consistent and heightened focus is.

Second, if we have managed to maintain our total number of objects, SPECIFIC objects have likely morphed into something else. We often end up with multiple basketballs or baseballs where there should have only been one. There is often lots of chatter once we stop the exercise and we start to ask one another 'what was that?' Lots of 'aahhhh's when people realize that a certain ball was something they didn't recognize during the game. When your partner made a specific gesture and you thought it was something completely different. It's all perfectly fine, as long as you were really focused on your partner, and really trying to observe the details they were creating.

Again, specificity is everything. And it starts from your actor's imagination— really SEEing the object, and the space. If you were working on scripted material, this is all the daydreaming and crafting you would do to build a character, to assign meaning to objects and words—all to more fully and truthfully engage with your partner and the circumstances of the scene. Actor's faith. BELIEVE it.

I should say that I have also seen productions where spacework was used to great effect to better tell the story. One in particular was a one-woman performance from Carey Mulligan in a play titled "Girls & Boys" written by Dennis Kelly. Yes, there was a full set and props, but it is a memory play and she would live out the story at times interacting with characters and objects that were not present. So, not only is spacework good practice for firing up the actor's imagination, it can also be practically applied stagecraft to better tell a story.

Actors are often quick to dismiss spacework as something that they will 'never actually have to do.' I say, if you build the skill of spacework, whether you ever improvise a scene or not, if you can create all those details and connections to something that does not physically exist in the space, and make it real for yourself and your partners, IMAGINE how those objects will come to life for you when you DO have that chipped cup from Grandma's tea service that is the only item you have left to remember her. Or you DO have that tattered leather-bound journal where you kept your secrets. Or you DO have that bright pink bridesmaid's dress from your sister's wedding. The skill of spacework serves you in profound ways and deepens your work, both scripted and unscripted.

Objects and environments and clothing help us create character and place. They are the visible counterparts to all the same details and clues we are working to create through spacework when we improvise. They can be just as alive and just as real for us. We just have to imagine and then COMMIT. We have to SEE it and BELIEVE it exists. No different than the belief that we are a certain character or in a certain place or telling a certain story from a script we've been rehearsing.

So, let's expand the work. At this point, I encourage you to put the book down and spend the next 24 hours witnessing objects and activities that are common for you. Be curious about everything. All the sensations and experiences we take for granted. If you make coffee, do you grind your own? Do you make it by the cup? By the pot? Where do you keep your coffee and your coffee maker? What does it smell like? Specifically. Not just 'it smells like coffee.' Does it smell smoky? Or rich? Is the smell strong or mellow? Is the grind fine or coarse? If you keep it in a canister, is the canister full or nearly empty? How do you scoop it? With a spoon? A little white plastic scoop that you keep in the canister with the coffee? Do you use filters? A pour over? Just like our observation exercise, the details seem infinite. Try to notice it all. What every object feels like in your hand. Its weight. Its temperature. Its size.

Close your eyes and replay the whole experience. SEE everything. Test whether there are details you missed. Then find a space free of the objects you need and recreate the activity using only spacework. Feel all the same details. Smell the same aromas. Don't gloss over the specifics. If one of your partners was observing you recreating this activity, would they be able to give you details? Would they be able to tell that the mug you drank from was red and not white? That it was 12 oz. and not a demitasse. Would they be able to describe your kitchen or your coffee maker? What you're wearing? Where you keep your spoons?

Consistency is really key. If you pull open a cabinet door, which way does it move? If you open it, did you close it after? Does the handle of the door magically come off, or does it move in the same path opening as it does closing? The clearer you can be, the better chance exists that your partners will be able to accept the offers as you intended.

Spacework & Environments

**TRY IT.
Do an activity with objects.
Then recreate the activity
with only spacework.**

Spacework eating and drinking can be tricky. Be sure to chew and swallow. And, although your mother would not approve, hold food in your mouth while you talk.

It bears repeating that we start with our own frame of reference. Our own experience. But ours is not necessarily the same as someone else's. You may live in a big house while your partner lives in a small studio apartment. Your door may be on the left, your partner's may be on the right. START with what you know, but always work with the understanding that even the most detailed spacework may be interpreted differently than you intended. And, do your best not to let it frustrate you. Your partner is not TRYING to derail you. They just observed something and applied their own frame of reference and understanding to it, and said 'yes.' Just like with the Sound Ball work, if it changes, work to find agreement, not to return it to its former state. Don't hold on to your own ideas and try to make your partner come around. Make a clear offer and then be willing to let it go in pursuit of finding agreement, however it comes.

Notice everything. Your bed. Your bathroom. What you can see out your window, if you have one in your room. Engage all your senses and deeply experience everything for a day. Then bring one of those activities to share with your partners.

Acting is about behavior. It's about the doing. As such, we involve ourselves in scenes and with our partners through activities. Activities and spacework ground us in the environment and in the scenes. Give yourself the gift at the beginning of any interaction to 'take in' the space. To set about DOING something. It will jump-start your imagination so you can lose yourself in the activity. You will see objects clearly and get immersed in the world you are creating. You shouldn't have to TRY. If you really DO the activity, you don't have to invent anything. And you don't have to worry about it being 'interesting.' You needn't look for problems. If you are cooking, you don't have to make a mess, or drop something, or accidentally cut your finger. Do your task, and do it well.

It always surprises me that, given the opportunity to IMAGINE doing an activity and creating it using spacework, people choose to be BAD at it. Why? Do it with confidence. You may be given the suggestion to perform surgery in a scene. You may not be a doctor in your real life, but why not be an excellent doctor in improvisation? You may not know the terminology or the procedures, but who cares? What you offer, what you create, is how surgery is done in THIS world, in THIS scene.

We don't want to fall into the trap of calling out everything unfamiliar. When we don't understand, we get insecure, so we start to make the scene about the fact that something is 'weird' or 'wrong' or that someone doesn't know what they're doing. "You're not a doctor!" Instead, we have to find the place where we say 'yes', and we do that by engaging physically and joining the activity. Mirror. Do what your partner is doing. Don't stand on the sidelines trying to figure out what's going on. Get in there and do the same thing. I guarantee you will find the answer faster by finding it together. Sidelining yourself is just your fear of getting it wrong. I say, there is no wrong unless you make it so. And making you look good is your partner's job, so they've got you. Go for it!

So, bring an activity in to share with the others. You don't need to 'perform' anything. You don't need to worry about entertaining us. We just want you to DO your task. If you catch yourself missing a detail or skipping a step, take a moment and reset and try again. Take the time to reestablish. As you get going, and as the others start to recognize what you're doing, I ask them to raise their hands. Once a majority have an idea what your task is, finish up what you're doing, and then let's check in. Let's see if we got it right. What did we see? What did we miss? What was that thing that you held when you did that other thing? Ohhhhhhh! What assumptions did we make? What assumptions did you make?

Often this brings the discussion back to the quintessential elements of any activity. What is absolutely clear? What distinguishes a blender from a coffee maker? How do we know it's coffee and not tea? How do we know you're making soup and not pasta sauce? What is the difference between chopping celery and carrots? The answer may not always be clear. And that's the point. We may be as specific as we can be, and STILL our partners may see something different. It's OK. Just agree and move forward.

Something else I notice when we are sharing these activities with one another is that it often takes someone quite a few beats to get to the actual activity. At this point, there is no pressure to speed through anything, but improvised scenes tend to be short, and the establishing spacework needs to be efficient. Here's what I mean:

Say someone is doing object work of brushing their teeth. They start by putting on their pajamas. Walking into the bathroom. Washing their hands. Drying them. Looking in the mirror. Opening a cabinet. Collecting items on the side of the sink. By the time they actually put brush to teeth (the ACTUAL, intended activity), we have gone about five or ten beats into the scene. Chances are, if this WAS a scene where one of your partners was going to enter, they would already have entered before you ever got to the toothbrushing.

You had clearly seen that this was YOUR apartment bathroom. It was nighttime and you were starting your bedtime routine. It is Friday so you don't have work tomorrow. You're wearing your Sesame Street pajamas. Whatever YOU see. But before the toothbrushing has even happened, your partner enters and identifies that you are at the kitchen sink. That there is a dinner party going on and she didn't know where you went off to. And all of those offers were based off what your partner witnessed. Perhaps there were some details you missed—that QUINTESSENTIAL bit of spacework that would tell your partner they were Sesame Street pajamas and not some other shirt or pants.

None of this is a problem. I just raise it to remind us that the offers come fast and furious, and we need to focus on getting to the good stuff when we do spacework. If your partner needs to know that you are brushing your teeth, then get to that. USE the toothbrush and DO the activity.

Now, it probably wouldn't matter, ultimately, because what we have already established is that if offers are not received as intended, we just agree with what was offered last and respond and build on that. You may have to pivot to the dinner party offer and say 'yes' to that. Recognize in those moments, (which happen a lot), whether your instinct is to hang on to what you had in mind, or if you are able to freely shift to the clearest offer. Would you, in the example we just shared, have insisted that the party ended hours ago and you are already in your Sesame Street pajamas? Would you call out your partner as wrong or crazy, or that she is dreaming, as a way to discount her offer and hold on to your own plan, so that you can be 'right'? Many people do, without even realizing they have that habit.

It can feel frustrating when your partner doesn't pick up on your offer. But, instead of blaming them for failing to appreciate your brilliantly executed work, be MORE brilliant by deftly adapting to what the scene and your partner needs from moment to moment. You may surprise yourself by having a lot of fun exploring an idea that wasn't originally yours.

In a later chapter, we will discuss the concept of justification, which is a tool we use as improvisers to help bring seemingly disparate or confusing offers into the fold. We accept something that feels inorganic, and we seamlessly weave it into the story. We don't reject it, we build on it and find out why it's important to the scene... More on that to come.

For now, keep exploring different activities. Do the activity in 'real' life. And then do it as spacework. This practice is essential to develop your imagination, to help you stay curious, and eventually it will require less of your attention. Object and spacework is so important to improvisation. It is the root of the who, what and where of the scene—all things that we must identify in order to be able to feel grounded and move forward with the story. But we need to get to a place with our craft that the spacework happens effortlessly. Our imagination can see everything in an instant, and once we have it, we can move in and through the space and handle the objects as we would with any of our daily routines. We don't THINK about how we make our coffee each morning, we just do it. Spacework can be like that, too. And once we get closer to that level of work, the more attention we can turn to observing other offers in the space. The more we KNOW, the less we need to discover, or remember.

Sometimes, we bring habits from our imaginary play as kids into our spacework without realizing. Carrying something with a closed fist, as I previously mentioned, instead of giving it actual space and weight in our hand. Slicing our fingers together in the air to indicate scissors instead of really shaping and moving our hands as we would if we were holding an actual pair of scissors. Pointing a gun by using our index finger as the barrel and our erect thumb as the trigger, instead of shaping our hand as we would if we had an actual pistol and had a finger on the trigger ready for our high noon shootout. Another common one is chopping things with the side of our hand instead of properly holding a knife by its handle. I tend to call out all these habits when I see them, because I think it's important to know that they exist, and to be aware that we often forget the reality.

This is not to say that every time you realize you have done some bit of spacework imprecisely that you should call it out. We all fall into the trap of being vague and losing specificity with our spacework. But that doesn't mean that when you notice it has to become a big dramatic moment. IF you were AC-

TUALLY holding a knife and handling it carelessly, you may cut your finger. But when you realize you were handling your space-object knife carelessly, simply adjust yourself to be more specific, rather than creating a problem, or saying 'It's magic! You cut right through your hand and you didn't even get hurt! You must be a ghost!' We simply want the activity and object work to ground us in a reality, not to take over the scene.

Personally, I think spacework is the hallmark of good improvisation. Watching improvisers standing still talking to one another is boring and unimaginative. And I think how much harder they are making it for themselves having to talk everything into existence—essentially 'commenting' and that's all. The players are not fully engaged. They are not connected to the world. In fact, they haven't even created one. We are left to assume that they are who we already know them to be. That this scene is taking place in this exact room, with these exact people. At this exact time. If improv and your imagination can take you ANYWHERE, why cheat yourself by choosing to play safe and imagining little to nothing? I say, get yourself into trouble. That's where the fun is.

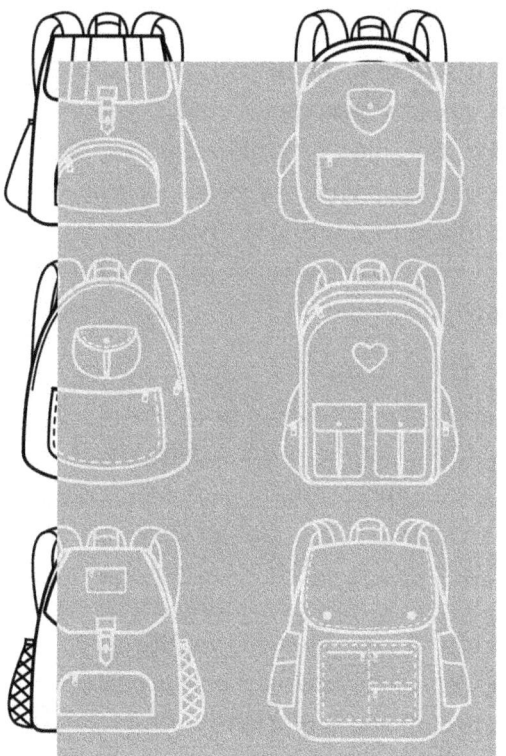

The beauty of spacework is that whatever you need is always within reach. Whatever object you require, you can create through spacework—as long as it takes up space, you really see it, handle it with integrity, and it doesn't just pop out of thin air. Although I'm not one for relying on improv tricks, I will often enter a scene carrying a bag or a backpack. Like Mary Poppins' carpetbag, a spacework bag can magically produce a myriad of useful things to keep any offer or activity moving forward. You'll have the tools you need right at your disposal, as if you KNEW you would need the objects all along.

ENVIRONMENTS

So far, most of the spacework discussion has been about objects. But, it expands to the larger world of environments. We can create vivid and real places through our spacework. And the same skills apply. We just need to SEE where we are, and then interact with the world.

It bears mentioning that although we are dealing with the reality we see and the reality we create in our scenes, sometimes object work can feel untruthful. We may clearly SEE a table in the middle of a large medieval banquet hall, but until we physically contact the objects and the space, it will be difficult (if not impossible) for our partners to see what we see. That means putting our hands out to show the height. Running our hand along the edge to show the perimeter. Walking AROUND the object to consistently establish the space it takes up. That it is solid and mostly immovable. We may think that if that table were physically there, we would not have to contact it so much. That's probably true. But it is NOT physically there, so we need to do the constant work of coming back to the objects over and over so that they stay present. Particularly large and immovable objects. Contact the space.

This would also suggest that **keeping it simple is the best way forward. Establish a FEW objects and use those objects repeatedly.** And, if you enter a scene, be sure that you interact with the objects that have already been established. Demonstrate through your spacework and behavior that you 'agree' that those objects exist and that they are important. There is no sense in creating an object in a scene that is not relevant or never gets used. It becomes just one more thing to be forgotten.

I think the impulse to create LOTS of objects comes from two places: first, we are used to having a lot of stuff around us. But in improv the only things that exist are the ones we clearly establish. Second, we are convinced that our world and our offers are not interesting enough so we keep inventing things. I say, let a few key items be enough. Build on the spacework offers the way you would any offer. Say 'yes' and see where it takes you.

The build usually comes from endowments—the same way you would if you were crafting something for a scripted scene. You would daydream a bit about what the objects mean to you. Why they are important. And let your imagination create some 'as if's to make the object more real, even when your prop physically exists. It's not just a picture frame. It's a frame your father made by hand. It has a nick in the corner from the time you threw it down after a particularly difficult argument with your dad. It is one of the only things you have left of his.

When we improvise, we can 'and' an offer by giving it endowments. We always START by physically contacting the object to define it. And then we can add verbal endowments as easily as 'saying what you see.' Once you agree that there is a photo frame, let your imagination REALLY see it. Every detail. And through a combination of how you physically interact with the object and what you say, we come to understand it even more clearly. "You repainted it pink! Your favorite color!" "You kept it! I didn't think you liked my gift." "It's dusty. And the picture is yellowing. This must be 100 years old! What a find!"

Adding some observational details, particularly those that would be difficult to establish through physical object work alone, can help make objects more real. In those cases, they start to give us clues about the characters and their history as well, but we will talk more about the 'who' later. For now, we are focused on the 'what' and the 'where.' What are you doing, and where is it happening?

Let's combine objects and environments into a fun game called Mission: Impossible. In this game, a player will enter a space. For this game, we will discuss ahead of time what type of space it is, so that we are not going in completely blind. So, let's say this is a luxury hotel suite. The place to start is always with what we know and what we expect to be true. Starting from something familiar and real means that you don't have to invent everything.

So, what sorts of objects and things would you imagine would be in a luxury hotel suite? A large bed. Luxury linens and bedding. Bedside tables. Lamps. A chandelier? Plush carpet. Maybe a balcony with sliding doors. A sofa and sitting area. A large screen TV. A big, tiled bathroom with a claw foot tub. Floor to ceiling drapery. A safe. A wet bar or mini bar. Phone. Coffee table. Paintings. Mirrors. Doors.

Although we all have different experiences and perspectives, if we can find a common denominator, it lays a good foundation for the scene. This is not to say that before a scene begins we always discuss the details. That's not what improv is. I am just saying that keeping it 'real' is a lot easier place from which to build than if you invent everything from scratch. There will be PLENTY to figure out, so try to reduce that number of things when you can.

One by one, a player is going to enter this hotel room—a master spy in search of a small thumb drive with crucial government secrets. First spy, 001, is going to establish the entry door, and one other object in the room through spacework. Does the door open in or out? Is it a key or a swipe card? Or touchless? Does the door make a sound? Does it close on its own? What type of handle does it have?

Your fellow players will need to pay close attention to your spacework details. The room does not change from person to person. We want to be sure that every player who enters interacts with the space in the same way, and that no details are missed.

So 001 entered, established the big king-size bed in the middle of the room, where she found the thumb drive between the mattresses. Then "WEE-OOO-WEE-OOO-WEE-OOO!!!" An alarm sounds. Quickly, 001 must hide the thumb drive in a new place, and get out of the room. She chooses to drop to the floor, pull up a corner of the bedside rug and tuck the thumb drive underneath. And then stealthily reopens the door, exits and closes it behind her.

Next up: 002. He must enter the hotel room using the door 001 established. He must look first for the thumb drive on the bed. But it doesn't seem to be between the mattresses where it should be. 002 looks around and notices the bedside rug. Aha! Sure enough, he goes to the floor, pulls up the corner and finds the thumb drive. "WEE-OOO-WEE-OOO-WEE-OOO!!!" 002 has to hide the thumb drive in a new place and get out unseen. He sees a floor lamp on the other side of the bed by the window, rushes around the perimeter of the bed (helping to once again re-establish its location and size), pulls off the lamp shade, unscrews the bulb, hides the thumb drive in the socket, screws the bulb back in, puts the lampshade back on, and gets out of the room through the door. Whew!

You see where this is going, and you see how much more difficult it gets as more and more objects are established. Soon we will have another room or two. We may have a balcony. We may find the thumb drive behind a mirror

next time, or on top of the drapes, or in the toilet tank. And before each subsequent spy finds the thumb drive, they must look in ALL the previous places.

One thing I like to point out is what happens to the spacework when the alarm goes off. We start to get sloppy. As soon as there is pressure to act quickly, we tend to lose all of the detail. You'll need to find for yourself what it takes to be able to act quickly and STILL give clear, unrushed offers. The objects that tend to be forgotten, once we get to Agents 009, or 010, are the ones that were never clearly established to begin with. From the first time we saw the object, no one was really sure whether 006 put the thumb drive in a bookcase or a minibar. It was too general to really identify because 006 was in such a rush to play the game and get out. You have to be able to do both, which is why we practice the skill.

So, if you were 007, who followed 006, and you were not sure whether it was a minibar or a bookcase, you have the opportunity when YOU handle that object to re-establish or add some detail that will help you and your partners who follow you to be more clear. So, you approach the object, after checking the other places it should be, and show us that it is indeed a minibar because you grab one of the tiny bottles of booze and take a swig before finding the thumb drive. That extra, clarifying detail will help your partners. I'll bet that all the spies who follow will now remember the minibar. We are all collectively relieved to have agreement about the object. One less thing to be unsure about.

As the game goes on, I find that the later spies tend to like to be more flashy than the earlier ones, too. Part of that is that they have just had way more time to think about what they might do when they get up. They also have a lot of pent up excitement when they finally get their chance to play. I just want to be sure that you acknowledge where you are on this continuum. Are you able to take in offers and give your attention to the moment WITHOUT starting to plan your own moves? Do you start to think about what you'll 'fix' or how you'll do it 'better?' Do you stop paying attention and start to imagine how well-received your clever idea will be?

Be honest with yourself. And do the work of staying present with your partners, even when you are not in the scene. So much of what I learned in acting class came from watching others. We see how they solve the problems of the scene, and are especially delighted when it is a choice that never would have occurred to us. Each person brings their unique self and perspective to the work, as do you. Get excited about jumping into someone else's offers and seeing where they take you. Just like when we were mirroring, by simply and generously following someone, we find ourselves moving in a new way. We have much to learn from one another through the collaboration of improv.

Object work in improvisation is DOING. But spacework may actually live more in the realm of BEING—in pursuit of 'living truthfully in imaginary circumstances.' There is never a need to be 'busy' with spacework, but you should always start any scene by engaging physically. When I see people stuck not knowing what to do next, it is usually because they are just standing there trying to reason it out intellectually. When someone is standing still, the imagination is being pushed to the back. Instead, we should connect with the 'what' and the 'where' through active spacework, and let the story reveal itself organically. Once you are engaged in activity, you forget about your need to make anything happen or to be interesting. **The being comes out of the doing, and the doing leads to change.**

When we are in acting class working on scripted material, we do our homework. We prepare before the scene. We spend time connecting to the material, the character, the place, the circumstances. And then what is the last thing we do before we enter a scene? We leave ourselves alone. We stop actively trying to craft, and we refocus on being present in the moment, and allowing each moment to lead us to the next. Activities keep us connected to the space and to our objective. And it is from that place that change emerges. It is why an actor who delivers the same dialogue night after night on stage, or take after take on film, can have a profoundly different experience each time. It is from the observation of the behavior, borne out of activity, that leads to these subtle (and sometimes not so subtle) shifts. Who knows what observation will drive a scene? Who knows how you will react next time? **Be open to each moment, and even when you are rehearsed and know EXACTLY what you will say and when, no one can guarantee how it will happen for you. How it will feel. How it will bring you to life.**

We've created an environment together in our hotel room spy game, but each of us worked individually. That's not usually how it goes in scenes. So, let's work a bit on sharing activities and objects and environments.

Someone should start an activity using spacework. Just like we did when we shared our activities for each other. Set about doing something, and get into the flow. Establish objects. Use them. Be clear. Really SEE the space and the objects. And then just DO your task. There is no pressure. No drama. We don't need problems and mishaps.

Before too long, let's have one of your partners enter the space you've created. Their sole objective is to JOIN your task. For your partner entering, they MAY know what you're doing, they may not. It doesn't matter, in the sense that even the most observant person will miss clues, or see something differently than you intended. What your partner IS going to do is to try to find agreement with you. They are going to engage with you and the objects. They are going to work with you on your task.

The best place to start, in my opinion, is with mirroring, especially if your partner is unsure what you are doing or about specific objects you've created. Perhaps you are a master tailor, and your partner has never threaded a needle. Regardless, they will TRY. And simply by mirroring, they can immediately join you in your task and continue to look for clarity as the moments happen—until you both find agreement.

It is not your job to TEACH your partner what to do, or correct their interpretations of your object work. **Your responsibility, when someone joins your scene, is to SHARE your activity with them.** That also means responding to THEIR offers. We want to maintain a reality in the scene, but we are early in the process and want to work on our adaptability, as well.

Remember to keep it simple, and don't over-invent. We don't need fifteen objects to keep track of when our activity really only relies on three. Use the objects repeatedly. Pick them up and put them down. Share them. Even better, handle the same object TOGETHER. If you are making up your bed, fold or unfold the sheets together. Take separate sides and explore how you can cooperate to make the sheet real. Or maybe you are cleaning, and you need to move the bed so that you can sweep underneath it. Move the bed frame together. One pushes and one pulls. Or you can try pushing from the same side. Solve the problems. Meaning: use your imagination to really see the object and to create its size, weight and function, and then handle it with integrity.

Don't create problems for the sake of drama. You are folding the sheet and it snags on something. You are moving the bed and you stub your toe. Or you huff and you puff but you can't move the bed. Not necessary. Again, the need to create problems is borne out of our deep sense that we are boring. And we have all seen way too many movies. Discover, by working simply, how fascinating things can be. Be curious and let the small things you perhaps never even noticed before be the things that capture your attention.

We have talked about mirroring a lot, but there is another part to mirroring that can also help us to engage physically in the scene. That's **complementing**—joining the same activity as your partner, and picking up some other part of it. If your partner established that she works in the laundry of a hotel and she is moving towels from the washer to the dryer, perhaps you join by holding a basket into which she can transfer the wet towels, and then hold it for her while she loads them into the dryer. Or while she is emptying the washer, you can empty the dryer and begin to fold the towels. You're working on the same task, just complementary parts.

What you'll want to avoid, particularly at the very start of scenes is that your partner goes to one corner, you go to another corner and you each start doing your own thing. I often give the example of cockroaches. When the light goes on, they scurry for the corners, each to save itself. In improvised scenes, on the other hand, always, always work together whenever you can. Scenes are so much richer if we establish a solid foundation of a what and a where, even though the story is rarely ABOUT the activity or the location.

Say you are given a suggestion that you work as a chef. To give you and your partners the best shot at building that strong and simple foundation, ask yourself 'where would this activity most likely take place?' There is no need to be a chef on a moon base. Or to be a chef at the local dump. Start with something 'obvious.' Why complicate things before you even begin? The only thing we know going into this scene is that you are a chef. We ALREADY have to discover what type of chef you are. What you are preparing in this moment. Where you are in the process. Where you are physically. If, on top of all that, you choose to be a chef in zero gravity because you think it'll be more fun, you are making it infinitely harder for your partners to know what you are doing and where you are. And then you'll spend the whole scene playing the game of trying to get the food where you want it to go in zero gravity. It would probably be a laugh, and you'll certainly use your imagination, but we don't want to get ahead of ourselves. Let's not compete in the Olympics until we've run a few local races.

All of our early spacework should be done without talking, as well. We want to avoid the crutch of being able to TELL someone what we're doing. "Hand me the spaghetti so that I can put it into this pot of boiling water on this stove in the kitchen of my apartment." Use your spacework to communicate those offers instead, and explore how you respond when someone inevitably misinterprets your intention. You hold out your hand for the spaghetti, and someone hands you chopped carrots, thinking you are making soup. What do you do? THAT is the skill to build.

You'll recall from our work creating activities for our partners, we talked about finding that quintessential element that will be the perfect clue to clearly distinguish your activity from another. Part of that is 'starting in the middle.' If your activity is to scramble eggs for breakfast, start cracking and scrambling the eggs. If you choose to begin by waking up, using the bathroom, washing your hands, checking your text messages, putting away the dry dishes from last night, taking out a bowl and a fork, getting out the eggs and the milk, the salt and pepper, a pan... My bet would be that your partner would engage after the first beat or so, which means that you may be coming out of the bathroom about the time your partner shows up. And, they would have no idea scrambled eggs were important, or about to happen. And chances are, whatever your partner offers in that moment will be more compelling (however simple or subtle) than what you had planned, and you will probably never get to the scrambled eggs.

Spacework can also help us establish the 'who' in our scenes. The way that we endow objects can highlight their importance and create clear relationships. If I establish a heavy, jeweled crown and I remove it from my head and extend it to you, you may show agreement by kneeling to accept the honor. We begin to see the majestic throne room. The tapestries with the family crest. From the object and the gesture, we can ask 'who might these people be?' If I was wearing the crown, we could safely assume I was the current king. If you knelt before me to accept the crown, we could safely assume you are my successor. My son or daughter.

Like all offers, we say you MUST agree. Yet, no one is telling you how you have to feel about it. You must accept that there is a crown and that I have removed it from my own head and am offering it to you. You agree that the crown is now on your head, signifying you are the new ruler. But, whether you WANT the crown is up to you. Whether you have a good relationship with the king is up to you. What you will do next, in response to the offer, is up to you.

But before ANYthing can happen, we have to build the foundation of the what, where and who through agreement. THEN we can begin to explore our responses and what they mean to the next moment of the story. Until we know what's 'real' in the world of this scene, who inhabits the world, who they are and how they are connected to one another, what they are doing in this moment, and where they are specifically, we're going to be unsteady. And the extra challenge is that all of those establishing elements need to happen pretty quickly. As we move into story and scenes, we'll find how eagerly we want to get to the 'drama,' and how little we have often established when that happens.

Let's do one more challenge around spacework that helps us encompass all three aspects of the platform (the what, the who, and the where): Freeze Tag. It is a fun warm-up, too, that can get us out of our heads.

Standing in our group circle, one person comes to the center and strikes a dynamic pose. No need to INVENT anything. You don't even have to have an idea. In fact, it's worth noticing how often we enter with a bold and specific idea, and have it promptly identified as something different than we intended. And then we have to immediately let go of our original idea and simply respond to the offer at hand. So, build the habit, in this game and in scenes generally, of just DOING. Engaging physically in the space, and seeing what happens. Give yourself permission to just jump in there and take a posture before your brain has a chance to stop you. It's excellent practice for NOT thinking and pre-planning. If planning and controlling is your approach, I am sorry to tell you that you will be disappointed more times than not when your idea takes a turn.

Once someone has frozen in their pose, as soon as you can get there, jump in and join them. I'll remind you that your most direct ways to engage are to either mirror or complement—either do the SAME thing, or find a way to join the activity through a supporting part of the task. If someone has taken a bold pose, prostrate on the floor looking like they are begging for mercy, I could lie down beside them and beg as well. I could mirror their physicality and their intention. (I could be wrong, of course, but 'begging for mercy' is what my gut tells me I see.) Or, I could choose to stand over my partner, wielding a sword to strike them down. Complementary postures need not always be oppositional, or have cause-and-effect relationships. Nor must they be linear, as though you are joining as assembly line. But they ARE related, and they ARE connected. Complementing SUPPORTS and builds on what you see.

Once we have a pair, let's keep rotating people in, for now. So again, without hesitation, I want a third player to step in and tap out one of the two frozen players. When a frozen player is tapped, they respond "Thank you!" and step back to the perimeter of the circle. The person who just entered, now takes a new pose to mirror or complement the remaining poser.

It doesn't have to be related in any way to the pose that came before. It doesn't have to be the next beat of the story. These don't have to be the same characters. They don't have to be in the same place or time as before.

Same as joining before you have a chance to think about what you want to do, tap someone out before you have a chance to think about which one you want to replace. We are trying to work the muscle of DOING, not thinking and planning. Surprise yourself with what you DO.

We can go on this way for a while. Tap someone out. "Thank you!" Take a new pose that mirrors or complements the remaining poser. Tap someone out. "Thank you!" Take a new pose that mirrors or complements the remaining poser. Inevitably we get to a place in the game where we start to slow down, as though players have already run out of impulses. I assure you this is not the case. But it does suggest that we get bored and start to apply pressure to come up with 'better' ideas than what we've seen so far. Or that our ability to focus needs strengthening.

I remind you that your partners need you. They need you to jump in. To support. To inspire the next moment with your response. Your offer. Sometimes, the need is more immediate than others. For instance, someone may jump in and find themselves in an awkward one-legged stance. (Good for them for not playing safe, and for not 'fixing' the predicament they find themselves in.) But, you can help your partner by either tapping them out, or by creating a complementary pose that offers some physical stability or support.

As an aside, (we haven't addressed this point yet), we should always be aware of physical contact and how to make behavior real while still respecting personal space. In fact, I ask my students NOT to touch one another in the early going. If there is to be physical contact, then there must be agreement from all the parties involved that it is acceptable and appropriate for the moment. Any gesture that you feel requires physical contact can be and should be performed, at this stage of the work, with SOME physical distance. It is possible, through our spacework, to gesture as though to hug someone, but to embrace without actually making contact. It may feel strange, but should not feel any more strange than spacework, generally. I just find it better to assume your fellow players DO NOT want the physical contact, so we need to give them a way to find agreement, to say "yes" in those circumstances. Once you have built sufficient trust over time, then physical contact may become a more common part of your scenework. For now, NO TOUCHING.

OK. Let's add to the game a bit. Same idea of one person striking a pose, another person jumping in to mirror or complement, and someone to tap out one of the posers. Once you jump forward, BEFORE you tap someone out, I want you to **say what you see.**

What is happening? What is the activity? What objects do you see? I am not asking you to INVENT. I am asking you to use your actor's imagination to visualize the scene and give us the details. Don't worry about being right. Just say what YOU see. No commentary about whether you like it or not. No judging. Just what you observe, based on the offers of the two posers in front of you.

How we express our offers is important. Build the habit of speaking about what you see as something that you KNOW to be true. You may find yourself using the phrase "I think…" a lot. See if you can choose words to express your offers with confidence and certainty. Your truth is just as valid as another's. "I see…" "I observe…" I know…" Others may visualize it differently, but that is not your concern. Your objective is always to be as specific, clear and certain as possible.

Based on what you identify the activity to be, WHO are these people? WHO would likely be doing this? Unless you see a spacewalk, they don't need to be astronauts, or aliens. We don't need to be clever or inventive. We're actually looking for the clearest relationship. It is OK to see two friends. Or lovers. Or family. Or coworkers. Or schoolmates. Additional details are helpful, always, but we don't need drama and we don't need story. We don't need you to tell us what one person did to the other that made them mad. We don't need you to create reasons for the pose. Just say what you see.

And give them names. Names can tell us a lot about a character. Perhaps they have a title. Perhaps their name suggests something about their nature. If the person you see is angelic, perhaps her name is Angela. Or Feather. Or Halo. I once used the name Milgret in a scene—some combination of Mildred and Margaret—and it captured that character perfectly. Don't THINK about it, just say what comes to you. Maybe you call the players by their actual names. That's OK. Maybe you use your friend's name or a sibling's name. Maybe you use your own name. It's all OK. Let's just add the detail so we can move ahead.

You'll find in scenes that using character names repeatedly is important. Not only does it help us find agreement, it builds reality and protects us from forgetting the names entirely. I have seen way too many improvised scenes where we spend wasted beats trying to answer why someone called someone the wrong name or forgot their name. **Just like with objects, repeated use is the key. If you keep it simple and keep coming back to it, you are way more likely to recall it.**

And then, based on what you've told us so far about what you observe is the what and the who, WHERE would this likely take place? If you see two best friends named Sarah and Ben flying a kite, they don't need to be doing so on the moon. The obvious truth is probably a back yard or a park. Why unnecessarily complicate the setup? My sense is always that it comes from that same place of insecurity about being uninteresting. Or not clever enough. But, you do yourself a solid to establish these elements of the platform clearly and quickly so we can get to what the scene is REALLY about—usually the relationship between the players. Rarely will the scene be ABOUT the who, where or what. But we need to establish these things before we can move on, as we will more clearly understand in the work ahead.

Once you have 'said what you see,' THEN tap someone out and take a mirroring or complementing pose, just as we did before. After focusing your attention on your partners and on describing to us what you see, hopefully you have forgotten any idea you had when you first stepped forward to tap someone out. Good! Just take a fresh look, tap someone and GO! "Thank you!"

ENVIRONMENTS

I-MAP-GINATION:
Take out a blank sheet of paper.
Draw whatever location you see. It may be the room where you are right at this moment, or it may be a place you can remember in vivid detail.
Use the drawing to create a location for your scene.

MEMORY MAP:
Observe a room in your home.
Go into another room and draw a detailed map of everything you remember. Now, go back into the first room and make a list of the details you missed, and be curious about why those things were either not noticed at all, or were forgotten.

ENDOWMENTS

SEE, PLUS 3:
Name a person place or thing and give three details about it/them.
Let your imagination really SEE it.
Build the habit of immediately identifying at least three details for each offer.

3

Story Building & The Shakeup

There is a danger as we move ahead. And that is that are going to begin using our words. I identify this as a danger simply because it tends to put us into our heads. We try to control the narrative by playwriting, instead of listening and responding. So, be aware of this trap as we take the next steps. Do your best to stay focused on your partners and the offers they give, and to resist the temptation to think ahead. 'When it gets to me, I'm gonna say "marshmallow" because I like marshmallows and I want to bring marshmallows into the story, and I think it could be funny.' The MOMENT any of your attention shifts to this type of planning and thinking, it inherently blocks your attention on others. You are no longer REALLY listening. We THINK we are. But, truth be told, not completely. We've got too many 'good' ideas brewing to give our attention to someone else. (Now I want a marshmallow.)

In the previous chapter, we discussed the elements of the platform of any scene—the who, what and where. We make these reality through our spacework offers. We use our actor's imagination to really SEE these details. And, essentially, we SAY what we SEE. We TELL the story of what is unfolding before us.

Let's start exploring story through its connection to agreement. Specifically, let's tell stories using "Yes...And." We'll make this one a pass-along story. Each player will add a little something to build on what was offered before. But, remember: the challenge is to make sure you LISTEN to the ENTIRE offer before you can move ahead. You can't have complete agreement if you only hear a part of the offer. The clever ideas we cook up in our heads tend to clog our hearing. So, we'll make sure, in this first story exercise, that we are focused on the habit of listening.

Let's arrange ourselves in a circle, since that form is very conducive to a pass-along story. One person will start the story with a simple observation, and make that offer directly to their partner, standing to their right. **Repetitions in our Meisner work begin with an observation. Scenes begin with observation. And this story begins with an observation.** Let's establish a basic truth and see where it takes us when we agree and respond.

"The sky is cloudy." A simple observation. All throughout this story, focus on just adding the NEXT detail, rather than trying to control it or push it in the direction you want it to go. We don't need to look for drama.

So, we have "The sky is cloudy." Now the next person is going to confirm they have listened to the offer completely by repeating what was said, in this form: by first saying "Yes!" "Yes! The sky is cloudy. And..." So we verbally agree by saying "Yes!" Then we repeat the last offer. THEN we add the next detail, building on what came before, and offer THAT directly to the next person in the circle. Begin to visualize the story as it unfolds. Really see the cloudy sky. Stay out of your planning brain. "Yes! The sky is cloudy... And it looks like rain."

Great! We're off! So the person in the circle who just received the last offer confirms they were listening by saying "Yes!" and repeating the offer. No need to start at the beginning every time—just the last offer made. The "And." "Yes! It looks like rain." Then turn to the next person in the circle and make the next offer. "And thunder clapped."

Next person: "Yes! Thunder clapped." [Turn to your partner] "And it poured."

Next person: "Yes! It poured." [Turn to your partner] "And water began to rise."

Next person: "Yes! Water began to rise." [Turn to your partner] "And it reached the rooftops."

Next person: "Yes! It reached the rooftops." [Turn to your partner] "And created a big lake."

Next person: "Yes! It created a big lake." [Turn to your partner] "And attracted many fish."

Next person: "Yes! It attracted many fish." [Turn to your partner] "And…"

We just keep going. Listening to the complete offer. Saying "Yes!" Repeating what we just learned, then adding the next thing. It is REALLY important to keep to the structure of the "Yes…And" story and to use those exact words in our offers. We are trying to build the habit of listening and agreeing FIRST, before we make any offer of our own.

Can you begin to see how we only need to add a little piece of information or detail? We don't have to explain the whole idea. In fact, I want us to get in the habit of leaving room for others. Let someone else build on what you offer. If you tell the whole story by yourself, that's only fun for you. And you are much less likely to be surprised by what happens. To me, the surprise is the fun part.

It is very common, when we start telling stories together, each adding our little piece, that we STILL try to goose things along. We don't believe that what is happening is enough, so we try to spark the drama. Or shock our partners. Or make them uncomfortable. In other words, we try to manipulate the story for our own amusement. I can't tell you the number of times in early storytelling that people vomit, or shit themselves, or die, or kill. Or become magical.

"The sky is cloudy" is enough. From that simple observation, we had a town flood, and a fish community form. And who knows where the rest of the story will go. Trust that a simple, organic offer is enough. We don't need that meteor to crash down for something interesting to happen. We need to invest in the story, listen, and see what unfolds as each person adds the next detail.

You also saw, in this first example, how we begin to lay the foundation of the who, where and what. It is natural for us to paint the picture of the world and to follow the thread of action. And our stories (and scenes) should absolutely be active. Our habits (good and bad) appear early when we begin telling stories.

Even in the "Yes...And" structure, you will find people trying to negate the offer they just heard. We are literally saying "Yes!" Yet they want the story to go their way, so they reverse the offer. Say, for example our story began as it did: "The sky is cloudy." And the next person responds, "Yes! The sky is cloudy. And it cleared up." Seems innocent enough, I guess. Weather DOES change. But, the problem is that even though the player listened well enough to repeat what was offered, they then went on to reverse the offer, as though it wasn't true to begin with. We never honored the offer of the sky being cloudy.

"But" is a telltale word for negating an offer. In fact, even as we use the specific words "Yes...And" we will hear some people say "Yes...But." As soon as you hear that "but," you know someone's offer is about to get killed.

Sometimes people are well-intentioned when they negate in group storytelling. When we encounter things that make us uncomfortable (like the aforementioned vomit and shit and murder, etc., that pop up), we often want to 'fix' it. For ourselves and for the group. I don't want to tell (or listen) to a story about poop, either. Yet we want to be careful, in these early stages, not to say that some negation is good and some negation is bad. I want everyone to play to the height of their intelligence. The bathroom, shock humor is a carryover of the 'improv COMEDY' connection, and we want to avoid it here.

Likewise, if someone or something dies in the story, some people want to reverse that. I say, see where the story goes. Let your actor's imagination work. Maybe this story will reveal to us what REALLY happens when our pet dies. Where they go and what they do. And if we stop and reverse course every time something gets uncomfortable, we will never see where it leads.

I often observe that our imaginations seem wired to create every TERRIBLE scenario. That, as actors, we tend to LOOK for the drama and the pain so that we can have an experience that brings us to life. That makes us rant. Or scream. Or cry. Yet, I also believe the imagination is equally capable of generating POSITIVE scenarios. Of seeing possibilities that do not end in pain and failure, or sickness, or death. What's wrong with exploring the AMAZING outcomes that could happen? We never get there if we can't get past the uncertainty and awkwardness of being uncomfortable.

With the "Yes...And" stories, it can be difficult to find the ending. They can seem to go on and on, and nothing may seem to happen. That's a good place to be, for now. I want us to be conditioned to be OK just adding the next little thing. Sharing the building of the story. Not trying to control it or make it what we want. By the time the offer comes around the circle to you again, it may be vastly different than when you last had your say. You can't drag the story back to where YOU left off. You only have the offer that is right in front of you. And, we challenge ourselves to keep our attention on that moment, and that moment only, by verbally agreeing and repeating the last thing said.

If you catch yourself paraphrasing, leaving out or changing certain words, that is an indication you are not fully listening. You are repeating what you WANTED to hear, or what was important to YOU. It is not your job to be the judge who decides which parts of your partner's offer were good or bad. You don't get to decide which parts of it are worth moving forward. Your partner's offer is as much yours as it is their own, and likewise your offer is not yours—it belongs to all the players. So share. Be generous. Listen and respond.

Now, I want us to work with a slightly more prescriptive story structure. One that has a few more guardrails to get us going in the right direction, to lay a strong foundation. And then some signposts to look out for along the way, to keep us all on the same page. It is, however, just a foundation. There are still infinite ways the stories can be created and colored. My colleague, filmmaker Christina Kallas, when we were working together at NYU, described screenwriting to me in a similar way: Each scene is like a box. And that box has a function in the collection of all the boxes. That box can be filled or painted with any number of options. Characters. Places. Things. Actions.

So it is in our improv storytelling. A beat can be whatever you can imagine, as long as it fulfills its function in the narrative. The story structure we're going to use next explores this idea, and in many ways becomes a map for our scenes.

These next stories are all going to start with "Once upon a time..." So the person who begins the story will start with those words, followed by a few details about who and where. "Once upon a time, there was a mouse named Charlie who lived at the base of a huge oak tree, atop a hill." No need to give us a paragraph. But in a few words, we now know WHO the story is about, and something about the world our character inhabits. He lives in nature. He is very small compared to his world. He is atop a hill.

I started this example with a non-human. Somehow, the words "Once upon a time..." put my imagination into fantasy or fairy tales. The story doesn't need to be fantastical to work or to be interesting. I could have started "Once upon a time, there was a working-class bus driver named Ralph who lived in a small Brooklyn apartment with his wife Alice." We know his name. We know he's married. We know where he lives. We know his occupation. We have a clue that he and his wife get by, but are certainly not rich. He has a blue-collar job.

This setup is actually a rip-off of another dated reference of mine: "The Honeymooners." If you haven't seen episodes of this (gasp!) black-and-white TV sitcom starring the incredible Jackie Gleason, do yourself a favor and get familiar. The point is: the who and the where can be ripped from real life, or even be your OWN life, and be a great setup for a story.

And, DO give us salient details. Particularly the character's name. Names, as I said before, can give us a strong clue about the character's nature. Or perhaps the era they are from. A woman named Tiffany may be from the 1980s. Whereas a woman named Mildred may be from the 1940s. Or a woman named Moonbeam may be from the 1960s. Angela-34X may be from the future. Think of opening lines from literature that succinctly set us on a path: "It was a dark and stormy night." Or "Call me Ishmael."

Best, in the early going, to keep the offers in third-person. Try to avoid saying "I." It actually makes a pass-along story very difficult to track if each subsequent person is saying "I." And characters are difficult to track generally when we use "she," "he" or "they." **Use names or descriptives as much as possible, so we can track the offers clearly—who is speaking, and to whom.**

So, once we have our opening, our "Once upon a time..." intro with a where and who, the offer moves to the next person. No need to repeat the phrase that came before, as we did in our "Yes...And" stories. But, maintain the same level of attention and really LISTEN before you build on the offer. The second person in the story begins their offer with "Every day..."

The goal of the second offer is to bring in the activity, the 'what.' Perhaps more importantly, "Every day..." serves to establish a routine. A pattern. And the routine should relate to the details that came from the start. Based on what has been offered so far, we may hear "Every day Charlie would wake with the sun and run down the hill to collect a grain of wheat."

Even though your 'I-know-what-I'll-say-that's-funny-and-clever-and-interesting' brain is probably firing away, the goal of each successive offer is to build organically and simply on what came before, just like in our "Yes...And" stories. Add what the story needs, not what you think would be the most fun or clever. Based on what we learned about Charlie in the first offer, it would be inorganic if "Every day Charlie put on his space suit and rocketed to the moon." Why? Because what's wrong with a mouse doing something a mouse would probably do? I am not discouraging you from imagining vast and varied possibilities. I just want to be sure that we build good habits first. And **one of the strongest habits for improvisers is to keep it simple.** There are already so many unknowns when you improvise, why make it even harder for yourself and your partners by upending reality from the get-go?

In fact, often in storytelling, locking into a genre can help keep you and your partners on the same page. If the story sounds like a romance, then there are certain aspects of romance stories that we can lean on. If the story is an American western, or sci-fi, we can use those tropes. If it is a children's fairy tale, or a pirate adventure, use those elements to build out the world and the action of the story. And the 'imagination' part of it is to really SEE the picture the story paints. **If you SEE it, then you don't have to invent it. You can simply describe what you see.**

Charlie the mouse wakes early and his task for the day is to run down the hill to collect a grain of wheat. The story could still go in many directions. We don't know why Charlie does this. We don't know why he runs. We don't know how long it takes him. We don't know what or who he passes on the way. But we have a simple and strong foundation of a who, where and what. Just like that scenic box my colleague described to me, each beat of our story has a function, and how we color it is up to us.

Alright, third person's offer. This one starts with "One day…" **We take what we know about the character and the world and the routine, and we break the pattern.** Again, what's different about today doesn't have to be a catastrophic event. It merely needs to interrupt the 'everyday' pattern so that we know what our story is about. What question needs to be answered. What idea we are exploring.

Knowing what we know so far, the offer may be "One day Charlie woke up late." Or "One day Charlie was so tired he couldn't run." Or "One day Charlie could not find a single piece of grain." Or "One day, Charlie opened his door to discover a grain of wheat on his doorstep."

We didn't need another character. We didn't need to chase some other thread. Or add something we saw in a movie once. It didn't need to be a catastrophic flood, or fire, or for Charlie to have some sort of injury. (That happens a lot for early storytellers… The way we tend to find drama is through some sort of injury, either physical or emotional.) Nor does it need to be something BAD.

Nothing is inherently good or bad. It is the reaction to the offer that defines it one way or the other. So don't assume you know where it's gonna go. (Another reason why you have to listen intently.) Stay with what you already have.

For this beat of the story, I like to use the analogy of a snow globe. You know, those little glass globes with the water and a little scene (usually a winter scene) inside. We can observe the world as it is (pine trees, a cabin, a clear day) and the characters (happy people, bundled up for warmth, children, couples) and the activity (skiing, ice skating, shopping, playing) clearly. But then we shake the snow globe and things look different. Something has changed. And now we need to explore the consequences of that change and how it effects what we knew to be true about the world and the people in it.

The change can be subtle. It doesn't take much to shift the world—especially if we accept the offers hard, and make seemingly insignificant things important. A flick of the hair, for example, may seem like nothing. Yet if we endow

it with significance and relate it to the story, it can have a huge impact. The whole scene may be about the consequences of that hair flick. And part of that significance comes in this "One day..." moment. We elevate the offer as though we say 'That's new!' 'That's never happened before!' Then we explore what it means, beat by beat, offer by offer, building on what came before.

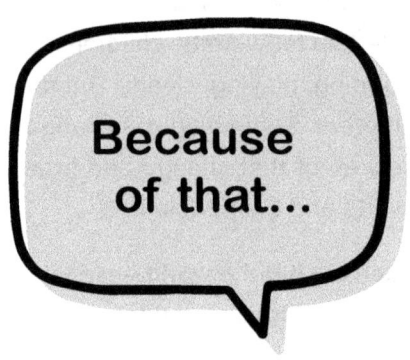

Which leads us to the next series of offers in our pass-along story: the "Because of that..."s. Let's take the last example from above and say that "One day, Charlie opened his door to discover a grain of wheat on his doorstep." The offer building off of that begins with a repetition, and finishes with an expansion of the offer: "Because Charlie opened his door to discover a grain of wheat on his doorstep, Charlie froze in shock."

Throughout the series of "Because of that..." consequences, we repeat the last offer, just as we did in our "Yes...And" stories. We want to be sure we build the habit of listening to the details of the offer before we move ahead with our own offer. So we repeat before we move ahead.

Next person: "Because Charlie froze in shock, Charlie made no sound."

Next person: "Because Charlie made no sound, he could hear EVERYTHING."

Next person: "Because he could hear everything, he heard a familiar voice."

Next person: "Because he heard a familiar voice, Charlie cried "Momma!?""

Next person: "Because Charlie cried "Momma!?" a figure appeared from behind the grain of wheat."

Next person: "Because a figure appeared from behind the grain of wheat, Charlie knew his mother had arrived."

Next person: "Because Charlie knew his mother had arrived, he ran to her and they embraced."

Next person: "Because Charlie ran to his mother and they embraced, they both cried."

Next person: "Because they both cried, the ground became wet with tears."

Next person: "Because the ground became wet with tears, the grain of wheat sank into the ground."

Next person: "Because the grain of wheat sank into the ground, it sprouted."

Next person: "Because the grain of wheat sprouted, wheat grew all across the hill."

It is very common, in the early going, to witness players hesitating before they add to the story. They listen and engage well enough to be able to repeat the last offer, but then SLOOOOOOOOWWWWLY turn to their partner, trying to buy time to think of what to say next. They scan the floor or scour the ceiling looking for the big idea. I point out to them that the answer is not written on the ground or in the sky. Part of the benefit of repeating, besides keeping us focused on listening, is that it is meant to keep you from planning ahead and thinking. Yet for some, this means they get surprised when they have to add their part.

At this stage, improvisers may suffer what I call the "paralysis of possibilities". When the next moment of the story could be ANYTHING, it can feel overwhelming. We feel the pressure to get it 'right', to find the 'best' idea, so we do nothing at all. We're stuck. And then when we realize we're stuck, we panic. We stall. We try to hide. 'If I don't make eye contact with anyone, maybe they won't see me. I'll look at the ground or the ceiling until I can find the answer.' Problem is, the more we dampen our impulses, the more space we put between the offer and the response, the harder it becomes to advance. We end up disconnecting ourselves from the story entirely. As I am sure you have experienced many times, as I have: once you lose your train of thought, it can be very hard to get back on track. 'What was I talking about?... It'll come to me...' Eventually, we will understand how to free up our responsiveness and ride the energy and momentum of the story.

There is no 'right' response to "Because of that..." And there is also no correct NUMBER of consequences. You just have to follow the story beat by beat.

You'll find a rhythm emerges of 'If that's true, what else?'—a sort of call and response. Based on what we know to be true from the last offer, what happens? What do we see? What is the consequence of that action?

And 'action' is the key here. Sometimes we don't know if our offers are good enough, so we equivocate. We stall. We unconsciously make INactive choices. You can often spot these stalls through phrases like "decided to", and "thought about", and "started to", and "tried to". In order to be truly active, these phrases would have to be followed by an action word. "Decided to run…" "Thought about running…" "Started to run…" "Tried to run…"

"Decided to" delays the action. If Charlie DECIDED TO embrace his mother, we need another beat to finish the action. "Because Charlie knew his mother had arrived, he decided to run to her so they could embrace." Why not just get to the action? Run to her. Embrace her. Why put in the step of thinking about it before the character inevitably does it? Actions get reactions. Thoughts and plans don't elicit a response because they are not observable. They are inactive. Charlie's mother probably wouldn't cry if Charlie was only thinking about hugging her. And, if she responded while he was thinking, she would likely be responding to his behavior (his pause or his hesitation), not the thinking itself.

Take a look at the book "ACTIONS: The Actors' Thesaurus" by Marina Caldarone and Maggie Lloyd-Williams and you see how many different, specific actions can be taken to advance the story. The most active behaviors are those that are directed at someone or something. "To think" is technically a verb, an action word, but it can't be directed at someone. I can't think you. I can't decide you. But, I CAN embrace you, or reject you, or kiss you, or fight you, or delight you, or frustrate you, or show you, or teach you… If there is a direct impact on someone or something, it is a stronger choice than a passive one. Don't delay the action.

"Started to…" or "tried to…" is a stall because it is not clear and definitive. It is a hedging of your bets. "Because Charlie knew his mother had arrived, he started to run to her so they might embrace." "Started to…" or "began to…" are phrases we use because we think our offer will (or SHOULD) be interrupted by some other more interesting turn. "Tried to…" suggests we are not sure the action is even possible and we are creating a problem to explain why. Instead of taking definitive action and running to his mother and embracing, Charlie only got started running. Or only tried to run. So what? Why couldn't he run to his mother and embrace her? He was about to trip? Or injure himself? And then a meteor might come down from the sky and crack open the grain of wheat, and aliens would come out and started vomiting on Charlie and his mother! Who... duh, duh, DUUUUUUHHHHH... is ALSO an alien!

The whole thing just spirals. And not because it is 'imaginative.' It is that we don't trust ourselves and the simplicity of the offers and the story. We have all seen way too many movies and read way too many stories to accept that a story about a mouse who is surprised by the arrival of his mother with a grain of wheat is interesting enough. But that simple thing CHANGED Charlie's entire world in that moment. The proverbial snow globe was shaken.

Your best bet is simply to listen, agree, and then take action. ANY action. You will never have a better idea than the first one that comes to you, because it is the one that happened in the moment. So, say it before it's gone. And before you have a chance to think about whether it's good or not.

Eventually, after we go through a series of "Because of that..." consequences, we get to a place where we are approaching the climax of the story. Once you have explored and expanded the consequences of the "One day..." shakeup until you can go no further, you've reached the "Until finally..." moment.

It is difficult to explain exactly what to look for in this beat, to be honest, because it will be completely dependent on the story you are telling. And how many consequences will occur before things have gone as far as they can go. Sometimes we stop too short and feel like we cheated the development of the story. Other times, it feels like we miss the climax entirely and the story restarts, or a whole new story begins.

It happens a lot, at this stage, that the story meanders down a new path. Instead of pushing to the climactic conclusion, we introduce new characters, or a new problem, or start a new adventure. If you think of it like a TV show, instead of wrapping up this 'episode', we are already on to next week's. These 'false restarts' in storytelling are very common. We don't think we've done enough, or that the story is interesting enough, so we press on and end up starting a new story altogether.

Try to stay connected to where you began—what you knew to be true, and what changed in that "One day…" moment. By the end of the story, we want to understand what we learned about the opening details. What was the event that set off the chain of effects? Today, Charlie didn't have to run down the hill to collect a grain of wheat. Over the course of the story, we saw, beat after beat, how each action led to the next, to the point where the grain of wheat sprouted and the hill is covered with wheat. Based on where we started, this feels like a big change to me, the ultimate result of that shakeup, and for my money presents a solid "Until finally…" opportunity.

"Until finally there were grains of wheat as far as the eye could see."

This leads us to the final beats of our story. Which are: "From that day forward…" and the moral of the story. "From that day forward…" sort of bookends the story by establishing the new normal. Charlie had a routine. It was shaken up. We witnessed the consequences of that until it forced a change. Now we return to Charlie's routine, but it, too, has shifted, if ever so slightly. "From that day forward, Charlie spent more time with his mother and less time fetching grain."

And "The moral of the story is: Love brings abundance." Or "The moral of the story is: Family makes life s-wheat-er." (You're welcome.) The moral is really just an assessment of what we explored or discovered in the story. What was the big idea? What was the 'question' of the play we were trying to answer? And it can't be known at the start. We discover it through the story. There would be no way to know when we met this mouse that tears would cause fields of wheat to grow. Or that his mother would bring him a grain of wheat today.

I specifically kept this example simple. Actually, I don't think you need to go much further to tell a complete story. The key is the foundation at the beginning, the shift, and the return to a routine, having learned something new. Too many of our stories seem to restart multiple times. Rather than stick with the grain of wheat and the daily journey, we find ourselves in a new place. Or encounter unrelated occurrences—the meteors of the story, as it were. These things inorganically stir up drama for the sake of drama, and the only reason we think we need them is because we don't think the story we're telling is interesting enough, or it's not the story we WANT to be telling. Again, release your need to control. It is energy and attention wasted.

We told this story as a bigger group. Let's see what happens when we tell a story, using the same structure, in smaller groups. Maybe two to four people. Start with the "Once upon a time..." opening with a character and place. Maybe try initiating a different genre, just to see how style can inform your offers. See how simply you can tell the story. Stay with what you know, and let the offers unfold organically, building to the "Until finally..." moment. Match each other's energy as a way to find agreement and to keep the rhythmic flow of the story going.

I cannot stress enough the need for keeping it simple in order to find agreement and to tell a clear story. Imagine it's as though every offer you make, you write on a piece of paper and you drop it on the floor. By the end of the story (or the scene), we want to have picked up every piece of paper off the floor. If the story ends and there are still lots of pieces of paper strewn on the floor, the story was too complicated. Too many ideas were introduced that were not essential to the story (what I call "over-offering"), or didn't directly build on the offer that came before (i.e. "inventing").

Why have ten objects if you only need two? Why mention grandma, if grandma is not in the scene? Why put the scene on the moon when the activity was to mend a dress? Complicated offers that require a lot of 'figuring out' will either get dropped completely because no one knows what to do with them. Or they will take over the story and the entire interaction will become about trying to justify the 'weirdness.' Do your best not to drop more offers in the story than you can focus on at once.

OK. Great! I imagine your experience in a smaller group feels a little 'easier.' Usually people find that having the offer return to them more quickly with fewer people in-between helps them to feel more connected to their partners and to the story. That makes sense. It is less common that we would have more than three or four people in a scene, anyway. But when you do, just like the larger group story telling, you see how the task of staying focused and giving your attention to your partners jumps exponentially.

If you are exhausted after improvising, it is likely because it IS exhausting to maintain intense focus for long periods of time. **This is an important skill of being an actor: to be able to bring your full attention to each moment. To be ever-present and available for your partners, so that YOU don't miss any detail. The 'smallest' occurrence could be the key to the whole story.** We have to MAKE it important by being curious and not dismissing an offer simply because we think we can come up with something 'better.' What's already in front of you is all you need. No need to invent anything. Let your actor's imagination take you to the world of the scene and then 'say what you see.'

Maybe try a couple more stories with your small group. Or try one with only two of you. How did it feel? What felt easier? More difficult? I'm not asking about the CONTENT of the story. Not whether you liked one story better than another. Focus solely on your experience of the process of sharing the storytelling with your partner within this structure.

Let's tell another story using this structure in small groups... with an additional layer. I want you to bring some spacework into the picture. I want you to begin an activity using spacework that you and your partners can share. Maybe you want to play a game of poker. Maybe you want to fold laundry. Maybe you want to clip coupons. Maybe you want to paint a chair. For this exercise, just let the activity be easy to share, and nothing stressful or overly complicated.

Something all of you can easily identify and join in on.

One person starts. Establish an activity. Share objects. Share the task. No conversation or talking. Just DO the task. And without much hesitation, like in Freeze Tag, each partner should join in on the spacework. Mirror or complement. Let the activity go for a couple beats and look for agreement about what you are all doing. "Test your theory," as I like to guide. Meaning: if you see something specific, DO that activity to confirm with your partners that you are, in fact, doing the same task. See if you were 'right.' Find your rhythm together, and give the task your attention.

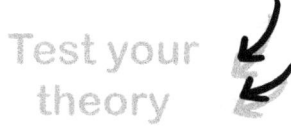

Once you feel like you and your partners are in a flow, working together, begin to tell a story using the "Once upon a time…" structure. I don't want the story to have anything to do with your activity. We are simply strengthening the skill of being able to maintain our connection to an activity and to the space, while the CONTENT of the scene (in this case 'story') diverges. Think about how much of your time you spend in your daily life physically engaged in one activity while your thoughts and your conversation are about something completely different. You are doing the dishes, but you and your spouse are arguing about how you make bad decisions with money and shouldn't have bought the most expensive peanut butter. (Or whatever.) The point is that **scenes are rarely about the actual activity. The activity just keeps us grounded. It is a completely natural behavior for us to bring to our acting. Even in imaginary circumstances, we can create a truthful reality through activity.**

See what happens as you let the story unfold while sharing an unrelated activity. Did your spacework become unclear? Non-specific? Was it harder to keep the story flowing? Or did having another activity to focus on make the storytelling easier because there was no room to THINK about what you wanted to say or what you wanted to happen in the story? There is no 'better' or 'worse'. We simply want to notice the behaviors that help us, and those that distract us.

There is a LOT that is happening when you're improvising. The offers come fast and furious, as I like to say. So, we need to understand what is required and what our natural inclinations are in order to be able to be as free and present as possible. This exercise is not a performance, but if it were in front of an audience, those watching would see everything that happens. So, you want to be sure YOU don't miss anything, either—a sort of balancing act of being inside and outside the scene at the same time.

Missed offers are unexplored offers, and we are inevitably left disappointed that we never discovered what a specific offer meant. (That piece of paper we dropped and never returned to.) Say that, in a scene, your grandmother was sleeping in a chair, opened her eyes, grabbed a piece of candy, popped it in her mouth and closed her eyes. But you were engaged making pasta for dinner and didn't see the candy offer. Just like Nora and those macaroons in "A Doll's House," we want to know what sneaking the candy means to the relationship, the narrative, and the world of the story. When something happens, it should be explored.

Now, try another story using the same structure. And THIS time, I want the spacework to RELATE to the story. In fact, I want you to physically ACT out the story as you're telling it. Engage in the space. Don't do and THEN tell. Tell AS you do. Really SEE the story come to life. Keep it in third-person, even if you are playing the character you are describing. Try to avoid dialogue, at this point. Describe, don't converse. Focus on ACTION.

Just like the mirroring work, see how seamlessly you can initiate and respond. Let the action happen AS it is being described—one should not precede the other. It should appear as though the action and the story are happening simultaneously. We are not able to distinguish, from moment to moment, whether the actors are following the storyteller, or the storyteller is describing what the actors are doing.

Usually, players find that this version of the storytelling is the most fun for them. That they feel the most fully engaged. That they can truly SEE the story. Yes! Every time you do a scene, try to summon that same level of engagement. Be fully invested. Fully present. When we move into scenes, you WILL be the character. It is a useful skill to have to be able to observe the story (as an audience would) while being PART of it—to absorb offers that are happening, even while you are DOING. Find out what it takes to be able to spread your attention, and then allow yourself to respond—not THINK, or plot, or playwright... ACT.

Let's keep exploring story, and give ourselves a new challenge. What if we told a pass-along story One. Word. At. A. Time? Each person in the circle will make an offer that contributes to the narrative, and the offer will be just ONE word each time it comes around. This exercise will let us explore a couple of ideas. First, it will make it painfully obvious how little control we actually have to bend the story to our liking. Second, we will begin to better understand how rhythm and flow help us in storytelling, and in scenework. And, we also get a deeper understanding of what it means to contribute what the story or scene NEEDS, even when we want to play a bigger role. We need to generously prioritize the story and the group above our own desire to be the focus and have the best ideas. Sounds like a lot for a simple storytelling exercise, but there is, as always, a lot there to be gained.

Since we were just working with the "Once upon a time…" story structure, I suggest we approach our word-at-a-time story in the same way. So, the first four players have a gimme:

First player: "Once…"

Next player: "upon…"

Next player: "a…"

Next player: "time…"

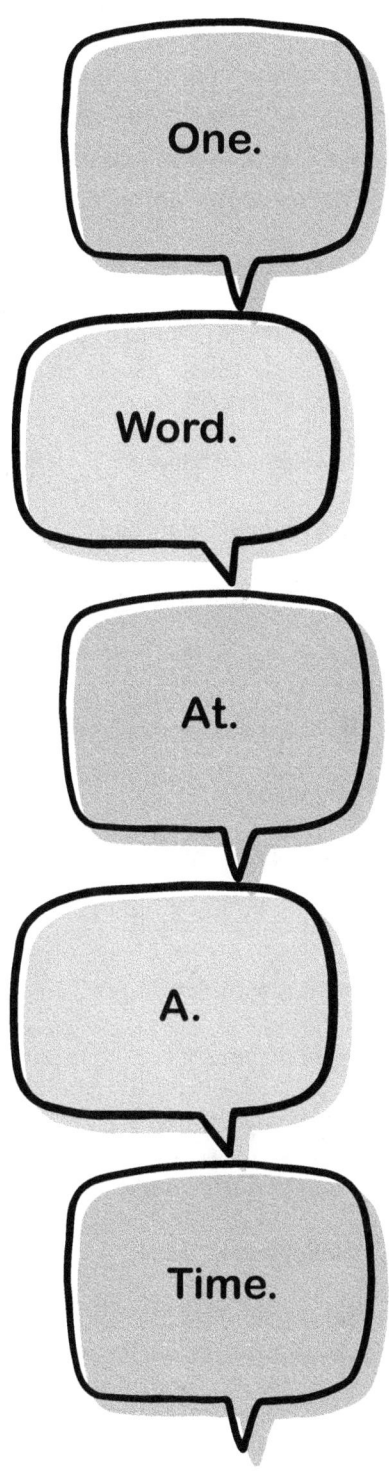

And then we continue, each person adding the next word. Hesitation will kill the momentum and make it much more difficult to offer the next word. Your first idea is your best idea. And, the truth is, if you are following the offers intently, your response should feel effortless. Language has a flow. If you stay with the rhythm of the sentence, you shouldn't have to THINK about what to say.

Next player: "there…"

Next player: "was…"

Next player: "a…"

Next player: "dancer…"

Next player: "named…"

Next player: "Isabella…"

Next player: "who…"

Next player: "lived…"

Next player: "in…"

Next player: "a…"

Next player: "small…"

Next player: "cottage…"

Next player: "in…"

Next player: "the…"

Next player: "shadow…"

Next player: "of…"

Next player: "a…"

Next player: "enormous…"

Next player: "castle."

Even in this first sentence, we see how many players added small joining words—they didn't get the coveted nouns and verbs and adjectives. They got the articles and the prepositions. The conjunctions. Although it is certainly helpful if all the players speak the same language, it's not necessary for anyone to be a grammar whiz. In fact, I'd caution you not to get sidetracked by grammar glitches. You'll notice one player said "a…" and the next player said "enormous…" Not grammatically correct, but we can easily follow the intention of the offer.

Be wary, as well, of the return of 'stinky face.' You'll notice lots of judgment in this word-at-a-time storytelling exercise. We are disappointed when one of our partners misses something we thought should have been obvious. We get frustrated when someone STILL wants to showcase their 'cleverness' and injects some inorganic idea into the mix—the verbal meteor. It's OK. We need to discover what our reactions are to these 'glitches,' because we will have to deal with them a lot. Rarely does a scene or a story go the way you think it should. So, **my advice is not to work for a result. Stay present in the moment you're in, which is the offer right in front of you, and simply respond to that.**

Depending on how many players you have in the circle, you may contribute only one, or perhaps two or three words to a single sentence. And when it comes around to you, you may find yourself seemingly only able to contribute the little articles and joiners. This may feel frustrating to you, but you are playing an important role in keeping the flow on the story going. It may feel like thankless and boring drudgery, but it matters as much as any shinier word. In sports, statisticians keep track of assists. Nobody wins a game alone, so be the proverbial 'team player.' You get the championship ring same as the MVP. Make your priority to do good work, not to be the star. So much terrible improv and acting exists because players are showboating and grandstanding instead of making their partners look good. If I can play that literal piece of trash floating in a pool, as I told you I once did, you can find a way to humbly support your partners and the scene, as well.

We continue one word at a time, following the "Once upon a time..." story framework, so the next two players will give us: "Every..." "day..." Then:

Next player: "Isabella..."

Next player: "leapt..."

Next player: "over..."

Next player: "the..."

Next player: "fence..."

Next player: "surrounding..."

Next player: "her..."

Next player: "yard..."

Next player: "and..."

Next player: "twirled..."

Next player: "and..."

Next player: "swayed..."

Next player: "through..."

Next player: "the..."

Next player: "darkened..."

Next player: "field..."

Next player: "where..."

Next player: "no..."

Next player: "flowers..."

Next player: "ever..."

Next player: "grew."

Sometimes it's hard to know when a shared idea is complete. Don't be afraid to end a sentence. A run-on thought can be difficult to track (as you've probably experienced many times in this book). So, when we can end one thought and start a new thought, it usually puts us back on track—not as a way to negate what has been offered, but to keep thoughts simple. In this case, we established Isabella's routine, and used what we already knew: that she is a dancer, so she probably moves like one. That she lives in a cottage, and that is where she is coming from. And that the castle casts a shadow, which probably makes it dark. And if it's dark, things don't tend to grow.

It can be especially helpful in word-at-a-time stories to let your imagination really SEE the story. If you can visualize the character and the world, and then get a sense of the style, the offers should come more easily. I know I sound like a broken record (Look it up.), but remember there is no need to look for drama. We don't need to create problems in order for something to happen. We simply need to make important what we already know, and then explore the consequences. 'If that's true, what else?' What do I SEE? And based on that, what happens next?

Before we get to the actual 'consequences' in our story structure, though, we have to shake up the snow globe. Something needs to interrupt the routine as we now know it to be. That comes with our "One day…" moment. So the next two players give us: "One…" "day…" Then:

Next player: "the…"

Next player: "field…"

Next player: "was…"

Next player: "so…"

Next player: "dark…"

Next player: "that…"

Next player: "Isabella…"

Next player: "could…"

Next player: "not…"

Next player: "see…"

Next player: "anything…"

Next player: "at…"

Next player: "all."

Whoa! Okay! Now we're cooking. Based on what we knew about Isabella leaving her home each day dancing toward the castle, and that the castle cast a shadow that darkened the field, something shifted today. We had our 'That's new!' moment. We don't know yet what it means, and we don't know yet what will happen. But, based on what we knew to be true, we had our "One day…" shift, and now we have the question of our story: what happens to a dancer when she can no longer see?

We want to find out, so we move into the "Because of that…"s. Since we are telling the story one word at a time, it would seemingly take us forever if each time we added a consequence we started with a repetition of the last offer. "Because…" "the…" "field…" "was…" "so…" "dark…" "Isabella…" "could…" "not…" "see…" "anything…" "at…" "all…" Instead, we can simply state the consequence, which is the next action of the story. BECAUSE of the last offer, what do we SEE?

Next player: "Isabella…"

Next player: "stopped…"

Next player: "dancing."

Great! A simple response to the offer of not being able to see. And one that directly relates to our character. (Notice how we keep using her name, instead of 'she'? Use names, it really helps us visualize and track the story.) So, that offer leads to the next offer. Although we won't actually SAY it, HEAR for yourself the lead up to the offer: 'Because Isabella stopped dancing…'

Next player: "Isabella…"

Next player: "listened."

Great! Another simple and completely understandable response. Really see Isabella standing there in the pitch blackness. Hear for yourself the lead in to the next consequence: 'Because Isabella listened…'

Next player: "Isabella…"

Next player: "heard…"

Next player: "the…"

Next player: "sound…"

Next player: "of…"

Next player: "hooves…"

Next player: "galloping…"

Next player: "in…"

Next player: "the…"

Next player: "distance."

Great! The result of listening was hearing something. Makes total sense. Our imaginations begin to color in the picture in front of us. We have no idea where each moment will go next. I only ask you, at this stage, to focus on the simplicity, and to avoid the 'meteors.' Don't go looking for drama. Let the details and curiosity about what you see lead you to the next moment. 'If that's true, what else?' 'If I were Isabella, what would I do?' Keep it active. We don't want to get bogged down in detailing how Isabella FEELS, or what she THINKS, and certainly not what she is 'deciding' or 'starting' to do. If she is scared, we'll know that if she runs. And, she doesn't need to START running, she can just RUN. Let actions move the story, the same way actions will move our scenes.

Like the story of Charlie we told previously, there is no way to say how many consequences will occur, how many offers will require further exploration and action to arrive at the "Until finally…" moment. The danger, as we discussed before, is likely that the story will restart. In this example, instead of following the simple thread of Isabella dancing her way into darkness and the series of consequences that build from that, we all of a sudden find ourselves in another place, meeting lots of other characters, going on lots of side adventures. Our simple story morphs into an epic miniseries. Never lose sight of where you start. Those are the details we want to button up by the end of the story. And once you've thoroughly explored and addressed them, you don't need to go looking for more drama.

Keep following the structure. At some point, we'll have "Until…" "finally…" followed by the resolution. (One word at a time, of course.) And then "From…" "that…" "day…" "forward…" where we learn what Isabella's new routine is. Maybe she still goes dancing toward the castle every day and now always takes a lantern. Maybe she still goes dancing toward the castle every day and is known for inventing the game of Hide-and-Seek. Who knows? But something has changed from her original routine.

And even in these word-at-a-time stories, I still like to hear the moral. So "The…" "moral…" "of…" "the…" "story…" "is…"

"Never…" "Stop…" "Dancing."

Or, "It's…" "Always…" "Darkest…" "Before…" "The…" "Lawn."

For our final story challenge, let's put ourselves back into the story. We'll do this with just ONE other partner, in pairs. This will be a word-at-a-time story, and we will be simultaneously acting out the story as we tell it. To give ourselves a little signpost, we're going to identify an object that will be important to the story. It will either lead to tragedy or triumph. Meaning: this object will be the reason the characters accomplish their task or not.

For our first go, let's say the two players work as plumbers. And where would a scene about plumbers LIKELY take place? A bathroom. A kitchen. Don't complicate it. Establish a space that is familiar. You have enough other challenges happening.

And, what is an object that plumbers would use? A wrench. A tool box. A plunger. For this scene, let's say that a plunger will lead to a triumph.

As you and your partner begin, start with the ACTIVITY. Find your rhythm together in your spacework. Make sure you AGREE what the space looks like and what task you are doing. Are you replacing a pipe? Installing a sink or a toilet? Unclogging a drain? As soon as you have agreement about the activity, then you can begin the storytelling. One. Word. At. A. Time, back and forth between you both.

"Once…" "upon…" "a…" "time…" "there…" "were…" "two…" "plumbers…" "named…" "Rebecca…" "and…" "Janelle…" "who…" "specialized…" "in…" "unclogging…" "bathtub…" "drains."

"Every…" "day…" "they…" "retrieved…" "item…" "after…" "item…" "from…" "their…" "customers'…" "drains."

"One…" "day…" "Rebecca…" "could…" "not…" "get…" "a…" "customer's…" "wedding…" "ring…" "out…" "of…" "the…" "bathtub…" "drain."

All of this is being told AS the action is occurring. The two players are busy with their activity. What is ACTUALLY happening is what drives the story. We are not cooking up the play and then acting it out. As before, we want the story and the telling of the story to be happening at the same time. Hopefully, if you and your fellow plumber took the time to establish your space and your activity, you should find a flow. (Pun intended.)

We can once again skip the repetition of the "Because of that…"s for this version of our story. You should still feel the lead-in, as though you were saying it. Remember, the consequences are responses that build on the preceding offer. BECAUSE Rebecca was unable to get a customer's wedding ring out of the bathtub drain, what happened next? Did Janelle try? Did Rebecca try a new technique? Did the plumbers fill the tub with water? What happened?

The next beat of the story will come from what the actors ACTUALLY do. Engage in the space and DO something. The story will tell itself.

So, now we only need to let our plunger be the source of the triumphant resolution to the story. By agreeing ahead of time that the plunger would lead to triumph, we have inherently agreed that it will solve the problem that the "one day…" moment creates (the shakeup of the routine). And in terms of this particular story structure, we have also inherently agreed that the plunger will be part of our "Until finally..." moment. If the plunger solves the problem, then there would likely be no further consequences.

Wrap up your story with a "From that day forward...", still acting it out as you go. And then give us the moral. Still one. Word. At. A. Time.

What was your experience of this story? Did you find a place where the words were just coming out of your mouth and there was no deliberation required—no hesitation? Were you able to follow the narrative? Did the action of the scene simplify the storytelling? Was it easier to see the story when you were immersed in it? Unless you are playing a specific game in a scene, it is unlikely that you would speak only one word at a time, but it underscores the give-and-take nature of offers, and our relative lack of control over what happens.

As we move into scenework, keep these story structures in mind. Begin to feel where you are in the arc of the scene. Are you still building the foundation of the who, where and what, or are you establishing a pattern? Has the snow globe been shaken? Are you following consequences? How do we know when we've found a resolution? And how do we know when we've collected all of our dropped papers and we can end the scene? It is helpful to have a sense, while the scene is happening, where you are in the narrative. Simultaneously, we need to be able to move ourselves out of our storytelling heads to engage physically in the action of the scene—doing, not telling.

Probably the most important anchor in the scene will be the "One day..." moment—the snow globe shakeup. Something that we will begin to refer to as the EVENT of the scene. And we will see how important it is to clearly establish the foundational rules of the world so we can know when we are breaking them. Once we accept a pattern-breaking moment as true, we make it important—make it the event of the scene. And, once we agree what the event of the scene is, we can stay focused on that big idea. Most of the scene will be an exploration of the consequences of that one event, similar to the storytelling structure. Remember, it need not be a 'meteor.' **Any offer that we can endow with a sense of 'That's new!' 'That's a game-changer!' 'That's never happened before!' can be enough to build an entire scene. We just need to BELIEVE it's enough.**

IMPROV AND THE ACTOR'S IMAGINATION

TELL A STORY

Once upon a time...
Set up the platform (who, where, what)

Every day...
Set up the pattern

One day...
Break the pattern

Because of that...
Follow the consequences

Until finally...
Find a resolution

From that day forward...
Establish the new pattern

The moral of the story is...
Answer the big question with the lesson learned

4
Energy Expansion & The Power of Pace

We have mentioned 'flow' and 'energy' several times. It IS a key part of improvising and acting. Wherever the offer is, there, too, is the energy of the moment—the energy of the scene. It is the thing that everyone is tuned in to. The thing that everyone is observing. And then the next offer, a response, an "And...", comes right out of the offer at hand. And the energy of the scene, or story, continues.

We are always trying our best to give specificity to our work, especially our spacework. The more detailed we can be with our imagining, the more particular our spacework becomes, which then requires less effort. If we can really SEE it, we don't have to spend any energy THINKING about it or crafting the details. We simply let those details be revealed.

Yet, I find that spacework is usually the first thing to go when an improviser begins to get overwhelmed with all the offers, and where she is in the story. There are SO many things to consider that our attention gets pulled from the underlying activity. And, without realizing it, we are stuck standing still trying to TALK and THINK our way through. This is why we spend so much time developing the skills of spacework which allow us to maintain our physical connection to the space and the scene, without needing to dedicate effort to it. It simply becomes instinctual, and we strive to maintain our connection—to be grounded in a place and grounded in an activity, whatever it may be. Remember, the scene is not usually ABOUT the activity, which is why I think it drops in importance as we move through the scene. You CAN do both. And, **the best scenes I see are those where the physical world stays as present and alive as the contact between the characters.**

And there is always more to observe. A former improv teacher of mine, Ralph Buckley, used to reference something he credited Mike Myers with saying about spacework. Something to the effect of 'it's not just a bottle of ketchup. It's a bottle of Heinz 57 ketchup.' The idea being: details matter. Your partners or an audience may not be able to tell you the specific brand of your ketchup after the scene has ended. But, those details and the application of your actor's imagination in this way, and to this degree, matter. They DO inform your character and the scene.

An improviser may start a scene where he is bartending. Specifically, his activity is making a cocktail. He is creating spacework with care. We SEE the mixers. We SEE the stainless steel cocktail shaker. We SEE the bar top. We SEE the martini glass and the bar rag he has over his shoulder. Then a coworker approaches the bar, collects her order and gives the bartender a little wink of thanks before she walks away. This was a "one day..." moment for him. He asks a fellow bartender if she saw what just happened. They begin to discuss it. Before you know it, the improviser playing the bartender has stopped spacework altogether. Instead of putting the behavior INTO the spacework, he dropped it to focus solely on how he was feeling and reacting to the wink gesture. We no longer see any of the details because he is not keeping them alive by using the objects and interacting with the space. If someone walked in on that scene at that point, they would have no idea where the bartender was or what he was doing.

Find a way to live in the details and to keep energy moving WHILE you give your attention to the offers that come, and the responses that follow. Why not USE the environment and the objects to explore your response to the offer? Did you think your coworker was flirting with you? Maybe you use your bartending skills to try to impress her next time she comes back. Maybe you write a message in garnishes for her to discover. Maybe you make her a special drink. Or write a love letter on a cocktail napkin. You see how putting your response into ACTION keeps both the world AND the story alive? It can feel a bit like trying to pat your head and rub your stomach while hopping on one leg. With practice, you can do all of these things simultaneously and sustain a full reality in your work.

So, where do we tap into this ability? I like to explore it by bending time—by taking whatever time it takes, and moving at whatever pace we need, to be able to see everything clearly. Let's call it the "Matrix approach". In "The Matrix" movies, and many that have been made since, a character is able to see everything in great detail, even things like bullets that are moving at the speed of, well, a bullet. The characters themselves are moving in regular time, yet it appears to them that everything has slowed, allowing them to avoid danger. To witness the details. To react without missing a moment.

Let's try it for ourselves by passing energy along in a circle. Everyone stand in a circle in a neutral position, just like we started our mirroring work. Feet planted flat on the floor. Arms at our sides. Shoulders relaxed. Head perched atop your shoulders, like there's a string from the top of your head to the ceiling.

One person is going to start by making a simple sound and a gesture. The sound doesn't have to mean anything, and the movement doesn't have to be anything recognizable. Maybe you lunge forward and shout "Yaaaaaaaaahhhhhhh!" You hold for a second, and you step back to your original spot in the circle. Your partner to your right will then MIRROR your sound and movement as PRECISELY as they can. Same duration. Same physicality. Same sound.

It bears repeating here that we are each unique. Try as I might, I may not be able to recreate a particularly high-pitched sound. Or inflexible as my limbs can be, I may not be able to lunge as far or as deeply as my partner. The point is to TRY. TRY to do it exactly. HONOR the offer your partner made by saying "YES!" and demonstrating that they had your full attention and that you were listening. You want to be able to repeat EVERY detail—perhaps a detail even THEY missed. 'I didn't even realize I was doing that!'

In this first round, EVERYONE in the circle will repeat EXACTLY what the originator offered. Once the sound and movement travels the perimeter of the circle and returns to the originator, the originator does their own sound and gesture one final time.

Then we move to the next player, who creates a NEW sound and movement. Maybe a spin in place and a "WHEEEEEEEEEE!" Then the partner to her right will repeat EXACTLY the spin and sound. It passes to the next person in the circle until it returns to the original spinner, and she does her own sound and gesture one final time. We keep going until every person in the circle has had a chance to create a NEW sound and gesture.

It cannot be overstated, I don't think, that having people repeat what you put into the world is very encouraging. We want to live in that world of "Yes" and know that our partners are leaving space for us, and that they are willing to pick up our ideas and run with them. It is a very lonely place to live, as an improviser, when you feel relegated to only do what others do because they are leaving no room for the possibility that someone else's idea has value. Like on a grade school playground, improv bullies will try to control the scene by steamrolling it with their own ideas, regardless of who else is there or what other offers are in the space, or even what the scene NEEDS. It comes, as it often does for bullies, from insecurity. The bully tries to control because they are afraid. But the group need will always win out in the end. So, continue to focus on elevating everyone's offers, and trust that they will elevate yours in return. Create your own world of "Yes!"

OK. Let's try a variation of this pass-along sound and movement exercise. This time, I want someone to begin by originating a new sound and movement. And, just as in the first round, I want their partner to their right to repeat that sound and movement exactly.

Now, here's the twist. I want the next player to repeat the sound and movement, and I want them to EMPHASIZE and EXPAND whatever they observed was DIFFERENT between the first player and the second player.

They were both ostensibly doing the SAME sound and movement. The second player was really TRYING to capture it all, with every detail. But, as I pointed out, we are all different. We have different abilities. Not to mention, UNEXPECTED things happen. We TRY to do the lunge, and find ourselves a bit off balance. So, we make a correction so we don't fall. The job of the third player, then, is to repeat the sound and gesture and further exaggerate the difference.

Sometimes the differences are small. Perhaps the player who repeated the original sound and movement went a little slower or faster. Perhaps their pitch was slightly higher or lower. Perhaps their lunge was a little deeper, or their spin more graceful. If you observe it, it's true. So, if you are the third in the chain, repeat the sound and movement and emphasize that change.

Be careful not to MOCK the player before you. We are not using this exercise to point out their 'mistakes.' We are merely highlighting that differences exist, and that those differences should be elevated and made important, particularly when they were completely unplanned. **Surprises are EVERYTHING in improvisation. Be open to the unexpected so that when it happens, and it OFTEN does, you are not thrown by it. Rather, you seize the gift of that change and lean into it.**

There is a difference between mockery and mimicry. Mocking comes from a place of our own insecurity. We fear that we will look silly if we simply do what our partner did, so we try to distance ourselves from it. We judge our partner's offer as 'stupid' or 'bad' and we let them know by making fun of them for it. We repeat, and we exaggerate, but it is done mockingly. Whereas, mimicry is, to paraphrase the old saying, 'the highest form of flattery.' Be excited to try something your partner created and offered to you. In a way, even if you think they looked silly, they have, in going before you, given you permission to do it, too. And, if others deem that you look silly, you are not alone. The ones who truly look silly are the ones who don't engage and don't try. Be fearless. Give yourself permission. Get yourself into trouble and see what happens. I think you'll be surprised. In fact, to mirror F. Scott Fitzgerald, 'for what it's worth...I hope you see things that startle you.'

One last thing on this point: In ANY spacework you do, live it as truthfully as your imagination is capable. Don't 'pretend' to do something. REALLY do it. Don't choose to be 'bad' at some skill simply to protect yourself and your ego from possible embarrassment. If you are cast as a doctor, be a convincing doctor. If your character needs to move a 1,000 lb. boulder, TRY. Solve the problem.

It's disappointing to see people choosing to be bad at what they do. We spend the whole scene dealing with the mishaps of the lack of reality, instead of getting on with what the scene is REALLY about, which is, nine times out of ten, the relationship between the characters. If you are really TRYING, then we can more easily move forward without having to comment on everything the character is doing 'wrong.' If it's done with confidence and conviction, it feels truthful. We believe that this doctor, even if her methods seem unconventional, knows what she's doing. The lure of the Dark Side—to make improv 'wacky'—is strong, so be sure you fortify your skills against the temptation. 'Complete your training, young Padawan.' ("Star Wars"? Look it up.)

In this game we are asking that the exaggeration be intentional. Not to add something new because you think it's funny or clever. **Let the exaggeration come from something you OBSERVED, not something you invented.** If the player before you lost their balance a bit, it would be a great thing to emphasize in your recreation of the sound and movement. But if the obvious change was the loss of balance, and instead you repeat the sound and movement and add a bit of the Macarena, that is inorganic. You are not actually elevating the gift your partner gave you. Instead you are bullying your own 'clever' idea into the mix. Likely something you pre-planned. There is no space for this type of work. You MUST put your attention fully on your partners and fulfill your duty of 'making them look good.'

We never want to get to a place where we are exaggerating solely for the sake of being ridiculous, either. At the root of every sound and every movement needs to be a truth. What am I doing? And even, WHO would do this and why? I DO want you to give yourself permission to lose control. In fact, I encourage it. But we also want to hold on to the truth of the moment.

Once the sound and movement has been repeated with an emphasis on the change, then the next player does the same thing. What was different between the two players that preceded you? What did you observe changed, if anything? The next player repeats the sound and movement, exaggerating the difference. Think of this new pattern as "One, Two, What's New?" and continue around the circle, letting each subsequent player observe and exaggerate what changed between the two players before them, until everyone has had a chance. To end this specific sound and movement, the originator does it one final time, doing their best to repeat the gesture that was returned to them—probably INCREDIBLY different than the original sound and movement. No stinky face! Do not judge what came back to you. Openly accept the gift your fellow players returned to you.

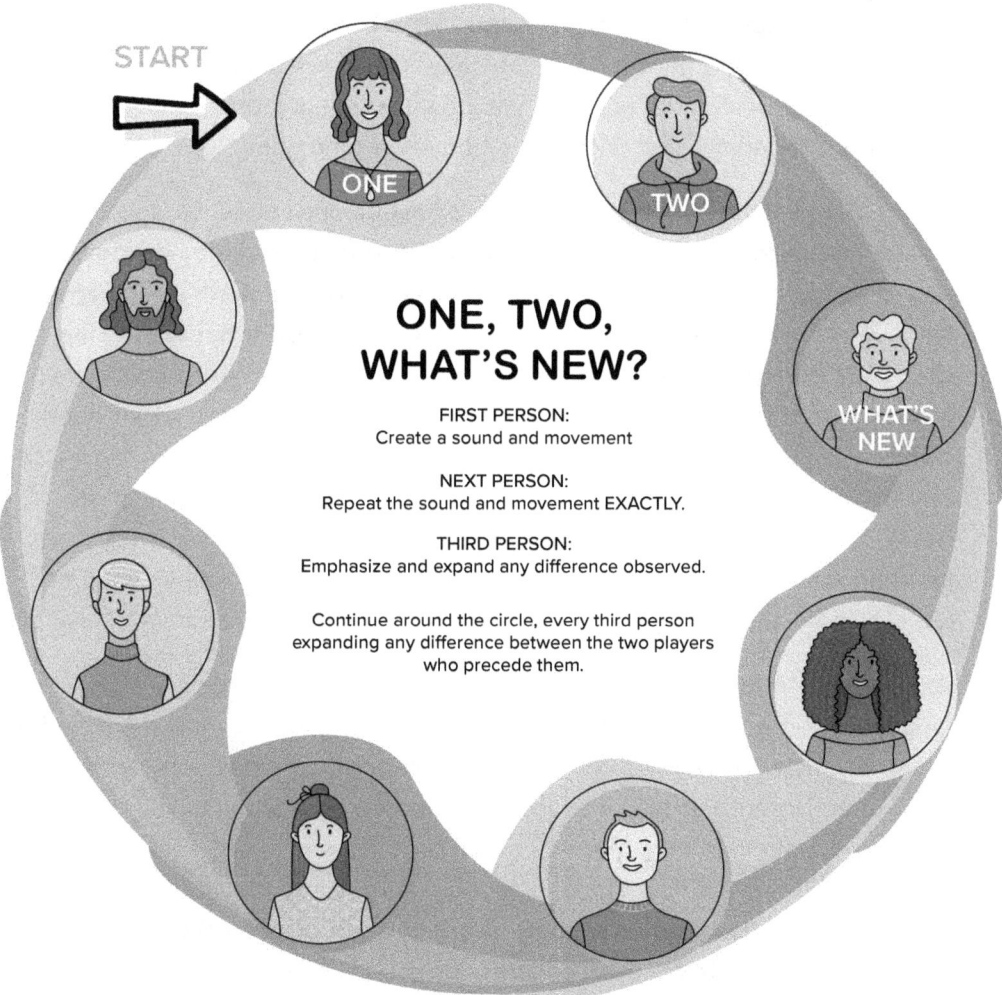

ONE, TWO, WHAT'S NEW?

FIRST PERSON:
Create a sound and movement

NEXT PERSON:
Repeat the sound and movement EXACTLY.

THIRD PERSON:
Emphasize and expand any difference observed.

Continue around the circle, every third person expanding any difference between the two players who precede them.

Then, just as in the first round, the next player will create a new sound and movement. Their partner to their right will try to repeat it EXACTLY, and then the third player in the sequence will repeat the sound and movement while emphasizing the change they observed—"One, Two, What's New?" That comes all the way around the circle. The originator repeats it one final time, in whatever potentially unrecognizable form it was returned, and the next player starts the cycle anew. Once everyone has had a chance to originate a new sound and movement, the exercise is complete.

Exaggeration highlights something about our offers, generally: what we put into the space may not be interpreted the way we intend. In fact, the response that is returned to you may be unrecognizable, as I said. That's OK. Simply respond to whatever offer comes to you. Offers change, organically. Once a moment happens, it is gone, and all you have is the next moment right in front of you. Do your best not to keep comparing subsequent moments to the moment it began. Usually, that originating moment is long gone.

So far in our exercise, we have completed a gesture and sound. Stopped. And then had the next player repeat in its entirety. Stopped. Had the next person repeat. Stopped. Etc. But **this is not how scenes go. We don't pause after every offer. The energy flows and is continuous. One offer begets the next offer, begets the next offer, and on and on.** So, let's send a sound and movement around the circle, but do so in a continuous way. You no longer need to wait until your partner has completely come to a rest before you begin to repeat the gesture and sound. Think of it like starting The Wave at a sporting event. One person stands from their seat, raises their hands over their head and then sits back down. Slowly other spectators begin to follow, until the 'wave' is moving around the perimeter of the stadium as other join in.

Start with the ethic of repeating EXACTLY, but know that organic shifts will happen. When something changes, don't force it into the movement and sound, simply ALLOW it to change. Let one sound and movement keep circling the perimeter. See how it evolves, naturally—no need to forcibly change anything. Just be a good observer and respond. Give yourself permission to follow the energy and flow of the movement and sound. Put all of your skills thus far into practice. Don't anticipate. Allow yourself to follow the impulse as it happens. No need to control it or plan what you want to happen, or what you

THINK would be 'fun.' Simply connect with what IS happening, and respond.

Now comes the time-bending fun. What if we could alter the speed of any activity to allow us to experience it in greater detail? To see things at the granular level and let those details be alive for us? We can! Here's your chance.

Same idea as we just experienced. We are going to send a wave of sound and movement around the circle, allowing it to stay the same or change organically—simply letting it flow. And then at a certain point, I will call "slow motion!" And when I do, I want you to, wherever you are in the sound and movement, proceed in slow motion. As slooooooooowwwwwwwly as you are able to go. Let the intention and the energy of the sound and movement continue, just at a slow pace, like we are watching an animation frame by frame. We want to EXPAND the details. EXAGGERATE the intention and the movement to wring out every detail. Even moving at a pace that feels 'normal' for an activity, we tend to miss a lot of the details. **Slow motion helps us see it all by giving us time to observe it more carefully.**

Often, when we first attempt slow motion, I notice a few things happening. The slow motion makes people tense up. Perhaps hold their breath. Observe when this happens to you. We never want to block ourselves when we improvise, and when we stop the natural flow of our breathing, it inhibits us. Keep the energy of the sound and movement going. The only thing that is changing is the pace.

The slow motion also has a way of changing the mood or the intention. Once a sound moves into slow motion, a cheerful tweet may start to sound like a dangerous growl, or a sad wail. Exaggerated slow-motion bird-like movements that were once delicate and light start to look like heavy, menacing ogres. Or devious witches. In itself, I am glad for people to have this experience. Whatever your imagination sees is perfectly valid. But we need to be aware that slowing down and expanding the detail does not equate to something menacing or bad. I think of a sloth. They don't appear sad, to me. Their slow, deliberate movement does not feel angry or aggressive. They actually seem pretty chill. Slow movement does not necessarily indicate malicious intent, or suspicious or sneaky behavior.

Slow motion also creates some physical problems you and your imagination will need to solve. If the movement is a leap in the air, how do you recreate that movement in slow motion? You cannot physically levitate yourself. There is no rope or bar hanging from the ceiling that will allow you to hoist yourself. You need to capture the INTENTION. How can you move your body in slow motion with the same energetic sense of lifting off the ground that you had when you actually jumped? Try. Solve the problem. Can you stand on one leg at a time and capture the feeling? I am a very physical improviser, and I LOVE seeing people solve the physical challenges of spacework, like flying, for example, when you cannot actually defy the laws of physics. To me, THAT's magic. THAT's imagination.

Once we have been in slow motion for a bit, allowing the sound and movement to continue around the circle, I'll call "regular motion." Then, wherever the movement and sound is in our circle, it continues to flow, just returned to its 'normal' pace. That's not to say that we revert back to its original form. If organic changes happened within the slow motion, BUILD from there. If we entered slow motion like a bird and are coming out of slow motion like a gorilla, go from there. Continue to let the energy flow around the circle, evolving as it does.

A few more times, we'll move in and out of slow motion. Each time, I want you to see how seamlessly you can adapt to the change. How MUCH detail you can observe and create for yourself and your partners. How you solve the problems that slow motion presents, and use them to allow your imagination to try something.

Part of the learning from the slow-motion work is not to immediately run from each offer in pursuit of the next offer. We have to be ready to find agreement about one thing, and allow ourselves and our partners the space to really expand it and explore it. 'If that's true... what else?' As we've discussed, our habit is that we are already bored with something before we've even really scratched the surface of what it means. We are so eager to find the next 'better' thing, instead of being curious about what we already see—the proverbial 'grass is always greener' syndrome. **Let what you have be enough. Don't feel the need to invent. Be focused and curious instead.** And then when you get to the "One day…" moment of the scene, you won't miss it while you are looking for something 'more interesting.' **We want to get into the good habit of taking one simple offer and exploring and expanding it until we feel we can go no further.** Far too many improvised scenes are littered with unexplored offers—like those slips of paper dropped on the floor and never collected.

OK, let's walk about the room. I just want you to find your own pace, your own rhythm. Whatever is happening for you right now. I don't want you to consciously DO anything. Just check in with yourself. 'This is how I walk. This is how I move through space. This is the pace at which I do it. What sort of mood am I in right now? What am I thinking about? How am I breathing?' Don't worry about others in the room. Don't crash into one another, of course, but there is no need to talk or say anything to anyone. No need to make eye contact or a joke. Just move about, and find your own rhythm in this moment.

Then I want you to walk quickly—as quickly as you can without running. Still you. Still you moving through space. Just at a much faster pace.

And, while you do this, once again, check in with yourself. 'What's happening to my breathing? Does this pace feel easier or harder than my original pace? Do I feel energized and focused and driven? Or do I feel hurried and anxious and chaotic? Do I feel like I am accomplishing something? Am I more aware or less aware of my surroundings? What happens to me physically when I move at a faster pace? Do I pitch my weight forward, over my toes? Do I bounce? Do my shoulders tense up? Do I lean forward? Do my arms swing more? Or less?' Observe everything you can about what has changed.

Then come back to your original pace. Does this pace feel slower now that it did before? What is happening with your breath? Did your mood shift? Do you feel a sense of relief or release now that you are no longer moving quickly?

Or does this original pace now feel lethargic and slow? Did moving at a faster pace illuminate any details in your imagination? Did you imagine yourself in a busy place, like an airport or train station or city street when you were moving fast? How about now? Is this a weekend walk in the park? Or a stroll home from school? I find that the imagination starts to kick up when we simply set about an activity—even just walking.

Now, this will likely come as no surprise, I want you to walk in slooooooooow-wwwwwwww-mooooooooooooshuuuuuuunnn. As slowly as you can go. Observe and expand every detail. How your foot rolls across the floor. Where your weight is in each moment. How it shifts. What happens when you are standing on one foot? Do you feel balanced? Does it create tension? Did your mood shift again? Are you now in that ogre-y place where you feel heavy and grumpy? Or is there a peace and freedom in being in no rush? Does having the expanse of time to really do something feel freeing? Or do you feel like you're walking through molasses? Do you feel frustrated and stuck?

Then come back to your original pace. How does it feel now? Do you feel a real sense of relief to be out of the molasses? Did you lose any of the detail you discovered when you came back? Can you still see all the specifics you observed when you were in slow motion? Is it possible to bring that level of detail into your spacework? Let's find out.

Find yourself a spot in the room where you can begin an activity. It can be anything, as long as it involves objects. Clean up your bedroom or your kitchen. Do the laundry. Build a canoe. Paint a canvas, or a wall of the house. Mow the lawn. Whatever. Just use objects. Activities like stretching, or dancing, or even reading may not be the best for this exercise. Choose something active with a few objects.

Set about doing your task. Get specific with your spacework—your objects and your environment. Really see where you are and really see what you are doing. And then simply do it. You don't have to craft any circumstances for yourself. You don't need to worry about how long it's going to take or what else you have to do. You have everything in your space that you need to be able to do your task. We don't need drama or problems. If you are sewing, no need to prick yourself with the needle. (And no meteors, please.) Put your attention on your task. Let it find its natural pace and rhythm.

Once we have settled in, and are completely focused on our task, I want you to now do the same task QUICKLY. As quickly as you are able. Keep in mind, you may have been doing some delicate work. It may be difficult to do it fast. But, try.

Check in with yourself, as you are doing your task rapidly. 'What is happening to my breathing? What about the details of my spacework? Are things getting messy? If someone were to look in on me right now, would they have any idea what I am doing?' In our Meisner work, we endow an activity with a 'standard of perfection.' Would you be able to say that you are still doing this activity precisely, or have you allowed yourself to lower your standards, simply because you are moving quickly?

And what about your intention? Does the shift of moving from a normal pace for this activity to a fast pace create any change in your sense of purpose? WHY you are doing this activity? Do you all of a sudden feel a time crunch that wasn't there before? Some REASON why you have to move quickly? In the Meisner work, we craft a time constraint for our activities, which includes the WHY. But, in this improvised exploration, I want you to see if the reason comes out of the doing itself, absent any planning.

If the work you were so carefully doing is now in shambles because you were rushing, say, what does that mean for your objective? If this activity needed to be done PERFECTLY, what do you do now? Hurry! Time is running out!

In this part of the exercise, be AWARE of problems that may arise from rushing, and how they are affecting you. (You drop a tool you were using and it makes you frustrated because now you have to put the object down to reach the tool, for example. Or you were painting a small pewter model and rushing caused you to knock over your paint, which made a mess and you want to cry.) But, for this exercise do not let those 'problems' derail you. If you realize that rushing would have caused a spill, simply adjust your spacework and keep going. I want you to be able to stay with your intended activity and not get sidetracked with a rush to the First-Aid kit. Simply acknowledge the truth of what would happen if you were to rush. And see what it does to you emotionally and for your intention.

Now come back to your original, 'normal' pace. Check in with yourself. Assess the situation you may have created by moving so quickly with your activity just moments ago. If you did make a mess, tidy and reset and keep going with your task. What is happening with your breathing? Do you feel relieved that you no longer are rushing? Or did you accomplish a lot when you were pushing yourself, and now this original pace actually seems slow? Do you feel empowered or exhausted? Stressed or relaxed? What about your intention? Did your imaginary reason for rushing disappear? Or are you simply more confident now that you will be able to accomplish the task?

Often, simply by changing the pace of what we're doing, our body responds, and our imagination kicks in to help us understand 'why.' Let it happen. Observe those changes, just as we did in the previous exercise. When those offers emerge, expand them. Explore them. Follow the consequences and discover what it means. This is what I mean when I keep saying you don't have to look for drama or invent anything in your head. You simply need to observe what is actually happening when you engage in the space and apply your attention to your task and your environment.

Alright, we're back to our task at our original, 'normal' pace. Keep going.

And now, (this will surprise no one), I want you to do your activity in slow motion—as slowly as you can go. I want to see EVERY detail. Feel every object's weight and size and temperature fully. Take in the room or space where you are doing your activity. What details do you observe NOW that perhaps you ignored before? The color of the walls? How brightly or dimly lit the room is? Is it a familiar place? Indoors? Outdoors? Are there any pictures or objects around? If there is a door or a window, is it opened or closed?

And check in with yourself. What is happening to your breathing? Your mood? Your intention? Do you feel burdened and bogged down? Or do you feel free to have the time and attention to really do a great job at your task? Just like our work in the circle, slow motion can sometimes cause us to feel sad or darken our mood—what was once flowing, now feels labored and ugly. There is no right or wrong here. We simply need to be aware, to observe, what is happening to us and to our spacework. Try to use the slow motion as a way to deepen your experience, and to expand your activity, moment by moment. Really see it. And be curious about each moment. 'If THAT's true, what else?'

And then come back to your original pace. Are you able to keep any of the new discoveries alive? Or as soon as we are back to 'normal' things become vague and non-specific again? Work to build the skill of being able to bring the space to life and treat it, and objects, with integrity, regardless of how fast or slow you're moving, or how you feel about it. Remember: you MUST agree. You don't have to like it. How you respond to any offer is up to you. But you must first observe it and agree it happened.

Let's try a couple more things before we end this exercise. Keep going with your activity. (You've been at it for a while now, so hopefully you are in excellent physical health if you chose a particularly strenuous activity.) Stay with it, just a few beats more.

While you continue your activity, I want you to, without letting the person know, begin to observe someone else and what THEY are doing. Keep at your own task, and simultaneously become aware of someone else.

What are they doing? Can you tell? If you were to drop what you were doing and go join their activity, what would you do? (Extra points if your answer is: MIRROR!) Based on what you observe about their activity, where would this be happening? Where are they? If you joined their scene, how would you enter? What objects do you see?

Do they seem happy with what they're doing? Do they appear to be good at it? What is their mood? Based on what they're doing and their mood, why do you think they're doing this activity? Let your imagination spark the answers. Don't INVENT reasons and explanations, simply OBSERVE and draw a conclusion. You may be right. You may not. The point is: be curious and inspired about what you observe, and then let the response happen naturally—nothing to cogitate. And know full well that you may enter a scene thinking you've got it all figured out, and STILL have observed something differently than what was intended. In which case, you start from THAT point, and work TOGETHER to find agreement about the details so that you can move forward (which can't happen until you've got a foundation on which to stand).

Do you wish you had chosen their task instead of yours? Given the opportunity to do ANY activity, did you choose something tedious and repetitive, while your partner chose to paint a masterpiece? Or play a game? Or do you see them wasting their time while you are doing something meaningful? How does that realization affect your activity? Does it make you work harder? With more ease? Does it make you happier?

When you shifted your attention to someone else and their task, what happened to you and yours? Did you keep your activity going with specificity? Or did you walk through the table you established? Or put your hand on a hot stove? Forget where you put down one of your tools? Or forget that you had a broom in your hand? **Build the skill of being able to keep an activity going, to keep the environment alive, while putting your attention on something or someone else.**

And, as you continue your activity, let me suggest that if you are observing someone, perhaps someone is also observing you. Would they be able to identify what you're doing? If they were to join your activity, how would you make space for them? What would you WANT them to do in order to help you? Would you be glad for the help, or rather finish it up yourself?

If someone is observing you, does it make you more focused? Does it improve your spacework, knowing that someone may be trying to figure out what you're doing and how to join your activity/scene? Do you all-of-a-sudden feel the need to impress this person? Why are they observing you? Do they have a crush on you? Does that change the way you do your activity?

Do you begin to show off?

ANY of these simple responses we make, from our own imagination, can affect our behavior. And when our own behavior changes, chances are our partner will observe a shift and respond in kind. Before you know it, the scene is flowing along, things are happening, and it all appears effortless because there is agreement in each moment as it comes. I need your offer so I pay attention to you, and you need my offer so you put your attention on me.

Now, wrap up your task. If you took objects out, put them away. If you plugged something into an outlet, unplug it or turn it off. Tidy up, and then exit your space. Maybe you remember one last detail you forgot to tend, and you can re-enter your space, do it, and exit again. It's good to get in the habit of clearing things at the ends of scenes—it shows respect for the work. If everything you created just disappears when your scene is over, there is probably more work to do to become even more fully invested in the reality of spacework. (Or maybe that's my improv OCD.)

Just like in our "Once upon a time..." story structure, scenes also have a 'shakeup', "One day..." moment—the event of the scene. And once we have built a foundation, we look for agreement about the event, and then use the rest of the scene to explore and expand that single moment, "Until finally..." we reach a resolution and a new normal.

Finding agreement about the event can be difficult, usually because we are still holding onto this idea that the event has to be something cataclysmic. It doesn't. Remember: that flick of the hair, if accepted and endowed with meaning, could be enough to set a whole series of consequences in motion. Be tuned in to the small details and the small shifts. Leave the playwriting to the writers. You are here to live truthfully in imaginary circumstances.

So, let's explore a scenic exercise where we can work together to find the event. It's called "Kiss or Kill." Here's how it works. You and a partner stand several steps apart, facing one another (what we sometimes refer to as a 'gunslinger pose'). Just a neutral posture. You don't have to DO anything. And there will be no talking at all for the duration of the scene.

We're going to start with a suggestion of an object. And similarly to how an object in our word-at-a-time shared stories led to a tragedy or a triumph, this object will be the source of a 'kiss' or a 'kill' moment.

Once we have the suggestion of the object, I'll ask you and your partner to approach one another until you are standing face-to-face—not nose-to-nose, but a conversational distance. Then, one of you will establish the object using spacework. If the suggestion was an apple, for instance, perhaps one of you had it in your pocket. Or you pick it from a tree. Or from a bushel basket on the ground. Wherever the object comes from, establish it clearly. Handle it. Observe it. Really see it. Make sure you both have a chance to make contact with the object. And while this is happening, keep your attention on your partner.

Here comes the crux of the exercise. At some point, based on the behavior and what you observe in your partner, we want to find agreement about whether this object is going to lead us to a 'kiss' or a 'kill'. Meaning: whether it will be the source of great joy and happiness and positivity, or, frankly, death. Once we've established the object itself, our primary task is to agree whether it's 'kiss' or 'kill'. And that decision comes organically out of the interaction.

Let's continue the apple example. You and your partner approach one another. Both seem to be in a pretty pleasant mood. Both are smiling. And then your partner picks a big red apple from a tree branch above your heads. We observe through the spacework that it's a fairly large apple. It has a stem and a leaf. Your partner hands you the apple. You brush it off and give it a little polish. Again, all the while keeping your attention on your partner.

And then we leave ourselves open for any possible shift. We look for an indication that things are about to get better, or they're about to get worse. And that depends on what you observe and how you respond to the behavior.

Let's say your partner reaches out a hand to take the apple back, and you hesitate. Or instinctively pull the apple away. We are not TRYING to provoke one another, but the observation of the slight hesitation may be enough for your partner to get upset and take further action. In that moment, the goal is for you BOTH to see that a shift has happened. And based on whether that shift is positive or negative, find agreement about how the scene will proceed—what the consequences of that change will be.

In this case, if your partner gets angry about your hesitation, it seems like the situation is going to get worse, which will lead to a 'kill.' And, in that moment, we both AGREE there has been a shift, an "event", which we will now explore in slow motion. From the moment you both agree, every consequence of that change is going to be done in slow motion, all the way through until the end of the scene. For a couple of reasons:

1) When we are improvising violence or aggression, we don't have the opportunity to rehearse what's going to happen, so we slow it way down so that we can be absolutely certain that you and your partner are safe and in total agreement about any physical actions taken. Remember, we are working WITHOUT actual physical contact, at the moment, so the spacework and the agreement need to sell the behavior. If you choose to strike your partner in the scene, you would never actually make physical contact, even in slow motion. Your partner's reaction, how they receive the blow, will sell it.

One of the first things we learn in stage combat is that the 'victim,' the recipient of the aggression, is actually the one in control—because without the recipient's acceptance of the behavior, it can't actually happen. If you are supposed to choke me in scene, you place your hands loosely around my neck, and it is MY grip on YOUR wrists that creates our physical connection. And it is MY behavioral reaction to the gesture that makes it real. That makes it appear truthful. So it is in improvisation, as well (minus the actual physical contact).

2) We are working on expanding and exploring offers. Once we have agreement about the shift, we want to experience every bit of what follows. It sounds a little perverse that I want you and your partner to enjoy your death, but this is what we actors are after. I want you to give yourself permission to have the experience, and to allow your imagination to see every detail. Someone slaps your face in slow motion and we want to see the impact (no actual contact, of

course). We want to see the spit fly. We want to see the tremor ripple through your entire body. Just like our circle exercise, let the movement exaggerate organically when in slow motion.

I regularly have to remind my students that there are no cameras in the classroom—no one is recording this. You don't have to scale down a 'performance' or act 'small' as though inches from a camera lens. This is not a performance. In fact, I prefer that you take things further than you think you should. You are exploring the expansion of details and emotions and movement and behavior, not rehearsing camera blocking.

We actors do ourselves a disservice when we become too constrained by the pursuit of 'truth.' We are so fearful of someone thinking we are 'overacting' that we never, even in a rehearsal room or a classroom, get to experience the full breadth of what we are capable. We THINK we are coming in at a 10*, but we are really only pushing 5, maybe less. Why settle for general dislike, when you have the opportunity to play with unbridled fury? Crank up the mechanical bull and find out what it takes to throw you.

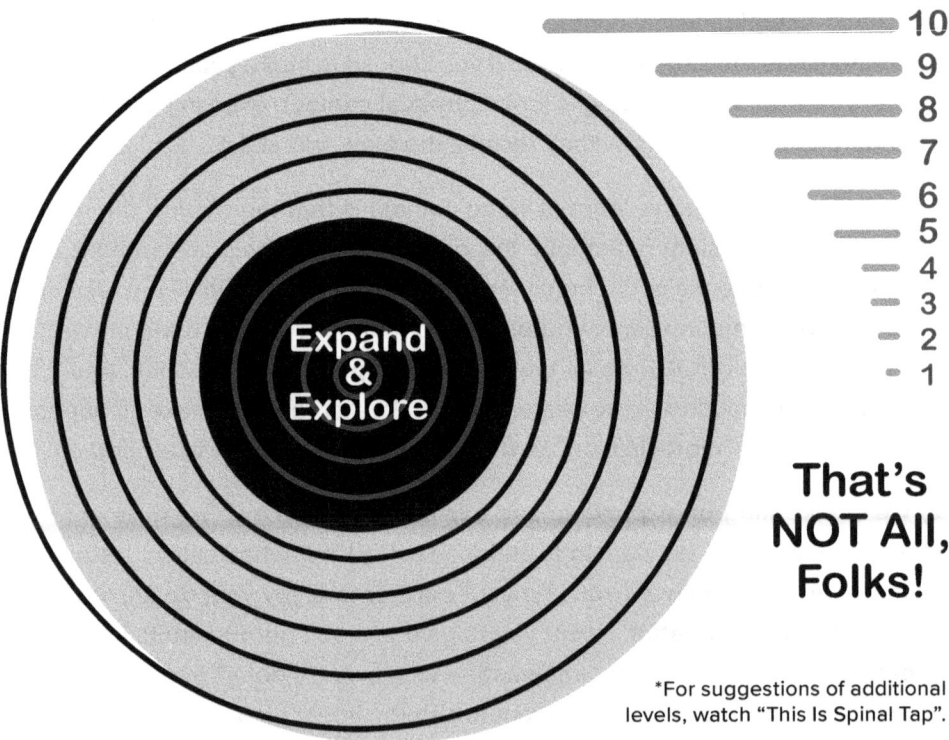

That's NOT All, Folks!

*For suggestions of additional levels, watch "This Is Spinal Tap".

Find out what it's like to experience something at a 10, so that when you need to feel that same intensity but your character can't SHOW it (or the camera doesn't need as much), you have that tool at the ready. Know that you can be brought to life, absent the grand gestures.

To be clear, we are not talking about "volume" or "size". Try not to frame your acting work in terms of scale. Those are TECHNICAL elements of your craft—skills which you will hone in rehearsal and through time spent on set or on stage, to fit the demands of a specific medium. What we want to explore and fully understand now is that great intensity can be achieved through silence and stillness as much as it can through noise and bombast. For now, in this work, remove the constraints of what 'shape' or 'size' your impulses take.

As a way to approach the concept of expansion, it can be useful to deal in extremes: 'if it is not all, then it is nothing'. This sort of black-and-white polarization has a way of raising the stakes of any offer. If you tirelessly pursue the maximum and accept nothing less, if you allow yourself to become intoxicated by the need, you may surprise yourself with the lengths to which you'll go to acquire something—a feeling, an object, a person, whatever. We rarely 'go there', to a place of obsessive intensity, because we are trying to make it safe and palatable so others don't think we're nuts. Screw it! Dive in fully, and accept whatever emerges, without judgment. You'll give yourself the experience, and you'll definitely give your partners something crystal clear for them to respond to.

OK, so you established the object, the apple. You both had a chance to make contact with it. You kept your attention on one another. And then your partner reached for the apple and you hesitated. Your partner took this as an aggression, and you can see it in his behavior. Because of that, we AGREE there has been a negative event, and that this scene is leading to a 'kill'. So, we shift into slow motion to explore the consequences for the remainder of the scene.

Using your imagination, how could the object of an apple lead to a kill? Perhaps, it is poisoned. Someone could choke on it. You could throw an apple at someone. Or beat them to death with it. (Like I said, it sounds dark to even write that, but this is acting, and we are using imaginary circumstances. We have to be curious. What would that be like? Is it even possible?) Someone could step on an apple and fall. Even the act of stealing the apple, or destroying the apple, could be enough to lead to death, as long as you responded accordingly.

One thing is essential to a 'kill' scene: **someone wins and someone loses.** Nine times out of ten, players choose 'kill' scenes over 'kiss' scenes. They interpret changes negatively, and then someone tries to control the scene by killing the other player. That IS the goal of the kill scene, of course, but my point is that we choose that path out of insecurity. We feel uncertain, so we take actions that give us a sense of power and control.

If you recall what I said before about stage combat, the recipient of the aggression has to AGREE to lose the fight. It is perfectly truthful and natural to resist and to fight back against aggression. But, in order for the scene to end, we need to get to the "Until finally…" moment—which, in the case of the kill scene is the final blow. Too often, the kill scene (all happening in slow motion, mind you) becomes a tit-for-tat aggression-fest, where the balance of power keeps shifting between the two players, when what needs to happen is for there to be agreement about who is going to die. Once the 'loser' accepts his fate, we can have all kinds of fun experiencing the consequences of each behavior.

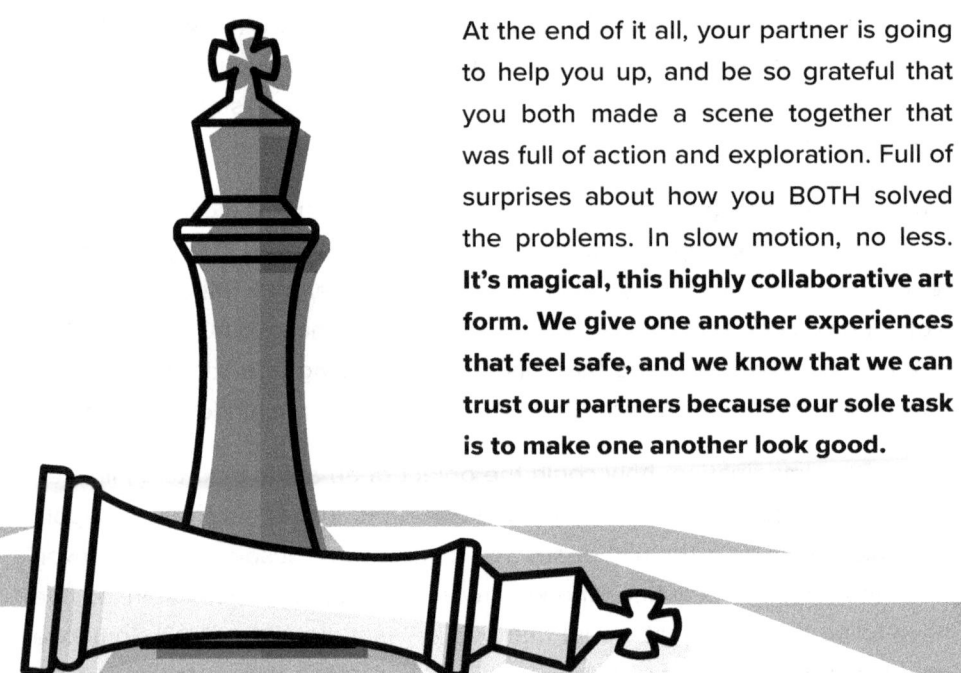

At the end of it all, your partner is going to help you up, and be so grateful that you both made a scene together that was full of action and exploration. Full of surprises about how you BOTH solved the problems. In slow motion, no less. **It's magical, this highly collaborative art form. We give one another experiences that feel safe, and we know that we can trust our partners because our sole task is to make one another look good.**

That same apple, and you and your same partner, could have just as easily moved into a 'kiss' scene. Everything starts the same way. We approach one another. We establish the apple. We both handle it. Your partner reaches out for the apple and, maybe this time, you playfully toss it to him. We observe in that moment a shift. Your partner saw this 'GAME ON!' attitude in the return of the apple, and he wants to play. So, we agree that a shift has happened, and we move into slow motion. Except this time it is clear that the scene is leading to a 'kiss'.

This is not to say that a "kiss" here has to be anything sexual or romantic. What we want to explore in a 'kiss' scene is something that FEELS orgasmic. That FEELS like ecstasy. And, once again, it is our acceptance of the offers that can elevate them to this degree. In fact, the previous kill scene could have become a kiss scene if your partner had interpreted the hesitation differently. If your partner thought you were being coy or flirtatious, wanting him to chase you for the apple, or beg you for the apple, you may have found agreement that the same hesitation led to a kiss scene. It is ALL in how you respond to the offers. You accept that they happen, that they are true, but how you respond is up to you. Just don't THINK about it. Do.

So, how could this apple lead us to ecstasy? You could play catch with it. You could do tricks. You could shoot it off someone's head with an arrow, like William Tell. You could share it. You could bake a pie with it. You could make a game of it and pass it under your chin without using your hands. You could eat it, and savor every crisp, juicy bite. You could use it to give a neck massage. You could buff it to such a high shine that you can see your beautiful faces in it like a mirror. Anything you can imagine. And, it can be fairly ordinary. **It simply becomes about dialing up your own enjoyment of what you observe. Let what you see be the most delightful, most amazing, most joyous thing you've ever experienced.**

A kiss scene will end when we explode with enjoyment—at the point where we couldn't possibly go further or we would literally burst. (At which point, I guess a kiss scene would turn into a kill scene? Ha-ha.) Your "Until finally..." moment in a kiss scene is the orgasmic moment—nothing held back.

Funny how we, as actors, seem to be hard-wired for the negative, heavy drama. I say: explore the POSITIVE possibilities, just the same. Not only things like getting rich, or sex, drugs and rock and roll. Use your actor's imagination to ask "What if...?" How can you take a seemingly innocuous occurrence and imagine it into something expansive and important?

A pinball machine is an apt analogy. An offer is set in motion, like the pinball. And all throughout the scene, like bumpers in the machine, you and your partners are ready to react. Not only are you READY to react, you are on high alert, incredibly sensitized. It will only take the slightest pressure to elicit a strong and specific response. Any small brush of contact is met with an impulsive, powerful push. There is no agenda—just pure response. We can never predict the direction the offer will take from there, but we can be sure that staying actively engaged, taking things personally, and responding boldly will create momentum in the scene and lead to further bold and clear responses. Energy has a way of expanding organically as long as we don't intentionally dampen it in order to shield ourselves and control the narrative.

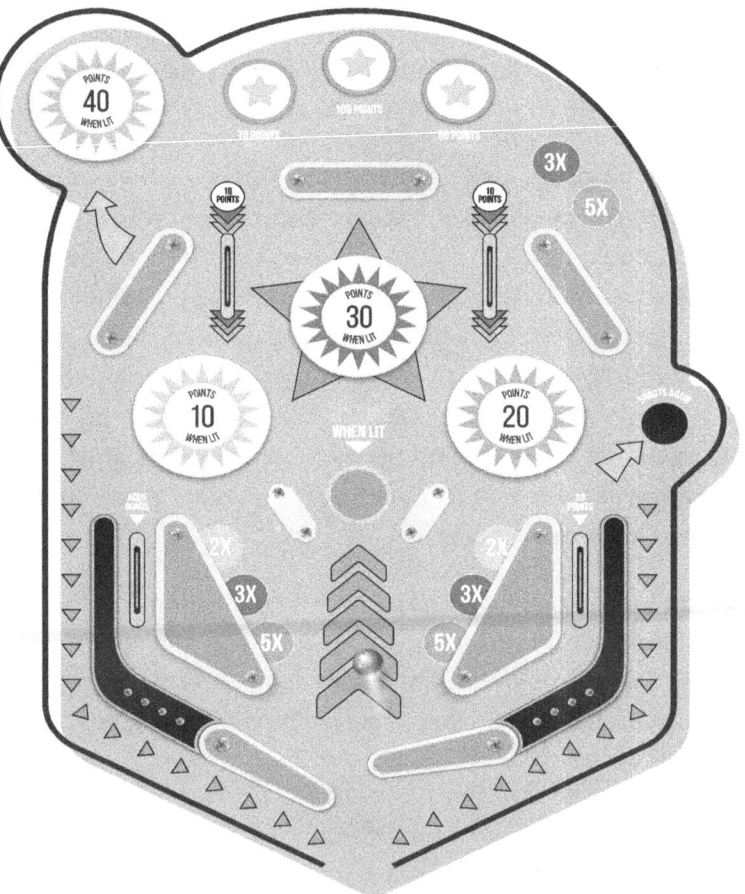

Say someone offers you a piece of chewing gum in a scene. Not a big deal, right? Well, what if your imagination tells you from that simple, casual gesture that this person is in LOVE with you. That simple and specific response sets the whole scene in motion. 'If that's true, what else?' Expand the consequences, offer by offer. Take action based on what you observe and what it means to you. Let the pinball continue to ricochet freely until you've won or lost.

There is no way of knowing how your partner will respond in each moment. Only once you act, will you see what actually occurs in response. Whether that piece of gum ultimately leads you to impossible joy with your newfound soulmate, or perhaps literally chokes the life out of you when you are rebuffed. And we can't wait to see every juicy detail. You've placed your bet. Now keep doubling down until you've hit big or gone bust.

In improvisation, you can forget about what's 'right' or 'wrong', and embrace the chance to explore ANY possibility, positive or negative. Improvisation is the place to explore 'what would happen IF...?' It is your opportunity to say the thing you shouldn't probably say, or do the thing you probably shouldn't do. Too often, I see actors stifle their impulses because they are concerned about how they might look, or what unplanned thing might happen that they didn't intend. They want people to think they are a good actor. And for most of us, 'good' acting means believable acting. Real. Truthful.

Yes...AND it has to include an element of imagination—even fantasy. You CAN behave truthfully in the most imaginary circumstances. If YOU believe it, however far-fetched, we will, too. We want to be surprised and delighted. We want to witness how you solve the problems. We watch and wonder, 'What would I do if I was in that situation?' 'What if that happened to me?' The answer, like the pinball, could go a million different ways. And, that's the key. **Explore. Expand. Turn off the critic that is judging your 'performance' and devote all your attention to the moment at hand. Say "Yes!" to any experience. Give yourself permission.**

5
Now You're Speaking My Language

Most all of the exploration we've done so far has been without dialogue. All due respect to playwrights and screenwriters, it's about what you DO, not what you say. I will always encourage you to DO FIRST...Speak if you must. And in improvisation, in particular, we have a tendency to depend on our language to solve the problems of creating something out of nothing and finding agreement, instead of our behavior. Remember, the DOING is everything.

Yet, our truth is that we talk to one another. We communicate verbally. So, although we shouldn't depend on it, it is completely natural to share dialogue. Let's wade a bit further into using dialogue, while continuing to build and emphasize our spacework and behavior—by working with gibberish.

Gibberish is made-up language. And as we improvise, we will create that language together. Languages consist of characters. Consonants and vowels. Languages have rhythm and melody and flow. Our intonation lets us know when a thought is completed. Or when it is emphasized. Or how to distinguish between homonyms. Even when to breathe. Gibberish is no different. It has a vocabulary. Each word has a meaning, even if we don't know the meaning yet.

But we are ABSOLUTELY using it to communicate ideas. Gibberish is not filler. It is not 'Blah blah. Blah blah blah. Blah blah blah blah.' Sounds and words are unique, and they communicate unique things.

Let's start by simply building words—stringing sounds together to create speech—and figure out how to really communicate. If you and your partner did not speak the same language, you would likely compensate with behavioral cues to attempt to communicate clearly. You may not know how to say "welcome" in another language, but you instinctively know how to behave to greet another person, and to be receptive and friendly.

I want you to start with your own name. Just your first name (or last name, or nickname) is fine, to keep it simple. Take the letters and sounds of your name and rearrange them to create a new gibberish name for yourself. For example, my name is Robert, so I jumble the letters and sounds and my gibberish name is Teboro. To assist with remembering this new word we've created, we are going to repeat it a bunch, and you'll attach a distinctive gesture to use every time we say your new gibberish name.

If, when you say your name, it sounds heroic, for example, then accompany your name with an heroic gesture. If your name sounds regal, perhaps a bow or curtsy. If your name sounds militant, give us a formal salute. The gesture doesn't need to be recognizable, but it is intended to help us remember your name, so it's best if it's clear and specific—maybe it has the same feeling or intent as the sound of your name. Likewise, it could be a gesture that indicates your personality. If your partners see that you like to dance or that you are a dancer, perhaps adding a balletic arabesque will help us easily identify the gibberish you.

Give us your name and your gesture, and we will all repeat it, just as we did in our mirroring work so far. **The best way to remember any offer and to keep it alive throughout a scene is to repeat it and to engage with it.** You will not likely remember something you hear once, with the multitude of offers happening. If you've ever been to a gathering where you didn't know others, how many names did you remember after meeting people once? Repeat. Make associations. Make something more significant with endowments and you are far more likely to remember it.

Each person in our group circle will jumble the sounds and letters of their own name and share it with us alongside their defining gesture. We will retrace and repeat the names and gestures to get them all into our bones.

Once we've introduced everyone, and repeated a few times, I ask for a volunteer who wants a challenge to give us ALL the names and gestures. It can feel intimidating but I insist you give it a try, mostly because I want to you to feel what it feels like to COMMIT to your idea instead of stopping yourself to decide whether you've gotten it exactly right. If you do something with confidence, we, your partners, WILL say "yes." It is not in our ethic to point out your 'mistakes.' Do your best, and as long as you are TRYING, we'll all adapt to the shifts, should they happen.

Each of us on the outside of the circle whose name you are repeating is there to help you, as we would be in any scene. We can mirror you or clue you to spark the connection. We WANT you to get it. We WANT you to succeed. As many times as I say it, it takes a bit of reprogramming for actors to be able to trustfully live in the space where everyone works together. We become so conditioned to think that others (other actors, in particular) want us to FAIL. That they want us to fall so that they can win. It may be true for some, but if YOU are a generous actor, you will attract other generous people who also want to collaborate, not compete.

Use the gesture as a way to connect to the name. I find that people are more likely to forget the word, but they usually remember the gesture. Allow your body to begin to move. If you find yourself moving, the name may come to your lips more readily. If the words aren't coming, keep repeating the gesture. Use your behavior to connect.

Once a few people have completed the challenge of repeating ALL the names, I like to do a little call-and-response game—a bit like a game of Marco Polo. Using the names and gestures we just created, one person begins by saying their own name with their gesture, and then calling the name and gesture of someone else in the circle. As soon as you recognize someone has called your name, you say your own name with your gesture and then call the name and gesture of someone else in the circle. And the pattern continues.

Players can tend to get a little stressed, worrying that they won't be able to remember everyone's names and gestures. We actors are prone to a kind of self-sabotage where we think if we don't remember EVERYthing, we won't remember ANYthing. I remind you that, if you think back to where we started with Whoosh Whoa, there is no obligation to use EVERY rule. All we need in any particular moment is ONE offer. So, if you find yourself getting overwhelmed with ALL the possibilities in this work, try to bring yourself back to the moment right in front of you. Don't worry about trying to do an entire scene in one beat. Take it moment by moment.

Ultimately, in this call-and-response game, we want to get to the point where the names and gestures are happening almost simultaneously—as soon as someone begins to call a name or make a gesture, the person to whom that name and gesture belongs should jump in. The people in this game who tend to get called on the most are those whose names and gestures are UNforgettable—usually that means distinctive and simple. But as we go on and some of the less familiar names and gestures are repeated, others will likely jump in.

In essence an entire interaction occurs, much like a scene, using only names and call signs. "Yes...And" is very much a call-and-response rhythm. You do. I respond. My response is an offer to which you then respond. And on and on it goes, like falling dominoes, until we follow the entire thread and can go no further.

In order to keep my streak of outdated references alive, when we start exploring gibberish I like to use an example borrowed from a Public Television show from the 1970's called "The Electric Company". Watch old episodes and see if you don't recognize a few famous faces. Rita Moreno and Morgan Freeman got their starts in TV with that show. The show had lots of different segments, some live action, some animated. A lot of the show had to do with basic skills of language and math and science.

There was one segment on the show where two silhouetted faces would appear, in profile. One person would make the first sound of a word, like "ch..."

ch...

...arge

charge!

and the other person would make the last sound of the word, like "...arge", and then both of them would combine the sounds and say the complete word together: "charge".

This is a fun way to build language in gibberish. One difference here is that we are not trying to make words we know from English or any other language. Rather, we want to create NEW words in our gibberish language.

So, one player makes a sound. "Bla..." The second player makes another sound. "...cloo." And then we ALL repeat the new word together. "Blacloo." The sounds don't need to be distinct syllables. The sound could have started "croo..." and finished "...t" making the new word "croot". The important habit to build here is to commit to the sound, regardless of whether it makes 'sense'. In this exercise, we are not concerned with the meaning of the words. Simply creating the words themselves.

It always helps if we can get the work out of our heads and into our bodies, so we'll introduce a rhythm we can snap along with—to avoid unnecessary hesitation and thinking. If you have no time to think, you are more likely to act, which is exactly what we want. There is no perfect answer. All we need is SOMEthing, and then we can take that offer and build on it.

Don't worry if you end up creating words that already exist. If we have been speaking a language for a long time, perhaps since we learned to speak, it is highly likely that sounds will follow other familiar sounds purely out of habit. It's OK. We're focused on the rhythm and building the skills of 'doing before thinking'.

Now take a couple of the new words you've created together, and let's add them to our vocabulary. Let's assign them meaning. Point at the floor. What's that called? "Hotma." Point at the ceiling. What's that called? "Clerch." There are three windows. What's one of those called? "Brob." Count to three. "Noch. Ting. Gloob." Count the number of hotma. "Noch." Count the number of clerch. "Noch." Count the number of brob. "Gloob." What color is the floor? "Pula." What else in the room is pula? The "flang" (chair). And the "hoff" (door).

By using these words repeatedly and applying a consistent meaning to each, we begin to build a usable vocabulary of gibberish. When a word is repeated that we 'know', we can then respond truthfully, just as we did with the gibberish names.

Funnily, sometimes our gibberish words bear not-so-vague resemblances to their English equivalents (or whatever language we all share, if not English). The floor might be "fluah." The ceiling, "seeglo." The color purple, "prollpah." It's OK if this happens. It is hard to break all the associations we currently have with language, and that's not even our goal. So, if your new word is a shadow of the old word, let it roll. The important thing here is that we use gibberish words in the same way we would use words we know—with meaning.

You may also find yourself habitually substituting words from other languages. If you are improvising in English, and happen to be fluent in Greek or Dutch or Japanese, try not to cheat by inserting real words from other languages. Sometimes our gibberish takes on the quality of a known language. My gibberish tends to sound Russian, although I only know a few words in Russian. ("Spasibo" comes to mind.) Some tend to sound Chinese. Or Spanish. Some sound like they are shopping at IKEA among the flurgs and hōokens. If you want to speak an Italian-inspired gibberish, be wary of simply stringing together words you remember from your last dinner out. "Spaghetti manicotti pasta ricotta fusilli roma pancetta bolognese" said with an Italian accent is NOT Italian gibberish. (It just makes us hungry.)

We can actually build entire phrases in the same way we built our "Electric Company" words. We simply combine sounds, and then use that string of sounds to communicate something specific.

Let's try.

One by one, I want each player to add a sound, until it feels like we have a phrase. So, one by one:

"Cha..."

"Ti..."

"Toe..."

"Ka..."

"Wah..."

"Mey."

> Cha ti toe ka wah mey.

We string it all together, and find its natural rhythm. "Cha ti toe ka wah mey." Say it a few times to get a feeling for it, until it flows naturally and conversationally. "Cha ti toe ka wah mey. Cha ti toe ka wah mey. Cha ti toe ka wah mey."

Try directing the phrase at someone. Put an intention behind it. Maybe even add their gibberish name when you address them. "Cha ti toe ka wah mey, Teboro." Are you telling them something, or are you asking a question? What does your tone and inflection suggest? Based on their response, it will become clear what you just communicated. Did your partner think you were scolding them? Did they receive it and respond as though it was a greeting?

Now I want you to use the phrase we just built to initiate a short gibberish interaction. Create a space object. It can be anything that comes to mind. A piece of jewelry. A chair. Some food. A car. Whatever. I want you to approach someone else in the circle, and give them this object as a gift. Use their gibberish name. Use your spacework to define the object for your partner. Handle it with integrity, and then give it to them. Your partner will find agreement about the object through their mirroring and their own interaction with the object. We can agree that we were given a necklace if we handle it delicately, and put it around our neck and admire it.

Avoid giving someone a gift that is boxed and wrapped, as a rule. Handing someone a box, or a letter, or a book puts a lot of responsibility on your partner to define the object. If you have an idea to give them a book, give endowments that will help them know what type of book. A paperback novel? A big encyclopedia? A magical book of spells and incantations? A small book of poetry? Their favorite storybook from childhood? They may not ultimately find agreement about what YOU see, but be as specific as possible, regardless.

And when you present this object to your partner (or to me, in this example), use the phrase we created. "Cha ti toe ka wah mey, Teboro." Which of those gibberish words is the name for the object? How do you make that clear? Is a necklace called a "wah mey"? If someone were to translate this phrase as they would any other language, what would each of the words mean? "Cha ti toe ka wah mey, Teboro." "Hope you like this necklace, Teboro." Your partner and you can further find agreement by repeating the word 'wah mey' whenever you refer to the object.

And your partner should respond. In YOUR language. KNOW what you want to say, and simply replace your English words with gibberish words. **You'll find quickly how important the INTENTION is to being able to communicate in gibberish. You have to REALLY say something,** not just babble nonsense to fill the air. We saw before that we don't need a lot of words, since the behavior can do the heavy lifting (literally). In fact, just saying someone's name and nothing else can communicate a lot. HOW you say it may be more important than WHAT you say. Whatever it is, make sure you MEAN it.

When you are interpreting someone's gibberish offer, focus on the behavior more than the literal words, as you would anyway, even if you knew the language. If someone told you "I love you" in English, you could interpret it a thousand different ways based on the tone, the behavior, and the circumstance. Same with gibberish. Read the behavior, and simply let the language flow in response. Say what you want to say. Just say it in a new language. And don't listen for drama that's not there. If things seem pleasant, don't insist on a 'kill' when a 'kiss' is on the table. Don't playwrite. Don't provoke. Don't fight what's there. Embrace it. (Without touching, of course.)

It's always useful, if you are able, to mirror the tone and style of the gibberish language your partner offers, as well. If it sounds Italian-inspired, mirror the style. If it sounds harsh or guttural, with lots of consonant sounds, mirror that. If it sounds melodic or poetic, like something from Shakespeare, mirror that. It is a reliable way to put you both in the same world of the scene.

If you were the one who used the gibberish phrase to present the object and initiate the dialogue, switch roles and give yourself the chance to receive. Create a new gibberish phrase, one sound at a time, with the help of your partners. Repeat it several times until it feels natural. Then your partner will approach you with a space object and communicate using the phrase. Respond, in their language, to what you observe. USE the object to be sure you have agreement about what it is and about any details you see. Don't just set the object aside and talk for the rest of the scene because you are unsure or unable to identify what you were given. In gibberish, language is not likely going to help you solve that problem. You MUST use your spacework and engage with objects if you ever want to find agreement about what they are. Do first, speak if you must. And when you do speak, say what you mean, and mean what you say.

Let's try a couple more things with gibberish. First, find a partner. We're going to use our "Once upon a time…" story structure to tell a story together in gibberish. Follow the structure, even replace specific words and phrases. REALLY communicate. Remember, behavior is important. Use your intention and energy to help your partner understand what you are saying.

Find common vocabulary. Especially your main character's name. Every time we hear "Charlie", we have some measure of agreement about who is doing the action. Anything that can be repeated should be repeated. KNOW, as best as you are able, what you are talking about. And one good way to help that is to keep it simple.

Lock into a style, if you can. If it feels like you are telling a romantic fairy tale, embrace the style and let the story flow. Although we never want to assume, using a genre or style does help put us in the same world of the story. There are certain tropes that you find in American westerns, or romances, or sci-fi. If it helps with understanding, use it. Find agreement wherever you can.

See how well you can follow the arc of the story. How do we know, in gibberish, when we are in the early set up? How do we know when there is a shift? How do we know when we are exploring consequences? How do we know when we've reached a resolution? Language alone will not be enough. So, explore what you and your partner do to get yourself on the same page at any given moment. Using your physicality, gesturing and engaging energetically are likely part of the solution.

Try telling a second story in gibberish, this time playing the characters. YOU are the actors in the story. See if being physically engaged helps the gibberish language to flow, and help you and your partner to tell a clearer story. If your imagination can really see it, chances are, when you talk about the story afterward, you will be surprised how many details you both knew, even though neither one of you knows the language.

Now, let's try applying our gibberish to more of a scenic game, and make some more discoveries about the role language plays—how we balance dialogue with behavior to make clear offers. This one's another guessing game called "What Are You Doing?", reminiscent of the spacework exercise we played earlier.

We'll create this scene with three players. In a minute, we will send one of the players out of the room so that we can gather some suggestions. Before that, let's run down how the game goes. We will get an activity, probably an occupation. So, let's say our players are all furniture makers, and specifically makers of painted wooden chairs.

What are some objects we would expect to see in a scene about makers of painted wooden chairs? Tools, like a lathe, paint brushes, screwdriver, drill, saw. Supplies like paint, wood, tarps, crates, screws, dowels. And where would an occupation like this likely take place? A wood shop. Great! There are so many unknowns to be solved once we get rolling, it makes sense to agree on the basic setup. This is NOT how most scenes will begin, of course, by discussing everything we know and plotting it out. But because we have not done proper scenes yet, it's important to give ourselves a solid foundation so we can get to the heart of the game. Which is this: one of our three players is going to leave the room so that we can jot down some ideas—three things the remaining players will need to get that person to do. And these three things are UNRELATED to the shared occupation we already know.

So, we send out our third player. What are three things the guesser will have to do that are UNrelated to the occupation of furniture maker?

"Do 5 jumping jacks." Great. Two more.

"Brush their teeth." Great. One more.

"Put on a tuxedo." OK.

Here are the ground rules about helping the guesser. You cannot do the activity for them, or before they do. So, you cannot start brushing your teeth and then encourage your partner to do the same. You CAN, however, provide them with REASONS to do the activity, and even provide them with the OBJECTS they'll need. So, if one of the suggestions was to ride a skateboard, you can't ride one yourself, but you can establish a skateboard and give it to your partner. You COULD do a parallel activity, such as roller skating or riding a bike, if you think it will lead the guesser in the right direction.

Once the guesser has done the activity correctly, we will give them a little round of applause so they know they've gotten it, and that they can move on to guessing the next.

The final rule is that IF you speak, you can only speak in gibberish.

A couple of hints about playing this game: If you are the guesser, your primary job is to engage with the objects and the space, and to make bold choices about what objects you see, and what your partners want you to do. If you go down the wrong path, they'll let you know, and then adjust themselves to tee you up again. Go for it! Set your imagination free and jump into the space and the activity. You already know these three things will be UNRELATED to your task. So, because they could BE anything, be willing to TRY anything.

If you are the two players guiding the guesser, WORK TOGETHER. You can get the guesser to do the three things in any order you like. But you better be sure you are both working on the same task at the same time. The two of you can build on one another's offers to lead the guesser in the right direction. The rest of us KNOW what the tasks are, so to us they may seem obvious—that your offers couldn't be any clearer. The point being: **your guessing partner may not interpret your offers the way you hope. So, be ready to adapt.**

Lastly, for all of the players, keep yourself grounded in your environment and your spacework. Use the occupation to help provide reasons for the unrelated activities. Maybe while painting the wooden chair, the guesser gets some paint on their face and on their teeth. This may eventually guide them to brush their teeth. And once they do the activity correctly and we give them a little applause, don't just forget about what happened, throw away the toothbrush and go on to the next task. Rather, try to fold the unrelated task back into the occupational activity. Maybe we paint the chair with the toothbrush now. Maybe we all smile broadly as we work to show how clean our teeth are. What we don't want is for the task to happen and then disappear. We want it to create a "Because of that…" reaction and lead to the next thing.

Beyond keeping the base occupational activity going, we are not putting any pressure on ourselves to have a story. Don't look for drama. Don't worry about a shift or an event. Just keep bringing your attention back to the occupational activity. You may find that there is a mini-event that leads to each of the three unrelated activities. In this case, those events are more of a 'reason' why the guesser needs to do each unrelated task.

Use your words—just be sure they are gibberish. Do your best to avoid compensating for lack of language with lots of pointing and indicating. Instead, put your physicality into your spacework. And when you DO say something, be clear with your intention which, as we saw a bit ago, can be very effective at eliciting a response.

It may all feel a little frantic. There will be moments of confusion. Your partner may make bold choices and STILL misidentify the targeted activity. Use the game to explore how we solve those problems—and whether we tend to depend more heavily on language or behavior. Usually, if most improv I see is any indication, our words are the crutch we too often lean on.

Remember, in scripted work, actors don't write the words. We ACT. We behave. We DO. And when there are words for us to speak, they are said with intention—which simply equates to more observable behavior. We want to build these same skills when we improvise—when we act without a script. And we do that by engaging our actor's imagination to engage in a way that makes it real for ourselves, our partners, and the audience. Whether we speak or not.

Last scene for our gibberish work, I promise. I want you to try "Film Dub." We'll need four players for this one. Two to be actors IN the film, and two to translate the dialogue from gibberish into English (or into whatever language you improvise).

Just like our earlier gibberish stories, it can be helpful here to lock into a STYLE. So, I like to ask for a suggestion of either a country in the world that produces film, or a genre of filmmaking. Brace yourself for loads of stereotypes here. At this stage, it's fine. For now, we WANT to have as many shared assumptions about the style as possible so that we can focus on the task of interpreting the gibberish, and relating it to the behavior. So, for example, if we get the suggestion of any East Asian country, we can probably expect some martial arts. If we get a suggestion for Film Noir, expect to see detectives and dames meeting on foggy nights under street lamps. Embrace it. Explore it. Mimic, don't mock.

The two players who will be acting IN the film will both be speaking gibberish—hopefully, gibberish that is influenced by the style, and also feels common to both players. We want it to feel like they are speaking the same language, one that they both understand. These actors should engage the space, using spacework and behavior to tell the story of this scene of the film. Remember, we need to know who, where, and what pretty much right off the bat. Focus on the doing. Talk only when you must.

The job of the two players translating, then, is to literally, word for word, translate what the actors are saying, as though we are reading the translated dialogue across the bottom of the screen. Try to match the actors' tone and energy. It will help with the translation. And, fight the urge to be funny or clever. Rogue translators like to mess with the actors—to make them say things they didn't really say. PLEASE, focus on listening and observe the scene AS IT IS. If one actor establishes that he has a single long-stemmed rose which smells sweet, and gently presents it to the object of his affection, the other actor, we don't need the translator to insert themselves by identifying the object as a dish rag. FORGET about 'wacky' improv comedy, and learn to enjoy improvising for TRUTH. Say what you see. Translate what you hear.

Pair up. One translator should translate for one actor, and the other translator should translate for the other actor. The more you can mirror the voice and quality of the person for whom you are translating, the better. Match their energy, too.

Beyond the challenge of accurate translation, we need to find a rhythm with the actors and the translators. Once an actor has finished speaking, we want to immediately hear the translation. Then the next actor can speak, and we hear, directly following, from their translator. Actors need to leave room for the translation while continuing the action of the scene. So, don't drop your behavior while you wait for the translation. Stay in the moment.

And LISTEN. Although the translators are TRYING to translate EXACTLY, offers may be interpreted differently than you intended. So, the actors need to listen to the translation, and then make any behavioral or spacework adjustments based on the verbal offer coming from the translator. If you handed your betrothed a rose, and the translator saw a daisy, adjust. Whatever the translator said is now the truth of the scene. Be ready to let go of your own ideas, while continuing to be as specific and detailed as possible with your spacework and your gibberish.

Translators should listen intently, as well. If you hear gibberish words being repeated, be sure to assign them the same meaning. This is especially important with names. When the actors say one another's names, we want to hear those translated every time. If a bit of gibberish dialogue is spoken with a particular rhythm or tone, match it. We want the translation to feel as though it is coming from the actor themselves. The more the translator can put themselves into the place of the actor they are translating for, the more aligned you both will be. Say what you hear, based on what you observe. Look for intention as a clue to the words themselves.

Don't worry about telling a complete story. You've got a lot of plates spinning, as the saying goes. And definitely don't worry about being interesting or clever or funny. Embrace the genre or origin country of the film suggestion and lean on what you already know. Then simply put your attention on the other person and respond to offers as they come. **The story writes itself if you simply and organically move from moment to moment, offer to offer—even in gibberish.**

6
Give & Take

There is an energetic call and response that defines improvisation, underpinned by the "Yes…And." This creates a shared responsibility and a shared experience in which our primary goal is to support our partners. I want to explore the give and take that's required. Of our focus. Of our energy. Of our attention. There is a balance, often difficult to find, that we need to strike between making a bold and clear offer, WHILE IN THE SAME INSTANT being willing to give up our own offer in service of what our partners and the scene need.

At every moment, we are looking for agreement, and sometimes that means 'losing,' as we saw in the Kiss or Kill exercise. Giving up your own agenda, your own idea, your own need for certainty and control so that the story can advance is exactly the place you need to be. The imagination is fully engaged, but we do not get locked into any one idea, and do not prioritize our own ideas over the offers of our partners. No one can move forward without agreement, and that also means agreeing where the focus of the scene is— what's important.

Let's warm up this muscle by building a machine together. Much like our Freeze Tag and our slow-motion work, someone will originate a repetitive sound and movement. If you are the originator, pick a movement that is easy to repeat for an extended period of time. Probably not a good idea in this exercise to be hopping up and down on one leg, or something else strenuous like sit-ups. Simply repeat a movement, as though on a constant loop. You could chop the air with a "Slooooooop!" You could move your hand and arm like a claw with a "Brrrrrrzshttttttt."

Once someone has established something, and with as little hesitation as possible, another player should jump in to mirror or complement the sound and movement. Don't THINK about it—get in and discover it by doing. One by one, the remaining players should jump in and add to the machine. Mirror or complement. If your imagination sees a particular function or need, add that. And then continue to repeat the sound and movement you create.

As each person joins, the group needs to absorb the addition. To find the rhythm of the group. To function together. To feel how to continue an activity while making space for other offers. Maybe one player's addition sparks your own imagination and you can adapt your sound and movement to create some clarity, for yourself and for your partners. Perhaps you had no idea what you were doing until someone hopped in and mirrored you. Once you saw THEM doing it, it became clear to you. This, again, is the power of observation—of putting your attention on your partners.

Once everyone has joined, we really want to coalesce. Listen to one another. Work with one another. Find agreement about the collective sound and function of this machine. Don't worry about 'figuring it out.' Let it reveal itself to you by doing. Repeatedly.

As a parallel to the pace exploration we did before, let's say this machine is now functioning, on a scale of one to ten, at a speed of five—right in the middle. What happens when we increase the speed of this machine to a seven? Find out. What adjustments need to be made? Does speed require more precision? More care? More specificity? Based on what you see, is it possible for the machine to perform its function at this speed?

What if we turn it all the way up to a ten? What is the fastest this machine can work? What adaptations do we need to make? Do we become more precise or less as we increase speed? What does that mean for our standard of perfection? Remember, we can't let ourselves off the hook with our spacework simply because it has become more challenging. Improv is perpetually about the exploration of "What would happen if....?" Using our imaginations, we dive in and discover what happens. There is no room for plotting and reasoning. We won't know how fast the machine can go until we crank it up and see.

Now let's bring the speed back to five. Together. Does the machine regain its stability? Does five now feel slow compared to where we began? Does your function within the machine become more clear after returning from the faster pace? Did you lose specificity and then regain it once the pace slowed?

Let's dial it down to a three. What lessons did we take from our prior slow-motion work? What detail do you see at this slower pace that was perhaps missed even at neutral speed? Does slowing down add clarity to your offers? Does it allow you room to really listen?

And, lastly, I am going to unplug the machine. As a group, I want you to agree how the machine powers down. Is it a linear machine? Does each part power down in succession? Or does every part power down at once? Is it gradual, or instant? What sound does the machine make as it stops? Again, we don't know any of the answers to these questions until we DO, together, and see. And we could play this game again with every player performing the same sound and movement and still have a different ending. It will all depend on what we agree is happening at that moment.

That in itself is a beautiful thing—to relieve yourself of the need for any particular result or outcome. We just go moment by moment, and the sum total of those moments is the result. We can't plan it. It simply becomes what it becomes. This should be freeing. It should be reassuring to know that you hold no responsibility for hitting any specific target. Don't work for the result. When you start by deciding where you want to end up, you immediately take yourself out of the present moment. And everything that happens will be measured against whether it is taking us toward our intended finish. Things NEVER go perfectly according to plan, so to me this sounds like a prescription for disappointment, scene after scene. Better to follow each moment closely, and at the end say 'that's exactly what was supposed to happen'.

Now I want you to move around the room, just as we did when we were exploring pace. Walk about until I can explain our next exercise. We are going to work on our give-and-take. In a moment, I will ask you to freeze in whatever place and whatever position you find yourself. All except one player who will remain in motion and add a sound (no words, not even gibberish, just a sound, like we did in Sound Ball) and will continue moving through space and repeating that sound until someone else TAKES it from them. Another player can 'take' at any moment by simply breaking their freeze and moving through space with a repeatable sound of their own. The sound and movement can be different than what the first player originated. The point is what happens at the precise moment of transfer between give and take.

We want that moment to be as instantaneous as possible. AS SOON AS the other player begins to move or make a sound, the player already in motion should FREEZE. The player NOW in motion, making a repeated sound, will continue until another player breaks their own freeze. AS SOON AS someone else begins to move or make a sound, they should FREEZE. We never want to have two players moving at once.

It sounds simple, but it is actually harder than it seems, particularly because the offers can come from anywhere. It is not easy in a group, where everyone is moving in different directions, to be able to take in everybody at once. But it's a great skill to build. To have eyes on all sides of your head. To be engaged in your own activity and still be able to observe and take in your partners, and to give up your own activity in service of the scene. **Be bold. AND be ready to abandon your own idea as quickly as you initiate it.**

It is interesting to notice in this game that very often when a player 'takes' (breaks their freeze and moves and makes sound), they EXPECT to be interrupted right away. This usually looks like hesitancy or lack of commitment. Someone 'takes' boldly and then gets quiet or stops moving because they anticipate someone is going to immediately step on their idea. Or there is a rush of embarrassment or self-consciousness because you are now the only one moving and making noise, perhaps in a way that surprised you. Build a habit that once you make an offer you commit to it completely, whatever form it takes. Follow your impulse until another offer comes. And don't back away until that happens. Own it, and let your partners respond.

This is how we take care of our partners: by not leaving them out there longer than they want. We don't have to 'save' anyone, but we should recognize when our partners need us, even if we ourselves are not 'ready.' We should always be able to jump in. It is our only purpose, after all: to make our partners look good.

What happens when two people initiate at the same time? You probably discovered this at some point. It is exactly like scenework, in this regard. You need to be ready to step up and make an offer in support of your partners and the scene. BUT, someone else may ALSO have an impulse at the same moment to make an offer. What needs to happen is what you discovered in the Kiss or Kill exercise: someone has to 'lose' so that the group and the scene can move forward.

We saw the same thing happen way back in our Whoosh Whoa game. At some point, two different people accept an offer that was only intended for one of them, and all of a sudden we have a 'splitter.' The offers (be they whooshes, whoas, zaps, whatever) start to move in two directions. I've seen groups and players solve this in different ways. Too often, the surprise of something happening for which we don't know the "rule" makes players freeze. They immediately redirect all of their attention to their logical brain and try to figure out what the 'right' answer is—and, in doing so, deny the impulse to simply respond. Your response IS the answer. There is no guarantee it won't lead to more surprises, and the game may even crash and burn. But, ACTION is always the preferable option to cogitation. Thinking is passive. It holds the energy in place instead of sharing it. **Only once energy is released can it elicit a response.** The only behavior we can observe when someone is thinking is probably just someone standing still.

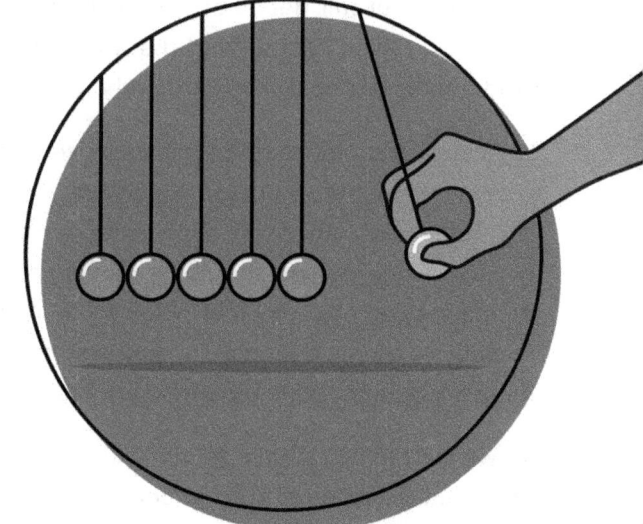

Let the game continue, and see how many times you can take. At the end of the exercise, the number of experiences you have 'taking' focus should be equal to the number of times you experience 'giving' focus. Because each time you take, your offer brings an instant response in which someone gives you focus. And when the next offer comes, you will immediately respond—you freeze and give your partner's offer focus.

You may begin to notice that certain offers are more successful than others at being observed, and creating the cleanest transition of movement and sound from player to player. Most people find quickly that bold and loud offers will get attention. But there are diminishing returns to throwing a tantrum every time you need attention. More importantly, we cannot expect every offer to be that obvious. Use this exercise to explore how pared-down an offer can be and still be seen and heard. Recall your work in the Point-Yes exercise. Is it about choosing to take when the energy is already near to you, making a clear transition? Is it heavily dependent on eye contact? Is it about making a particularly unique offer, in terms of the movement or the sound? Is it about dynamic change?

What about intensity? Not scale or volume, remember. As we saw in our exploration of slow-motion and expansion, intensity comes from the specificity of the intention. If the behavior is clear, attention will be paid. My mother would not raise her voice or become aggressive to make a point when I misbehaved. She would get still, get quiet, get close, look me right in the eyes… and I KNEW before she even said a word that I needed to change my ways. Strong and bold offers are not always loud and big.

Let's start another round of this exercise, and this time I want you to create a repeatable gibberish phrase. KNOW what you are saying, just say it in gibberish. Same rules otherwise apply. One person should be moving at ALL times, but ONLY one person should be moving at any time. Communicate. You can be expressing how you feel. You can be making an observation. You can be secretly cursing me for making you do this exercise again. Whatever. A movement and a repeatable gibberish phrase, one person at a time. Give and take.

As we start to use language, the exercise begins to take on a new dimension. I find that movements start to become more purposeful. They organically become more aligned with the sound we are making. And we use our movement to support our intention—what we are saying that we want others to hear.

So, let's push that idea. Start to DIRECT your gibberish phrase and the energy of your movement TOWARD someone. It doesn't mean you need to rush up to them and scream in their face. But, CHOOSE someone who you think NEEDS to hear what you have to say, and try to get through to them. You can physically move in their direction, keeping in mind you may be interrupted by someone taking focus, causing you to freeze. Who knows? Maybe they are directing their energy and words toward YOU, in response to what you just offered. Maybe their character felt you needed to be corrected, or stopped.

All-of-a-sudden, a scene-like quality starts to emerge. We don't speak the same language, but there is a rhythmic call and response happening in the give and take. When someone takes, we instinctively connect it to the offer that preceded it. In essence, we believe it to be the response to what happened. And because we are only moving and speaking one person at a time, we can clearly follow the thread.

And if in the middle of your movement you are interrupted, and you only made it a step or two toward the person to whom you were directing your energy, notice whether the next time you take, you pick up where you left off, or whether your intention and the focus of your energy has changed. I'll bet it is the latter. Once a moment happens, it takes real resistance and disconnection to stay locked into your own plan instead of staying present in the moment. We must give our focus to the scene and our partners. Imagine each offer as that sound ball from our earlier exercise. See it moving through the space, from person to person through the scene. Follow the energy.

As you repeat your gibberish phrase, you may find, as we did before, that your intention is changing. You may be using the same gibberish words, yet in response to a flirtatious approach from another player, the words soften. Or, after an aggressive run at you by another player, your gibberish words are full of intention to fight. Or to flee. USE your words. KNOW what you are saying, and at the same time realize that it is not actually the words that are doing the work—it is the behavior. Listen, respond. Listen, respond. This habit will serve everything you do as an actor—both scripted and unscripted work.

As a sort of scene emerges, so, too, does an environment. Simply by knowing what we're doing, what our action is, our surroundings and our circumstances take shape. Our imaginations can't help it. We make associations, and we see details as they emerge. If the exercise has been particularly cacophonous and we get closely clustered together, the world takes on the quality of a busy airport or train station, perhaps. If the exercise has been quiet or slow, we may imagine ourselves in a dark forest, or moments before a surprise party. Heed your imagination. Allow yourself to really embrace the connections. And, I'll point out again that none of this is about INVENTING. Simply see what you see, and explore that impulse.

Alright, one final round of this give-and-take exercise. Let's see what happens when we do the same thing (one person moving and speaking at all times, and ONLY one person at any time), and use English words (or whatever language you improvise in) to create a repeatable phrase. Your phrase doesn't need to have anything to do with the phrases you hear from others in the room. You can, in this case, decide ahead of time what it is your phrase will be. Or, just let it come out of your mouth the first time you 'take'. I am certainly not encouraging the habit of pre-planning, as a general rule, but in this version of the exercise, it's fine, and maybe even helpful.

Start out simply moving and speaking your repeatable phrase, and then freeze when someone else breaks their own freeze to move and speak, as you have done before. After everyone has had a chance to establish their phrase, then we can begin to direct our energy and words toward another player. You'll see how the call and response comes into play. Now that we KNOW what we're saying because we speak the same language, you'll begin to hear those phrases that match your own, and those that are in opposition. Unlike the last round with our gibberish phrases, DO NOT CHANGE your phrase. But DO apply different intentions to try to communicate responses to others' energy and phrases coming your way.

Your phrase may be a rhetorical "Why do I have to do it?" Someone else may be repeating "Laundry will be dry in fifteen minutes." Still another: "Walking is good for your health." In and of themselves, the phrases do not feel contiguous. But, when they are paired with a direction of energy and intention, and someone RESPONDS to an offer with those words, it takes on a more sensible quality. We automatically create context, and make connections that help the seemingly unrelated phrases make sense. It is STILL the behavior doing the heavy lifting, but the words begin to take on greater importance.

So USE whatever phrase you have to really communicate something when you next take. In fact, if you observe someone who you think will be open to your point of view and what you have to say, try to group up with them. 'Find your people', as I like to say. See if you can get everyone in the room on your side using solely that phrase and its accompanying, changing intentions.

Once again, the very nature of the give-and-take begins to create story—one offer leading to the next, leading to the next—as we follow the energy of the scene. Just like we followed the consequences in our story structure. Eventually somebody wins and somebody loses, and we find our resolution. Keep going with your English phrases and movements, and see if the group can find an ending to the 'scene'.

Like Freeze Tag, what do you see happening? Who are we to one another? Where are we? What are we doing? Does someone need our help? Do we need to band together to pray? Or to build a dam? Feel the energy and the sound and the motion of the group.

Let your movement continue to be more driven by activity, rather than just being random. Let's see if we can use our mirroring and spacework TOGETHER in this final round of give-and-take to find the end to our story. It's harder in a larger group, but agreement will get you there.

I particularly love watching people in this final part of the exercise. It really becomes quite magical as the story takes shape, and the group agrees, moment by moment. Still moving and speaking just one person at a time. Each person contributes so little each time, yet the group and the story advances. By passing the energy seamlessly between us, everything is revealed. And because we are bound to one another to agree, it seems as though we had pre-determined how it was all going to go.

Let's try one more scenic exercise to look at giving focus and taking focus. This one is called, aptly, "Entrances and Exits." This is one we can play with half a dozen players or so. The more people you include, the harder it may become. But if you are feeling confident after these last group exercises, be my guest.

Here's how it works. We'll define an environment (a where) and the threshold or doorway through which players can enter and exit. For this game there is only one way in and out. When we were spying our way through a hotel room earlier, and in most scenes we create, options exist for other ways in or out. For this one, it's important there is only one.

Once we've defined where we are and how to get in and out, the challenge of the game is simple: enter and exit as many times as you can before the scene ends. Here's the catch: in order to make a successful entrance or a successful exit, you MUST have the full attention of every player currently in the scene. If someone turns away from you before you have exited, your exit doesn't count and you have to return to where you made your last offer and try again—the same offer or a new offer. Likewise, you may not enter the scene unless every player currently in the scene gives you their attention. In this game, 'attention' usually equates to eye contact. You'll know whether or not you've been

'successful' because those of us watching will give you a little round of applause, as you would hear in a sit-com each time a big entrance or exit is made. We'll keep track of the number of your entrances and exits (each counts as one point), and at the end we'll see who has the most. If you win, your prize is that you will be identified as the person with the most entrances and exits. Quite an honor.

One challenge worth noting that comes up for us in this game is that improvisation is NOT competitive, it's collaborative. So, what happens when we add a competitive scoring element? If your successful entrance or exit is dependent on your fellow players, and they are also trying to score entrances and exits, wouldn't they want to prevent yours and rack up their own? Perhaps. But here's why that won't work: If everyone solely looks out for themselves, NO ONE will be able to score.

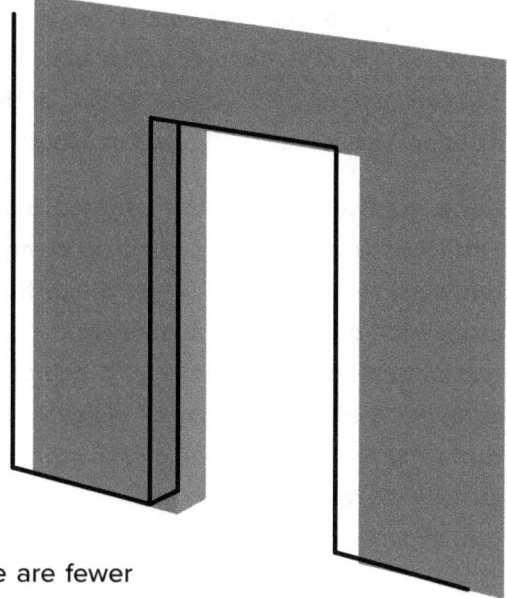

So, why not look for opportunities to collaborate on entering and exiting? Go in pairs, or groups. Find moments when there are fewer people in the scene because that means fewer people whose attention you need. Begin to see how making an offer to enter or exit that is IMPORTANT to your partners will likely help its success. If the scene is set at a birthday party, and someone needs supplies, volunteer to go, or go together. Or ENTER the scene with something that is needed. Time for cake? Carry it into the room together. Ultimately, USE the circumstances and offers of the scene to advance your entrance and exit goal. **I think you'll discover quickly that offers that only serve YOUR agenda are difficult to advance. Whereas, offers that bring something the scene and your partners need will be welcomed.**

Fight the temptation to block your partners or get payback for any previous slight. Competitive streaks can get ugly. It may feel fun to withhold your attention while one of your partners is trying to enter or exit. But, your momentary 'win' will not amount to much when the scene grinds to a halt. And if you set the precedent that your agreement is conditional, you can bet that others will make YOU pay for their agreement. Embrace the challenge and try to collect the most times in and out—and realize that, just as in any scene you will ever do, you can do nothing without your partners, nor they without you.

The first entrance is a gimme, since the scene is empty of other players. Cue the applause. One point.

You'll begin to discover what types of offers work and which ones don't. Shouting from the threshold may work. But if anyone who wants to enter or exit (which means EVERYone) shouts at the other players, that tactic will lose its effectiveness and just result in a loud, chaotic scene.

Once, several years before I started teaching improvisation, I was playing Entrances and Exits with members of my theatre company. We were in the rehearsal room next to Center Stage theater where we were rehearsing a production of "360", an adaptation of "La Ronde" which we had developed and written as a group. Ironically, one of my fellow founding members, Amy Schumer, took the 'exit' part of the game to the next level and actually left the room entirely while the rest of us continued shouting over one another. It was too chaotic, and a lack of collaboration can be frustrating, as I'm sure you've also experienced.

It wasn't until years later, even after having spent two years together in Bill's acting class, co-founding a company, and working on many projects together, I came to know that Amy and I share introversion (and a lower back tattoo) in common. And that game, the way I had set it up, was understandably too much, so she exercised a little self care and slipped out. (Of course, I tease her that introversion had nothing to do with it, she probably just had better things to do.) Eventually, I also came to understand how to lead the game differently from the way I was taught—that the focus of the exercise is really about the opportunity for collaboration between players.

Competition CAN be a useful element of an exercise, I've found, in that it shows us we are capable of greater focus and intensity than we often bring to our work. When something's at stake, we tend to dial in. It becomes important to us. See if you can use your imagination to bring those high stakes to your scenes, absent the need to 'win the game'. We're looking for quality of offers, not quantity. Volume is not the same as intensity. And chaos is just drama for drama's sake.

Remember, we are looking for dynamic shifts. Have you ever been in a group which is quite loud, and then you approach, saying something, but no one can hear you? What happens next? Well, if your intention is clear, I'd bet the group gets quieter because what you have to say seems important. Action and intention are always going to help you more than words (or volume).

I think that really sank in when we were doing the give-and-take round with gibberish.

If you ever went to camp, counselors have loads of tricks to get a boisterous group to focus. Try starting a rhythm by clapping or snapping or creating a familiar gesture and sound for others to repeat. One by one, others will likely join in. When the goal is to get everyone to focus, I find that nothing gets us zeroed in and grounded like a shared activity.

Or, walk up to a loud group and say "if you can hear me, say 'yes.'" Keep repeating this until one, then another, then another, respond "yes." Most people like to feel like they belong, even when the 'belonging' is little more than doing something simple that everyone else seems to be doing. So, all you need to do is get agreement one person at a time. It tends to ripple out pretty quickly from there—especially in a room of improvisers and actors. Sometimes we just need a little reminder that we are there for one another, not ourselves.

How might the offers change in Entrances and Exits if we added a door that could open and close? Or required a key, or for someone to buzz you in or out? Does that require more focus, or less? Does that allow for an entrance? Or hinder an exit? What pattern of behavior emerges? Does everyone make the offer of knocking or ringing a doorbell? If there was only one key or buzzer, would that automatically increase cooperation? Embrace the elements of the space and of the scene (the 'rules of the world') that help the group find focus.

There is one last thing I want to ask (and, perhaps the most important takeaway from this exercise): what happens to the scene ENERGETICALLY when someone enters or exits? What do you notice, besides a smattering of sit-com-style applause?

An entrance or an exit changes the dynamic of the scene. If there were three people and now there are only two, that is an obvious physical change. But what significance did the person who left have for either or both of you who remain? Now that they're out of the room, can you finally confess your secret crush? Or tell your partner you think their fiancé is all wrong for them? Does that person's exit give you a chance to discuss your feelings toward them?

More simply stated, perhaps, a birthday party with two people paints a different picture than a birthday party with ten people. Or a hundred. USE all of these changes. USE the energy shift of an entrance or an exit as you would any other offer. Take it in. Respond to it accordingly. Let it be important.

Maybe as soon as someone exits you miss them. You want to leave, too. You worry about what will happen to them. Then, they return with the punch bowl, and you are more deeply in love than you ever knew. Let the change of an entrance or an exit create your next offer, responsively.

Sometimes a scene can't move forward until someone exits, if only for a moment. We need their absence to be able to make endowments that we were unable to make in their presence. This doesn't mean every time someone leaves a scene you blurt out some secret. But the instinct is a good one—that you use the exit to build on what we already know. We add details and endowments that deepen the significance of the players and the scene.

And, here's a cool thing about improvising: even when you are not currently in the scene, you can still observe the offers being made. Players on the sidelines should always be looking for the opportunity to bring the scene what it needs. And if characters and objects are being mentioned in the scene, you have a built-in opportunity to make an entrance as that person or with those things. This is yet another way we can collaborate on the Entrance and Exits challenge, and in scenes, generally—by setting others up with opportunities to join. If we are talking about grandma in our scene, we probably want grandma to make an entrance at some point. Your partners helped you, and in turn you help your partners by playing grandma.

There is a move in improvisation referred to as the "Canadian cross." (I'm not sure why it is Canadian in origin, exactly. Probably because a lot of improvisation came from Canada. Or, that Canadians are known for being polite and kind and generous people.) This is when a player makes an entrance to give the scene a gift—something that could benefit the scene. The intention is not to stay in the scene, nor become an essential character. The sole purpose of the Canadian cross is to enter, make a relevant offer and leave.

Maybe the scene is taking place in a hotel room, and a couple is on their first shared vacation and feeling a bit shy. All-of-a-sudden, the bellman pops in with a bottle of booze, compliments of the hotel, and leaves. There is no guarantee where the offer will lead, ultimately, but the players should definitely not just ignore what happened and go back to whatever they were doing before the bellman entered. The player made the Canadian cross because they observed the offer of shyness, and brought an offer into the scene for the other players to explore. 'What would happen if two shy, awkward people alone in a hotel room let their inhibitions drop?' Allow yourself to get into trouble and see.

The scene does not have to become ABOUT the bellman. The couple doesn't need to recognize or know him, or have history of some torrid extra-marital affair. It was simply an entrance/exit gift. Look for similar ways to support your partners when you are not the focus of the scene. I guarantee **entrances/exits will change the energy of the moment, regardless of what happens next.**

7
What's This Scene About?

We've done a lot of skill-building to this point. And much of the work has been exercises or games. We keep talking about scenes, or referring to the exercises as being 'scenic,' but when do we create an actual, honest-to-goodness scene? Well... Now.

You'll recall our story-structure work here, as we get started building scenes. Specifically, the need to establish the who, what, and where in the first few beats. We need to know WHO the characters are, WHAT they are doing and WHERE they are. Collectively, we refer to these foundational elements as the "platform."

The platform establishes the baseline for the scene. The routine. The "every day..." This is very important. Primarily because, when improvising, we MAKE the rules of the world for each scene. We can ASSUME, to start, that the rules of the 'real' world apply (gravity, the way people speak, walk, behave, etc.) until proven otherwise. Sometimes offers seem unconventional. In improv, we can accept any minority circumstance as the majority circumstance. If my partner enters the scene hopping on one leg, for example, I don't need to immediately call it out. "What's wrong?" "What happened to you?" "That's weird!" We can't jump (pun intended) to those conclusions early in the scene. Until we have confirmed what rules apply, and what constitutes 'normal', we simply accept these offers as true. Hopping on one leg is how my partner moves, and as such, should not be confronted as being some sort of defect. In fact, if the offer of hopping on one leg happens early in the scene while we are building the platform, my best bet would be to mirror my partner's offer and begin to move that way, myself. **If I mirror, I instantly put my partner and myself in the same world. 'This is how things are.'**

Get all the platform elements out early in your scenework, through physical and verbal offers—in particular, offers that establish and endow. 'These are our names. This is how we are related. This is how I sound. How you sound. This is our job. This is our activity. This is where our activity is taking place.' Maybe some other circumstance. The state of the world. Life is good. Life is hard. We're rich. We're destitute.

Once again, we are not looking for drama early in the scene. We simply want to get our foundation established. 'Drama' is like a plot point—like something specifically intended to create a problem so that the scene can be 'about' something. Before we even know anything about these characters or this world, we don't need you to enter the scene in a rage, accusing your scene partner of cheating on you. That's a provocation meant solely to manipulate the scene and your partner. It comes from insecurity—concern that our world is not interesting enough as it is, or that the scene won't be exciting enough.

What makes the scene engaging is how deeply the players invest in it. If we allow the moments to happen, and we accept the offers with importance, the scene will unfold itself. It may not be about what we saw in some blockbuster action flick last night, but SOMEthing will happen. And if you are invested, it will be fascinating to watch. No meteors required.

Think about a play or movie you've seen, or a book you've read, one in which you didn't connect to the characters or the story for some reason. Why? What was missing? Probably, you couldn't find agreement with the context. If we don't see ourselves in the world or in the characters, our imagination won't allow us to suspend our disbelief to go on the ride. If it doesn't seem truthful, we probably won't trust it.

Likewise for improvised work, we have to establish context. We need to know the rules of the world we're creating. What and who we care about. What's at stake. What matters. What's REAL. We can't come out of the gate looking for the unusual, inventing problems to address, and calling out everything and everyone as 'weird.' Even if the world we create is unlike our own, we can still engage with a truthful humanity that feels universal. In order to get to that connection, we first establish how things work in THIS world. **We use our imagination and apply all our skills—spacework, storytelling, mirroring, give-and-take, "Yes...And"—to build a solid base for our scene.** We need to be sure that we are creating a clear, full, and compelling world and characters from the start.

Improvised scenes commonly begin with a suggestion—like at an improv show where an audience is asked directly for an idea to get the scene started. Maybe we ask for the who, where, or what.* Maybe it's more thematic: "Give me an emotion." "Tell me your favorite color." Maybe it's more occasional: "Name a significant event in your life." Or locational: "Give me a place you can get lost." Or situational: "What's the nicest thing you ever did for someone?" In improv comedy, a suggestion is often a setup for the joke, or a game-style challenge to play. Whatever it is, the suggestion ultimately becomes the seed from which the scene sprouts. And even if no initial suggestion is given, you'll make offers in the opening beats of your scene to fill in any unknowns.

So, let's build a scene, focusing on building the platform, without worrying about the story. I want us to actively reject any drama. For now.

Every scene begins by engaging physically in the space. Create objects. Use them. DO something. Make offers that define you, your task and the location. Remember my mantra: "Do first...Speak if you must." If my students begin a scene by talking, I ask them to start again. Build this habit. You'll thank me.

By simply engaging in an activity, we uncover our foundation. If we observe you cooking, we know WHAT you're doing. From there, by observing your be-

*See pages 236–241 for additional scene-starting inspiration.

havior, the objects you create, and the way you contact the space, we gather details about WHERE and WHO you are (from the looks of it a professional chef in a very busy kitchen of a fancy restaurant). We see that you are tired. Or happy. Old, or young. Confident, or harried. We see what you're wearing. How you move. Each of these offers strengthens the foundation.

Take your time. There is no pressure (EVER!) to get to the 'good stuff.' This IS the good stuff. SEE it clearly. Engage fully. Make it real, for yourself and your partners. Channel the lessons of slow motion to see if you can fully expand the elements of the foundation. 'If that's true, what else?' The more complete a world you create, the easier it will be to build a solid scene on top of it.

Try this with a partner. Take turns starting a scene with an activity. Make it a goal to have the most boring scene ever. We don't want anything to 'happen.' No drama. No picking a fight. No break-ups. No cheaters. No cutting your finger. Just do your task—like we did when we first started doing spacework. Let your partner have a few beats to establish an activity, and then, whether you know what's going on or not, GET IN THERE. Mirror or complement. Engage in the space. Join the world.

Build scenes this way a few times. Then try building some scenes where you give yourself a specific part of the foundation to focus on. 'This time, we're gonna focus on the where.' Next time, focus on the what. After that, focus on the who. Each time, really layer on the endowments.

You can use your words, just make sure that everything out of your mouth is an OBSERVATION. Nothing subjective. No judgments. No provocations. "You look happy" is different than "What are you so happy about?" "This room is dark and dusty" is different than "You should open a window and clean this place, for once." In both of these examples, the former is an observation, while the latter is clearly designed to instigate. See how long you and your partner can go simply building out the platform, focusing on different aspects.

I think most people find it easiest to build out the activity. We can define so much of the 'what' simply by DOING. Endowments for an activity might include WHY you're doing this activity ('I am preparing for a party.' 'It's my job.' 'I'm on vacation.' 'This is a hobby.' Etc.)—essentially, your circumstances.

The 'who' then comes organically out of the activity. Once we know what we are doing, we ask ourselves: 'Who would likely do this task?' I say 'likely' because there is no pressure to invent anything. If you are cooking, you don't have to be a cook AND an astronaut. No need to further 'spice things up'. (Pun intended.) You don't have to be a celebrity chef in the final round of an intense reality show cooking competition. It's enough to just be a competent cook, even if you are simply preparing a meal at home. Always be good at your task.

Add endowments about the 'who' to further define your character's traits. (Creating character could fill another whole book. For now, let any 'character' choices you make be some version of you, or someone you know well.) Is this person sloppy or neat? Kind or mean? Happy or sad? What is their worldview? Do they believe people are generally good? Or do they think the world was designed solely to make them miserable? Let us see it in your behavior.

If you change clothes or undress in improvisation, you do not ever take off your actual clothes. Use spacework to show us how you undo the buttons and remove a shirt, sleeve by sleeve; Spacework to show us you are putting on a big parka as opposed to a neat cardigan sweater. As long as you SEE it, and keep the offer alive, we will accept it and see it, too.

Same goes for your hair, or your jewelry, or accessories—spacework only!

How you show us who you are will extend to physical characteristics. How this person moves. What they sound like. Even what someone is wearing. If you clearly establish that you are wearing a blue chiffon prom dress, we will see that dress on you, and not the jeans and t-shirt you are ACTUALLY wearing. The 'character' can just be YOU in that blue dress. If you establish you have thick glasses, or that your hair is long, we will accept these endowments to be true, regardless of how you actually look or dress.

For my money, the most important element of character endowments is RELATIONSHIP—how you and the other characters know one another. Are you related? Are you coworkers? Best friends? Married? What is your history? How long have you known one another? What do you like and dislike about each other? What was the last gift you gave your partner? Where did you both grow up? Go to school? What shared experiences do you have? What would your character say is this person's best quality? Why do you choose to stay connected? What traditions do you have?

History really rounds out a relationship, and builds stakes in the scene. As I said before, scenes are rarely about what activity you're doing, and almost always about what is happening BETWEEN the characters. What they need from one another. Why they matter to one another. These types of endowments are golden. And it is so satisfying to watch improvisers build and agree, in the moment, about their shared history. Say "yes" and add the next detail. 'If that's true, what else?' And don't be afraid to own unflattering endowments.

In fact, let's do a quick exercise around relationships. Walk around the room as we have done for previous exercises. Find your own baseline. No need to DO anything. Just move about.

Now, without letting the person know, I want you to identify someone else in the room who, for the purpose of this exercise, you LOVE. This is a person who means more to you than anything or anyone else—a person who you would die without. You never want to let them out of your sight. Got that person in mind? Good.

As you keep moving about, and again without letting the person know, I want you to identify someone different whom, for the purpose of this exercise, you HATE. You can't stand this person! You wish you had never met them. And you hope you never see them again after today. Got that person in mind? Good.

Now, here's your task. I want you to find a place in the room where you are as physically close as possible to the person you love (NO TOUCHING!), and as physically far away as possible from the person you hate. Find the place where you can satisfy both objectives simultaneously. Is it possible? Try.

IMPROV AND THE ACTOR'S IMAGINATION

TRY IT: LOVE/HATE
Copy this page and cut it into individual game pieces.
Lay the pieces on a table and see if you can arrange them to
find a solution where all the relationships are all satisfied.

Every player has made a choice about who they love and who they hate, and is working toward that objective for themselves. What happens? It becomes immediately clear that one person's choice directly impacts another's. When the person you love makes an offer which moves them away from you, you respond by following. You NEED to be close to them.

But what if they are also moving closer to the person you hate? How do you successfully pursue one goal while losing another? It's important here to be incredibly clear, just as you were very specific with your activity when we were speeding it up. Really try. Acknowledge that you have to make compromises, but don't just let yourself off the hook. In scenes, if you decide that nothing really bothers you, you will stunt your responses. In this instance, taking something personally will motivate you. Be bothered that the object of your affection is moving away from you, and work to solve the problem. And when your mortal enemy nears, respond accordingly and move away.

This game creates a really dynamic 'scene.' Just like watching Freeze Tag, we start to see alliances form. Which people are friends and which are foes. Someone emerges as the 'popular' one, while one or two others find themselves alone in a corner, seemingly unaffected by the moves of anyone else.

We'll let this go on for a while, and at some point, the movement will likely slow. Why? Probably because people are tired of trying to solve something that appears to have no solution, rather than because we think we've cracked it. We think: 'Well, that person's no SO bad.' Or, 'I'll manage without my soulmate.' And then, just when we think our end is near, someone will realize their enemy is too close, their hatred is rekindled, and they'll move away. That single offer creates a ripple effect that sets the entire group in motion again. It's like our never-ending stories that somehow keep restarting.

'Until finally', we'll just call it, and everyone can freeze where they are. How did you do? What was your compromise? What relationships HELPED you with yours? Did the person you love also love you? Or was it the opposite—did the person you love hate you? Were you left on the outside with no lovers or haters? What was that experience like? (NOTE: Be sure to hug it out after the exercise, especially with the people you 'hate'. No hard feelings. And thank the people who 'hated' you, for giving you a juicy offer to respond to.)

Whether you were adored, loathed or snubbed, we can see that without knowing anything else about your partner, **ONE clear idea about ONE specific person is enough to create a relationship dynamic. Making a simple choice about how you feel about your partner can drive an entire scene.**

Imagine you are cooking dinner at home with your roommate in this scene. You are simply setting about your activity, and you need some pepper and salt. But your roommate, who you HATE, is standing in front of the salt and pepper shakers. This will inform your behavior. Do you forgo the spices and eat an unbearably bland and inedibly unseasoned meal? If you decide that you don't REALLY hate them in this moment, that they aren't THAT bad, then you will probably just give up. But if you explore and expand your choice, and see where it leads you, maybe you aggressively grab for the shakers, which is sure to elicit a response from your roommate. Or perhaps you ask them to leave the room to grab something so that you can get access to the shakers.

Put ALL of that feeling and intention and energy INTO your activity. Did you 'win' because you duped your roommate into leaving the room, seasoned your meal and returned the shakers before your partner reentered, none the wiser? Then, let's SEE that you won in the way you shake the salt and pepper. Show off. Celebrate victory with your behavior. If they won't leave, on the other hand, that will certainly elicit a response, too. And having made that simple, specific choice about love or hate colors everything.

Don't bog yourself down with an entire dramatic backstory and reasoning for why you love or hate this person. If you were doing a scripted scene, you would have time to do your homework and prepare, and then bring all of that work with you into the scene so that it's there if it should come up in you. But, when we improvise we have to craft in the moment. Which means we don't know the 'why' until it happens. Simply by acting on an impulse like love or hate, the responsive offers that flow from it will fill in the details. **Improvisation shows us how to make split-second choices and experience them as fully as we would if we had crafted them beforehand.**

Through our continued practice of agreement and acceptance, we can overcome uncertainty and create our character and our history as the scene happens—even when everything in us wants to resist. If, in the midst of Salt-and-Pepper-Gate, for example, you are accused of wrong-doing, instead of fighting the person or getting into an argument, try accepting the offer as the truth. You DID do the terrible thing they say you did. You WERE being an asshole at the party. You DON'T pick up after yourself. In 'real life' we always want to defend our character, much as we defended ourselves from aggression in our Kiss or Kill scenes. But improvisation is the world of 'What if...?' I say, BE what they say you are. ACCEPT the unflattering or negative endowment and see where it takes you. 'If THAT'S true, what else?' People do bad things all the time, usually for reasons they feel are justified. So, let's accept the bad thing and discover the WHY. How's it gonna turn out? If we believe this character, if we connect to them and their truth, we can't wait to see what happens.

OK. Let's play another game addressing the 'who' of our platform. We'll play this with a simple deck of cards. Without looking at the card, I want you to pick a card from the deck. Don't look at it and don't show it to anyone. Once everyone has a card, you can hold your card up against your forehead so that your partners can see your card, but you cannot.

Now I want you to interact with each other, and make verbal or physical offers that give your partner a clue as to what their card is. (For this game, let's say that aces are low, and king is high.) If someone is low, and you think you are high, then reject them. Or tell them to do some menial task for you.

If someone is giving you an offer that suggests you are lowly, ACCEPT the endowment and behave accordingly. I like to say: **"Test your theory." If you believe something to be true, CONFIRM it by accepting the offer and responding accordingly.**

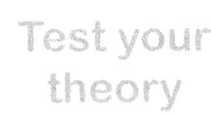 

Whether you are high or low, find your people. Find others who are low or high and see how they respond to you. Don't give away the game by TELLING someone they are lower or higher than you or someone else. Don't tell them what number they are by pointing to someone who has their same number and exclaiming "You're twins!" Behave and respond. Interact with as many others as you can to really confirm your place in the hierarchy.

Then, I want you all to form a straight line facing me, with the highest card to my left and the lowest card to my right. Don't discuss it. Don't push someone else into the right spot. Just find your place in the line in the order you believe is correct. Once everyone has picked their spot, I will give everyone ONE chance to move. You don't have to, but if you think you're not yet in the right spot, you may move ONCE. After everyone has their one chance and we're settled in line, look at your card.

Did you get it right? What were the offers that were most helpful to you? What confused you? We often see, in this game, that those on the extreme highs and lows find it easiest to know their place. While those in the middle numbers—fives, sixes, sevens, eights—have a tougher time knowing where they fit. Also, clusters can be hard to place. If there are several of you who have the same card or very similar cards, it can be hard to know where you stand.

This is all about STATUS. And, status can be a really great building block for relationships in scenes. Endowing that someone is very high- or very low-status is going to inform your behavior. You are going to act very differently around a king than you would a two. USE that. ACCEPT your position and then 'test your theory.' Behave clearly and boldly as you are cast. Be rich. Be poor. Be a genius. Be a fool. Be happy. Be jealous. Let your status help define who you are, and respond accordingly.

I suggest playing this card game a second time. And give yourselves a location or event, like a high school reunion. Endow one another with clues using the environment and the circumstance. "You were the most popular kid in school." "Once a loser, always a loser." "OMG! MY BFF!" "Go get me a cup of punch." Once you've interacted with everyone and found your people, line up again high to low.

How'd you do this time? Who had the biggest change from last round? We're you a king last round and this time a three? What was that like? Or did you get the same card as before? How did the circumstance inform you? Just like Love/Hate, making a clear status choice will help you set up a solid start to your scene. Someone is not just KIND OF better than you, they're a GOD! Someone is not just KIND OF annoying or KIND OF unsightly—they are AWFUL and REPULSIVE. Being EXTREMELY specific will help you find agreement so the scene can move forward.

What's This Scene About?

TRY IT: STATUS
Based on all the offers below, what card do you hold?
(Answer is at the end of the chapter—no cheating!)

No problem! Absolutely! Your wish is my command! Anything you say!

I can't be seen with you. Get lost!

Let's grab a bite... This time <u>you're</u> paying.

We shop in the same stores, but the clothes look better on you.

The final part of the foundation is the 'where', which I believe also comes organically out of the activity. We simply ask ourselves: 'Where would this activity likely take place?' There can be many answers to that question, for sure, but we want to find the answer that we can all agree upon quickly. **Building and endowing the 'where' is very much about contacting the space and saying what you see.** FEEL the nappy velvet drapery. Let the environment be very tactile for you. A dirt floor will evoke a very different response than cold polished marble. A cheery yellow childhood bedroom will have a distinctive feel.

And NAME the places where you are. Why just be at a school when it could be "Evermore High School"? Or "Holy Trinity Grade School"? Why just be in a park, when you could be at the "Topiary Gardens in Northside Park"? An ice cream store doesn't have to be plain vanilla. It could be "Mrs. Scoop's Ice Cream Emporium"—the place where you and your partner went every day after school when you were kids. Again, specificity is everything.

All of this foundation work relates to the story structure we explored before. We need to know who, where, and what to establish the world and the routine of the characters—the "Once upon a time..." and "Every day..." of the scene. Why? So that we can shake it up, like that snow globe.

Having clear, specific foundational offers gives you a simple blueprint of where the scene can go. Just like stories, we start in a familiar place so that we have something solid to build upon. Where you start is a good indication of what can change. Like in Kiss or Kill: you were alive, now you're dead. You were together, now you're apart. Someone wins, someone loses. If someone is high status at the beginning, there is a ripe opportunity for them to lose their status in the scene, explore the consequences of that, and find a resolution. They may return to their original status (or not), but we will have learned something. They and/or the world will have changed in some way.

If you start a scene in love with someone, be open for any offer that causes you to question your devotion, or to turn hateful toward the person. Even if it has never upset you before. Then we explore the consequences of that change. Why today? Why now? Either we return to love or we don't, but something will have changed "From that day forward…"

The shift can be small. It is our deep acceptance of the offer, and our expansion of the consequences, that will elevate its importance. You and your best friend are having dinner after seeing a movie. Your friend leans in to hug you, and impulsively kisses your cheek. That's new! That's never happened before! 'I knew it! We're not just friends… She's in LOVE with me!' Whether you are correct in your assumption doesn't matter. What matters is that you accept FULLY, and then test your theory by responding to the offer you observed.

We have to let our actor's imagination take over and ask "What if…?" We don't know how the scene will go, and certainly don't know how it will end, but RISK BIG. Make the leap. Test your theory.

How do we know when our foundation is solid enough for us to move ahead? In our stories, we know within the first two beats ("Once upon a time…" and "Every day…") that we have the who, what, and where, and an established routine. And, by the third beat ("One day…"), we have the shakeup. But in scenes, there is no specific number of beats to create the platform, which also means we don't know exactly when the shakeup will occur. We have to be able to distinguish between offers that are part of our 'routine'—what we know to be true for our characters and their world—and those offers that disrupt.

In scenes we refer to the shakeup moment as the EVENT—it's the first offer that breaks the routine. The event focuses our scene. Once we find the event, we know what the scene is about, and we spend the rest of the scene exploring the consequences, until we reach our resolution. Much like our Kiss or Kill scenes, we are looking for that moment of agreement about what happens next. That point at which we agree a shift has taken place, and our commitment to explore that idea—in the case of the Kiss or Kill scenes, the slow-motion ecstasy or death.

Let's build scenes, then, and see if we can find agreement about when the event occurs. In fact, in this round of scenes, the scene will end as soon as we find the event. We won't continue into consequences, or find a resolution.

Start the way you have so far. DO first. Establish an activity. Let your imagination add details. What do you see? Be specific, and interact with those elements. Remember, in improvisation we are creating everything from nothing, so some additional physical contact with the environment and the objects is probably necessary to truly communicate what your imagination sees. Some things may be impossible to communicate without words (color, for instance), but you should still SEE it all—it will infuse your behavior in ways you don't even realize. Take your time. There is no rush to get to anything.

If you are the one joining your partner in the scene after they have initiated an activity, get in there and DO something—join them in their activity. And, as always, if you have no idea what they are doing, GET IN THERE ANYWAY—mirror or complement until you both find agreement about what you're doing. For the person who originated the activity, that may mean having to adapt what you envisioned in order to find agreement with your partner. If you are the joiner, TRY to join the activity already in progress rather than start your own activity—channel your What Are You Doing? exercise. Remember, in that game the guesser's job is to engage physically and to make offers so that their partners can respond—to confirm they're on the right path, or to try a different tack.

Unlike our What Are You Doing? work, however, your partner in a scene is not going to tell you you're 'wrong'. Instead of working to get you to do a specific, pre-determined activity, your partners in scenes are going to try to find agreement with you—even if that means adapting (or abandoning) the original activity. Don't throw away EVERYTHING you built in the opening moments—it'll be even harder to find agreement about an activity if BOTH of you are starting anew. Rely on your mirroring. Do the same movement, and you WILL find the 'what'. I promise.

So get on the same page about the activity as quickly as you can, focus your attention on your task, and simply **DO the activity.** You can use words, of course, but don't depend on them. And certainly don't start spouting drama or provocation. Remember what gibberish taught us: behavior is everything.

And then focus on offers to help define the world—to build the platform of your scene. **Find agreement about who you are to one another, and who would do this activity.** Build history. Say 'yes.' Agree WHERE this is happening. Contact the space. Move through it, and handle objects with integrity.

As this continues (as long as it needs to) with the platform getting stronger and stronger underneath your scene, let your awareness turn toward finding the event. **Based on what you know to be true, what breaks that pattern?**

For now, we are simply working on 'finding the event'. So once you have agreement that a shakeup has occurred, that the routine has been interrupted, I want you and your partner to end your scene. That's as far as you need to go, for now. Show us you both agree the event has happened, by stopping the action to call "Scene!" TOGETHER.

It may happen quickly, or it may take a while. What I find happens a lot is one of two things: 1) Players come out right away playwriting and stirring up drama before we even have a platform established; or 2) SEVERAL potential events happen and the players don't accept them deeply enough, and therefore don't find agreement that an event has even occurred.

Say, for example, a scene begins with your partner angrily exclaiming "I'm breaking up with you!" We don't yet know where you are, what you're doing, or even who you are to one another. The only thing we know, at that point, is that your partner is angry, and you are dating. There is nothing at stake, and we have jumped ahead to a manufactured 'event' without knowing anything about the world or these characters. Maybe this is actually their routine: they break up all the time. Maybe THAT's the pattern. But, I think we've got a better shot at a solid, truthful, and grounded scene if we build the platform first.

Or, say a scene begins as we practiced. We've got an activity and plenty of specific offers to add detail about the platform who, where, and what. We now know that these characters are best friends since childhood. They are also roommates. The scene is taking place in their living room, and their activity is decorating the room for a party they are hosting tonight. It is the first party they've had in this new apartment. Their names are April and Chantal. As they continue with the decorating, we are discovering more and more details about their history and the environment. They are working hard, and Chantal pauses to put her hair up in a ponytail.

That last beat may seem like a 'nothing' moment. But, if April acknowledges the offer and gives it significance, ('That's new.' 'That's never happened before.'), THAT could be the event. "You never wear your hair up." Or, "You look really good with your hair that way." Or, April responds by stopping to put her OWN hair up. The challenge, as it is with EVERY scene, is to AGREE what that event is. In the early work, players let seemingly insignificant moments like this pass, one after the other. As a result, the scene seems to be going nowhere. And, because we feel like nothing is happening, the pressure to stir shit up and create drama builds exponentially. We want to avoid this. **We want to be so tuned in to one another that we can agree when a shift happens, however 'small.'** What makes it an event is that a) it breaks the pattern we have observed so far, and b) we make it important and give it focus.

The magic of the event is often that it is the 'mistake.' We are simply focused on the doing, and then something unplanned happens. It doesn't have to be a 'problem' or an accident or an injury (or a meteor) but it IS, in itself, a change. A surprise is, by its nature, not what was intended. Somebody sneezes. What does that mean? What is your response? You say "Bless you." THAT could be the event—IF your partner responds in a way that makes your own response important. And IF you both agree that the shift has happened. Your partner feels like you were flirting with them when you said "Bless you." Their behavior changes. THAT could be the event. We could spend the rest of the scene exploring the flirtation, or the misreading of the intention. We don't know how it's gonna go until we follow the moments, and we can't do that until we agree what the scene is about—what the EVENT of the scene is.

Try building scenes and calling your scene when you agree on the event. Do it a bunch of times. Do you find that the events happen sooner the more scenes you try? Why? Are you getting more efficient at building a platform? Or, are you and your partner more acutely aware when the event happens? Perhaps both? Or are you still short-changing the platform and jumping to the drama?

The event doesn't have to be anything extraordinary. What matters is our agreement that it happened, that it's important to us and to the scene, and that we are going to explore the consequences together. Often, I think players let events pass because they don't think the event is 'good' enough. Or 'dramatic' enough. I'd argue that anything can be interesting if the improviser invests in it. We are fascinated to see how someone responds to an 'ordinary' event. We can relate to the circumstance, and we, as actors especially, ask ourselves 'what would I do in that situation?' The magic of improv is the delight we feel when we witness someone solve the problem in a way we would not have thought of or expected—not because they are TRYING to invent some unusual solution, but simply because we are all inherently different and approach things uniquely.

I think about sit-coms a lot in this work. The characters in sit-coms are often broadly drawn—they are more archetypal. Yet, they are also incredibly relatable—we see ourselves in these people, regardless of whether we are truly alike. And then, like improvised work, we want to witness how these relatable characters in relatable circumstances navigate a situation (i.e. event). What often makes it comedic is that, despite their best intentions, the characters try just a little bit too hard. Or want something a little too much. Or dig themselves a hole trying to protect their image, their reputation, whatever. Their exploration of consequences borders on the extreme. We laugh because, although we relate, we insist that WE would never get ourselves in a mess like that. We distance from the character's worst traits, yet we laugh along because we know at the end of the 22 minutes everything's gonna be okay again. (Until the next episode, or course.) And the next time we see these characters, we will have even more history to add to the platform—and the pattern will be broken yet again.

"Scene!" Once you feel like you are finding the event more easily, begin to create scenes where you move past the event into the consequences. Let your "One day..." moment lead you to the "Because of that...".s. And then look for a resolution. That will take you through the full arc of a scene.

Just like your stories, be aware that you want to stay focused on ONE event and its consequences. You don't want your scene to restart over and over because you keep finding NEW events. We too easily get bored with what we have created and start to look for something 'better.' What you end up with is a scene, to use my previous analogy, that is strewn with little slips of paper full of abandoned and forgotten offers littering the floor. Ideally, you want to leave the scene the way you entered it: with nothing. That means keeping it simple, and staying focused on exploring and expanding ONE event. Not the 'best' event, but the event you all agree on FIRST. That's enough, so go with that.

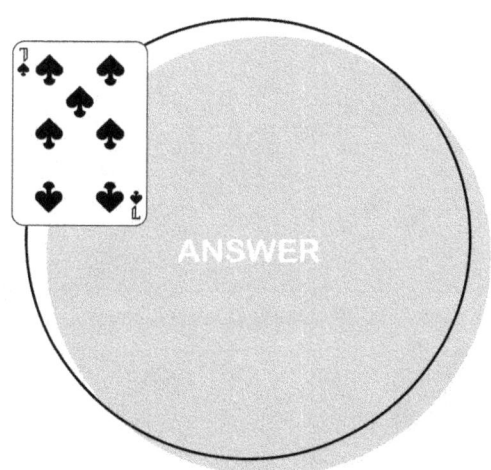

ANSWER

TRY IT: STATUS
Based on the offers on page 176, did you guess where you fit in?

8
Making Sense of It All

One thing we've come to know, at this point: When the unexpected occurs, we embrace it. We mirror it. We elevate it. We avoid dismissing offers and occurrences that we don't recognize or understand. Instead we LEAN into them. We work together to find agreement about what the offers mean. We adapt, instantly.

But what happens when an offer feels particularly incongruous? Maybe our partner gave an offer that they had cooked up in their head that doesn't seem to have anything to do with the scene. Maybe we misheard or misinterpreted an offer and responded boldly, as we should, yet inadvertently made a right-angle turn. What if, despite our best efforts, we introduce an offer that is anachronistic? (Technology often finds it way into historical scenes, for example. What do we do when King Louis XIV gets a phone call?) We are not intentionally inventing any of this. As I have warned you previously, stay away from the 'wacky' improv offers—those offers that are purely intended to muck things up so that the players have a problem to solve. A game to play. Or, worse, something to COMMENT on and point out as 'weird,' often just to get a laugh. Don't fall for it. Focus on truth. Put your attention on the scene and on your partners. THAT's where the 'answer' is.

And yet, skilled as we may be, shit happens. And we need to be facile enough to be able to integrate an unusual offer into our scene, and avoid letting it derail us. If our event is that an older sister is leaving for college today, a day ahead of schedule, THAT'S what we want to explore and know more about. THAT'S what the scene is about. Yet perhaps you forgot some of the environmental space work you and your sister created, and you walk through a wall. If our goal is to create a truthful reality, we need to understand how that is possible, without that 'mistake' dragging our scene down a different path. We don't want to lose everything we built while we comment for the rest of the scene about how you are a ghost, or the walls are made of Jell-o. In a word, a lot of the work in improvisation is about JUSTIFICATION.

Justification is the tool we use to help fold seemingly unrelated elements into the scene—hopefully without denying everything we already created. 'No I didn't.' 'It was a dream.' 'I didn't know.' 'You're a ghost.' 'You're a witch.' 'It's magic!' These are convenient 'excuses' improvisers often insert as a quick fix to a lapse in spacework or listening, and each is some form of negation, denial, or destruction of the reality we've built.

When we played What Are You Doing?, once the guesser correctly identified and performed the unrelated activity, I asked you to fold the activity back into the scene. That was justification. If you are plumbers and the guesser needs to do ten push-ups, how does completing those ten push-ups serve the scene? What does it mean? Why does it matter? That's the task of justifying.

A lot of short-form improv comedy scenes are just games of justification, in which we purposely challenge other players to make sense of wacky suggestions and offers. The incongruity IS the scene. It is just a cooked-up problem to solve, and we laugh and applaud when the solution is revealed.

Justification can be very satisfying. There is a wonderful tension seeing something happen that COULD derail the scene, and then watching deft improvisers seamlessly blend the offer into the story. When an unexpected thing happens, we don't know what it means in the moment, so it creates confusion. Yet, once we find agreement and understand how the offer relates to the scene, we wonder how we ever got to this point of the scene WITHOUT that offer—it actually becomes essential, in many cases.

The tricky part of justification can be knowing WHEN to explore a stumble, and when to dismiss it and move on. An improv purist would say that EVERYthing that happens is worthy of further exploration. I agree that every offer is important, IF that offer was purposeful. Sometimes unintended offers, like walking through walls and tables, are simply borne of us having A LOT to focus on, and momentarily dropping our awareness, or getting sloppy with our listening or spacework. Forgetting a character's name is a very common hiccup. These types of 'technical' blips will happen a lot, regardless of how skilled we are, or how engaged our imagination is—no matter how hard we work to treat our environment and objects with integrity.

So, how do you decide? I say, ANYthing that happens in the space should be addressed, but it doesn't have to take over the scene. If you call someone the wrong name, the next offer can be a quick justification. 'That's my maiden name.' 'I prefer you call me Angela.' Or you simply accept the last offer, and use THAT name for the rest of the scene without any further focus on it.

Some offers DO carry more weight than others, and could instantly drag the scene off into drama. 'Why did you call me your ex-girlfriend's name?' 'You're drunk!' 'You're high.' 'You're dying!' If we respond to a simple hiccup with a loaded provocation like these, it makes something that we could forgive-and-forget become the focus of the scene, instead. Think of this like a basketball game: we would call the foul, reset, and continue with the game. Scenework is much the same—usually best to quickly justify minor lapses and move on.

Let's try some scenes that explore justification. We'll start with a scene called "No Questions".

Before we set up this scene, we need to address questions, generally, as they relate to improvisation. Up to now, I haven't really called out when you ask questions in scenes. Yet, much like negation, and trigger words like 'but' and 'no,' I encourage you to avoid asking questions in your scenes. Why? Because a question puts the responsibility for the offer onto your partner. If you hand your partner a box or a letter and  don't endow its contents or add detail, you leave your partner to define it. Why, if you already had the idea to give your partner a gift, would you not add some detail about WHAT the gift is? If you felt the scene needed a gift, you MUST have had some impulse as to what the gift could be, and why it would be important in this moment.

Same with questions. If you observe that your scene partner looks angry, there is a difference between ASKING them WHY they are mad and making an observational offer. We want to focus on the latter. If you already know your partner is angry, based on their observed behavior, let your imagination define the details and inform your response. If your partner is angry, does your imagination tell you that it's your fault? Based on what you know about your partner, what tends to upset them? Then you can make a clear offer. 'You're mad at me because I never remember to take out the garbage.' 'You always get mad like this when you're hungry.'

Remember how, when we were telling stories, I was encouraging you to make it active—to avoid stall words like 'decided to', 'started to', 'thought about', 'wanted to', instead of just getting to the ACTION? Asking questions in a scene is the same. **Questions require two offers to introduce something, whereas we can accomplish it in one—AND have a clearer offer.**

For example, your partner is cleaning the apartment. You observe that your partner is angry, and that their anger seems to be directed at you. You ask your partner: "Are you mad?"

While continuing to clean, your partner replies: "Yes."

So, you ask: "Why are you mad?"

And your partner replies: "I'm mad at you for forgetting to take out the garbage again." Or, "You know I get mad when I'm hungry."

If you make an observation instead of asking a question, your partner can simply accept the offer and respond, without having to fill in the blanks. "You're mad at me because you had to take out the garbage AGAIN." "You're mad because you haven't eaten all day." And then we can move on and discover more. Instead of "Why haven't you eaten?" we can offer a detail that 'and's. "You don't need to diet. You look great!" "I know how hard you've been working to get the apartment ready for my parents' visit. Let me get you a snack."

Questions reveal our insecurity. We don't have confidence in our idea, so we hedge our bets, and make our partner do the work. We fear our offer will be rejected. Or worse: evoke stinky face!

So, let's practice NOT asking questions, with a focus on justification. We will start a scene as we have done—no pressure for anything to happen, or for it to be 'interesting.' At this stage, I still say 'try for the most boring scene you can'. Use your skills to create an activity, do the activity, create objects and a clear environment. Know who you are to one another. And let the scene unfold.

BUT... When someone asks a question in the scene, we will alert them they have asked a question by hitting the buzzer. Once the buzzer has sounded, whoever asked the question is given a full 30 seconds to justify their exit. Once they exit the scene, they cannot return. So, they better make it count. No one else may speak during the exit monologue.

For the person who asked the question and is now exiting the scene, remember what we talked about regarding entrances and exits: they change the energy of the scene. They create opportunities for new pairings and information to be revealed. So, rather than focus on how you 'blew it' by asking a question in a scene where we are trying to avoid questions, use your 30 seconds to help your partners. Leave gifts. Raise the stakes. Make endowments. Make a confession, perhaps. And, above all, JUSTIFY why you have to leave at this moment, and why you will never return.

(As an aside, you'd be surprised how many times, even in a game that is SPECIFICALLY about NOT asking a question, someone enters the scene and a question is the very first thing out of their mouth! We don't even realize we have this habit, but we do. How many times have you approached someone and the first thing you say is "How ya' doin'?" or "What's up?")

Your exit doesn't have to be an emotional, loud tirade about how you hate everyone else. (Although that works, too.) **Raising the stakes is not the same as raising the volume. Intensity can be found in small, quiet moments just the same.** Reveal something to your partners before you go. Tell the truth that you hadn't been able to tell them up until this point. "I always loved you." "I never liked that sweater on you." "Before I go, I want to you have this..."

You may also be surprised how many additional questions you ask in your exit speech. It's OK. At this point, we want to focus on building something to leave behind when you go. So, let 'er rip, questions or not!

Many times, players become self-conscious when they are given the floor to themselves, even for only 30 seconds. They freeze up, stand still and start TALKING. **Something that can help is to stay engaged with the space, physically.** Spend your exit speech collecting your things. Packing a suitcase to leave. Finishing your task. You can put all of your intention into your activity and keep the space and the objects alive for your partners who will remain after you are gone. This should relieve some of the pressure we often feel when we are on the spot. See if you can embrace the moment and, with your attention on your task, just let the truth come out. Justify your exit.

For those who did NOT ask the question that led to this exit monologue, your role is a little different. You still want to stay engaged—don't let the activity stop while you wait for your partner to finish and go. But your primary focus in this moment is to be affected. Take it in. Receive the gifts and endowments they are leaving behind. You may find yourself wanting to reply to what your partner is saying—to defend yourself against some attack, or accusation, or revelation. Don't! Let them have their say, and just absorb it.

And then once they are gone, ACCEPT the gifts they gave you, clearly and boldly. Admit that what they said was true. Let it inform your response. Above all, DO NOT let their exit be dismissed. "That was weird!" "She's crazy!" "She's drunk!" No. What they said was TRUE, whether you like it or not. So DEAL with it. Make it important and let it propel the next moment of the scene, until someone else asks a question, and then the cycle repeats.

Once every player but one has asked a question, monologued, and exited, I encourage the remaining player to ask a question so they can experience the exit monologue, too. Often, I find it useful to have the last person sort of sum up the scene—to ask the universe a big philosophical question connected to what we just witnessed. "Why does everybody leave me?" "Why can't we just love one another?" "What does all of this mean?" "What is the world coming to?" And then keep the space alive while they justify their own exit.

There's another justification game I like to play which I just call "Birthday Party". It's a scenic game, as well. In small groups, choose one person whose birthday it is. We are going to throw them a party. And bring gifts, of course.

Because the challenge of this game is justification, I am going to ask the people attending the party to decide their gift ahead of time. If you were bringing a gift to a party in real life, you would have to acquire it ahead of time—and an improvised party is no different. (Also, I don't want your gift to be influenced by the gifts others bring. You'll see why in a second.)

Start the scene as you would any other scene, with activity. Of course, we already have a few elements of our platform. We know it's a birthday party. We know whose birthday it is. We know that we each have a gift to give. But there are plenty of other details you can fill in. Names of the other guests. Theme of the party. Where, specifically, it is taking place. Introduce objects and environment and history, just like any other scene. The party doesn't have to be elaborate, or overly complicated. Just be clear, and find agreement so that we can get to the good stuff: the gifts!

One by one the party guests will present the birthday person with their gift. Just as we did in previous spacework, handle it with integrity. Probably better if your gift is not wrapped, or is wrapped in such a way that it can be demonstrated what it is through spacework. Remember, handing someone a box puts the responsibility on them to define the object. And, in this case, we want our recipient to be able to focus on their skills of justification, not to invent an offer, or have to guess.

If your are the birthday person, interact with the gift, as you did in our previous gibberish exercises. (You can use English here, or whatever language you improvise in.) USE the gift, so we know we have agreement about what it is and what it does. And JUSTIFY why this is the perfect gift for you. Perhaps it has to do with your personality. Or you already collect these objects and wanted this one which you don't already have. Or you love the activity for which the object is used (tennis, or poker, or cleaning). "This gift is perfect!" 'And here's why...' "You know me so well!" What we DON'T want is to react with "That's weird!" and then set the object aside. **Remember, the answer to uncertainty is to engage with it, and to work together to find agreement. Don't dismiss things—make them important. Endow. Clarify.**

One by one, the gifts are given. And each time the challenge of justification increases. This is why I want you to choose your gift ahead of time. If you don't, it's likely that one of two things will happen: based on the gifts already given and what you have learned about the birthday person, you will either a) choose something that organically fits with what is there. Or, b) you will choose something 'clever' or ridiculous in an attempt to intentionally outdo your partners' ideas, and to make the justification harder. No need. The challenges of justifying will come—we don't have to invent problems.

So, as another object is introduced, how do you use BOTH of these objects? How do they BOTH define you? How do they relate to one another? How can you put them to use together? What about three objects? Four objects? (How many guests did you invite?) Keep all of the objects alive throughout the scene—Wear them. Use them. Share them. And also keep the party itself alive—Eat cake. Wear party hats. Be together in the space.

Once all the guests have given their gifts, and the birthday person has justified them all, you can end the party and move on to the next person. Identify who will be next, and start a new birthday party for them. Try a new theme, or a new environment, so that each party feels unique and requires us to find agreement, rather than being a repeat of things we already know. Each time, before the next party begins, choose what your gift will be.

This game is useful for justification, and perhaps even better, it helps us build the good habit of responding to offers with acceptance and positivity. It is a good balm for chronic stinky face. **If we can move forward in scenes with the assumption that an offer is there to HELP us, then we are less likely to be thrown by it. And less fearful about any uncertainty.** If we are excited and curious about offers, and allow our imagination to integrate them into our scenes, we are well on our way to some fun and free improvised scenes.

Embrace justification as an essential skill of an actor and improviser. Our imagination is always searching for connections and meaning in what we see and what we do. And in improvised work, we need to kick our imaginations into high gear to first define those offers clearly, and then endow them with meaning and purpose. ANY offer could be the catalyst for the rest of the scene. So don't dismiss something simply because you don't recognize it at first glance.

Justification is not always about objects or platform elements. It also comes into play with behavior. Let's explore this with some scenes that restrict our words. This should further reinforce how important behavior is in scenework—and how we shouldn't depend too heavily on our words. Remember my mantra: "DO first…Speak if you must." We want the work to be firmly planted in the gut, and not in the head.

Let's start a scene with two people. A third person can be on deck, in case an entrance is needed. Start the scene with an activity, and make offers that help fill out the world and the relationship. Again, use your behavior and what you observe in your partner—the less you invent, the better.

Here's the challenge with this scene: You can speak, and you can use a language you both understand. But the game is "3-Second Delay". So one person can say as much or as little as they need. But once they STOP speaking, their partner may not respond verbally until a full 3 seconds have passed.

This is not to say that you freeze and wait to restart your action until you can say something. What we want to see is how we JUSTIFY the silence. WHY can't you respond right away? Is it something that takes time to process? Can you use the silence to build your reaction in your activity? If what your partner said to you was upsetting, let us see that reflected in your behavior.

Sweep that floor more aggressively. Let us see your anger rising in you physically. Or tears welling up. Or see you counting to ten before you respond, just like your therapist advised. Or simply staring at your partner, trying not to show them how hurt you are. Or doubling down on your activity in an attempt to prove to your partner that you're not bothered. (Although, we absolutely know that you are...As this character, you are a terrible actor!)

Let the silence propel you forward. FEEL what it's like to not answer immediately. What opportunities does that create for you as an actor? When you have the TIME to expand the moment, just as we found in our slow-motion work, what does your imagination see? If you thought you were at 5 on the anger meter, can those three seconds get you to a 10? Remember, intensity is not necessarily about volume or scale—you don't have to come out of every 3-second delay shouting or ranting. But DO come out of the three seconds more focused. More specific.

It will be difficult to stick to the 3-second delay, but be strict. Maybe you will find that you don't need to speak AT ALL after the 3 seconds. MORE delay is fine, but 3 seconds is the minimum.

Our daily habits from the 'real world' are hard to break. Particularly with negative responses, we immediately jump into attack mode. We stop listening, and try to talk over one another. We fight to defend ourselves. If you apply our learning from our Kiss or Kill scenes, maybe what you will discover in your 3 seconds is that what you wanted to respond to with negativity, you actually recognize as the TRUTH. Your partner told you, based on how carelessly you're cleaning the room, that 'you're irresponsible and you don't try.' You're hurt and you WANT to argue back. You want to shout, "No, I'm not! YOU'RE the one who's irresponsible!" Instead, maybe in those short 3 seconds, you have an epiphany—a realization. 'You're right! And here's why...' Let us see your resolve mount in those 3 seconds. Emerge from the silence already in action. Pack a bag to leave for a better adventure. Open the curtains and let the sun shine in.

Silence is only empty of words—not action. There are plenty of offers to be observed in the silence. In fact, give yourself the challenge sometime of doing an ENTIRE scene without speaking. You can still tell a complete and compelling story, creating rich environments and characters, without speaking a word.

IMPROV AND THE ACTOR'S IMAGINATION

Here's another scene to try. This one also uses word restrictions to help us build our justification skills. It probably has a better name, but I call it "1-3-5." This is a three-person scene. It starts, as all our scenes do, with an activity. DO something. Then we build the who, where, and what of our platform, based on what our actor's imagination sees, and what we observe in our partners.

This time, each player is allocated a specific number of words—either 1, 3, or 5—which we assign before the scene begins. For the entirety of the scene, each character can only use their allotted number of words every time they speak. If you have 5 words, no one else may speak until you have finished your 5 words. And then you cannot speak again until another player has used up their allotment. Players do not always need to speak in the same order, but they must limit themselves to their allotted word count, and no one may speak again until another player has finished.

This is a great game for exploring justification. If you play with abandon, you will find that you very often run out of words before you have finished your thought. So, what do you do? ... Justify. SHOW US with your behavior why you stopped mid-thought. We're you overcome with emotion and unable to physically SAY the words? Did you have second thoughts about how your partner would react to what you were about to say, and thought it better to NOT say it after all?

You can also find a rhythm working together. Maybe someone finishes another's sentences. Maybe every time you speak to the person with 1 word allocated to them, you set them up for 1-word responses. You are JUSTIFYING the word restriction by INTEGRATING it into your scene. Your partner speaking only in 1-word sentences is not 'weird'—it's absolutely normal.

Note how you interpret the word restrictions—what response they evoke in you. If someone doesn't finish their thoughts, are they keeping a secret? Are they planning a surprise party for you and are afraid they are going to let it slip? Or does it make them seem suspicious, like they are not telling you the truth? Let your imagine color your responses. And put that into your behavior. Don't start an interrogation—"What's going on?" "What are you up to?" (We just explored why questions are not helpful.) Rather, DO something. Test your theory. Start searching the room for clues of hidden party guests. Drop hints about what you hope you get for your birthday. Or, if their behavior makes you suspicious, look for surveillance cameras.

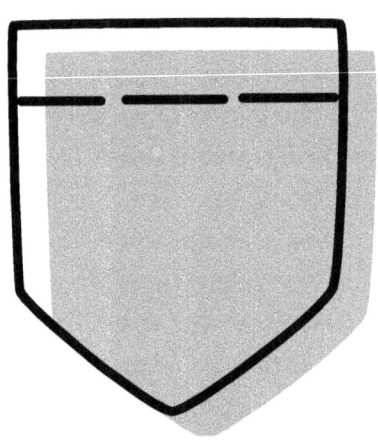

Alright, one more go at a justification scene. This one is known by various names, but I call it "Pockets." The idea is fairly simple: we'll get some suggestions of sayings, or phrases, or lines of dialogue. and jot them down on pieces of paper. Each player will take two of the phrases, randomly, and stick them in their pockets to use at some point in the scene.

The suggestions can be pretty much anything, even a question, if one comes up. Maybe start by collecting and writing down well-known lines from books or movies. And maybe common sayings. Or bits of advice your mother or a friend might give you. You only need a few per scene, so just collect enough so that we don't know which phrases each of the players is going to get. We also want enough so that the players can't remember all the lines they've heard, and won't be able to anticipate anything.

The scene begins, as all scenes do, with activity. Then we build the platform. Look for a shift. Observe. Listen... All the good stuff. And then at some point, you reach into your pocket and read whatever is on the paper. THAT is your next line of dialogue.

What follows is the justification. We want to incorporate that line, however odd it may sound at the moment it's said, into the character and into the scene. Say 'yes' to the line. Embrace it. And use it to propel the scene, just like an entrance or an exit would, or like the 3-second delay did in our previous scenes.

Sometimes, the line will present a familiar justification challenge: introducing a different name than the one we have established in the scene. If you pull out "Luke, I am your father" and your partner is not named Luke, it can throw you off track. As always, do your best not to reply with: "You're crazy!" Or "That doesn't make sense!" **The whole point is to understand why it makes PERFECT sense, and why it is important to the moment, and to the scene.**

In Pockets, in particular, you may be able to help yourself by giving a bit of a set-up before you pull your next line. Set-ups like:

"If you remember one thing when I walk out that door, know that…"

"Her dying words were…"

"Your Honor, I believe it was you, in the case of *Daly v. Periwinkle*, who wrote…"

None of these set-ups reduces the need to justify and fold the lines into the scene, of course. What the set-ups do is create a little bit of context—that it's NOT just coming out of the air—and provide some cushion for something that may sound particularly out of place. There is no guarantee that an attempt at a set-up in any situation will help. But in Pockets, it may.

Sometimes, you'll barely have to justify at all. It is often delightful and surprising (even shocking) how perfectly some of the lines seem to fit the scene when they are read aloud—as though they were scripted for the moment, when we know clearly they were not. Chalk it up to the magic of improvisation, group mind, and to our natural inclination to make sense of things. We are constantly making connections and building context in order to bring understanding to our circumstances.

Once each player has used their lines, look for an ending to your scene. Or perhaps the last line you read already magically created the perfect button to end the scene.

The point of any of these 'games' we layer onto our scenes is to get us out of our head and off of our habits. When we have a challenge or a task that occupies our brain, we tend to BEHAVE more freely. And we tend to focus harder. And to be more attentive. All of these things make us better actors because they force us to be present. Because we don't want to miss anything! Our partners need us. And we never know what offer is coming next, nor which offer is going to launch us ahead.

Justification is not about 'explaining things away.' It is about folding the offers into the scene, and endowing them with significance and purpose. USE what you have. It saves you from having to INVENT. Don't think. DO.

Despite how it may seem, justification is not something you should dread. It's not some onerous task. In fact, some of the most magical moments I have witnessed in improvised scenes have been how perfectly a seemingly unrelated phrase or offer has fit the moment. The unexpected and surprising bumps in the road keep you sharp—keep you paying attention. You respond, make adjustments, and drive on.

9
A Few Things I Learned Along the Way

Improvisation IS acting—the two are one and the same. They employ the same basic skills. And demand the same attention and focus and generosity. They both ask us to put our attention outside ourselves and to work tirelessly to find the truth of the moment. Then, to let it unfold...unanticipated moment by unanticipated moment—script, or no script.

So, then, why improvise? Why not just always know what's coming next, and prepare for it?

Because **improvisation is the key to your actor's imagination.** Improv is where you explore the "What if...?"s. The unknowns. Everything that's NOT in the script. You use your imagination to put impulses into action to discover what uniquely brings YOU, the character, and the world to life. So that you can see it, and make it real for yourself, your partners, and an audience.

I have witnessed too many unscripted scenes where the actors 'prepared', and had 'circumstances', and 'backstory', and 'objectives' (all the acting buzzwords), and then didn't ACT on any of it. Nobody tested their theory. There were no consequences. It all amounted to a masturbatory exercise in playing a mood or an emotion based on some idea they had about the character or the story. What's the point of going off script, if not to see 'what would happen IF...?' And then to DO IT and see.

Improvisation gives you the tools and the space to DO the thing you didn't think you could or should do. SAY the thing you didn't think you could or should say. Even to ASK the question you probably shouldn't ask. Until an ACTION is taken, until an offer is made, we can't move forward. We don't know what the event of the scene is. We don't know what question it is we're trying to answer. And we can't get to the consequences if we never shake the snow globe.

I hear this actor-y inaction defended in two ways: Either it's in the name of 'dramatic tension'. (Translation: stall. See also: delay of action.) Or, an actor whips out the excuse that it didn't 'feel truthful'. Which is another way of saying, 'I wasn't able to figure out why I could or would do that.' It is an intellectual exercise disguised as acting. The actor wanted to game out the scene and couldn't figure out how to get the result they wanted. We know from our work that you CAN'T know what's going to happen until it happens. You are wasting your time if you are looking for the 'best' move, or the 'guaranteed' result. And MORE time doesn't help. We say, 'don't work for the result at all'—it is NEVER the goal. Just make an offer so that your partner can respond. And then, you respond to THAT offer. And, that's how it happens. Moment by moment. DO, and the 'why' will follow.

Hesitancy or inaction is about our need to control. And it really comes to light in improvisation. We don't like uncertainty, so we try to control it—manipulate it, and worse, manipulate others. Often, this manifests itself in demands. "Stop it!" "Shut up!" "Don't do that!" "Be quiet!" "Sit still!" "Don't you dare!"

In improv, these are flashing signs pointing you in a direction: to DO exactly the thing that you are being told NOT to do. If a particular action is such a threat, we WANT to see what happens. We WANT to test the theory. To find the truth. And improv is the perfect place to explore it, with impunity. There will be scenic and narrative consequences for any action, of course, but we can't know what they are until we watch them unfold. What are you waiting for? **Get yourself into trouble and see what happens. And, certainly in improv, don't let someone ever tell you that you CAN'T do something.** 'Oh yeah? Just watch me!' They'll thank you for it. They can't ACT until you do.

YOU, OR THE CHARACTER?

How we talk about our work, and the words we choose are important. I find that when we discuss exercises or scenes afterward, there is a lot of fear of 'getting it wrong'. So, in order to look good, we distance ourselves from our choices—we say "I think..." when we talk about our observations. No. What you saw is what you saw. What you felt is what you felt. You KNOW what you witnessed. I encourage you to respond with "I know..." There is no risk of being wrong—'wrong' doesn't exist in this work. It may not be exactly (or sometimes even remotely) what one of your partners saw. But, at some point you MUST have found agreement, or you would not have been able to go on with the scene. OWN your responses. Respect your imagination and your impulses. It is a difficult habit to break, for sure, but continue to work at letting go of any worry about what is going to happen next. You only have this moment. Listen. Be present. Be clear, for yourself and for your partners.

In acting work, I also prefer that we speak in the first-person about our characters. In improvisation, we and our character are inextricably linked. We may not always like what we do, and will regularly insist "That's not ME!" when we want to distance ourselves from our character's worst traits. But, in service of the work, we should endeavor to identify as closely with our character as possible. In doing so, we better understand our own instincts, and we have a better shot at being able to be truthful, regardless of who we are playing in any role.

Actors often covet being cast in the roles of villains. These tend to be complex and intense characters who create drama, cause trouble, and drive plot. (And get the most dramatic death scenes!) Yet, in order to effectively and truthfully play any antagonist, you MUST be able to identify with their motives. Bad people do bad things, but they always seem to do those things for reasons they believe in. If you play a murderer, you can't just play the stereotypical crazed killer who is one-dimensional. No one was a killer before they killed. So, what is their world view that led them to this behavior? What do they TRULY want or need? Probably not solely to kill things.

And identifying with a character is not the same as condoning their behavior. Remember, as with any offer, the point is to agree that it is the truth as we know it in this moment. Whether or not you like it is irrelevant. Same with characters: you don't have to like them, but you need to find agreement about their truth.

(As I said previously, creating character encompasses so much that it requires another entire volume of explorations and exercises. But, we at least touch on it here because it IS an essential element of our scenework.)

Watch that you are not making excuses for characters, simply as a way to distance yourself from something you don't like or don't understand. If your partner behaves in a way that is erratic or 'bad' or unusual, there is a tendency to say "He's crazy!" "He's drunk!" "He's high!" "He's stupid!" "He's never done this before." **What we are trying to do in this work, however, is to rewire our responses to embrace offers with understanding, not judgment.** Again, by agreeing an offer is true, we are not necessarily aligning with it morally or otherwise. You don't have to like it. You just have to agree it's true.

If you immediately distance yourself or dismiss offers that you don't like, you are cutting off half of your options. Why not use improvisation as the opportunity to explore a different point of view from your own? In an improvised scene, why not join the baddy and get into some trouble together? We know, from our prior work, that there is no commitment beyond THIS moment. A few beats later into the scene, you may discover you are not a baddy, yourself, and the scene takes a turn. Or, perhaps you out-bad the baddy and THEY have a change of heart when they see their behavior amplified in your own. We don't know until it happens. So, why limit your possible experiences?

Generally, when playing characters other than the 'real life' version of you, the rule of thumb is to play them with dignity—to elevate them, rather than denigrate. We don't want to see you playing a character in a way that telegraphs to us your opinion of them. We want to witness for ourselves. It is common for people to play characters with judgment, even when they don't realize they are judging. It is no different than 'commenting' on the offers of your scene that don't make sense to you. You call them out, solely to be clear that "This is not ME!" Watch for your own tendency to give your characters stinky face.

If your character is a child, play a smart and capable child. If your character has a difficult job, be good at it. Do not create 'dumb' characters as a way to avoid your own discomfort. When we are getting our feet under us, there can be a tendency to choose clueless characters because that is how WE feel. We worry that everyone will see that we don't know what we're doing, so we try to hide behind an inept character. I say COMMIT, and we will go with you—it's much more interesting and satisfying to see someone try, than not try. You don't want to fall into the trap of explaining away the consequences of the scene to save some feared embarrassment.

Choosing to play 'dumb' often leads to a 'teaching scene', which we should also try to avoid. Status can be helpful, as we've seen, and it is perfectly acceptable for one character to have authority and power while another character is relatively powerless. Such dynamics are often the root of the shift that happens in the scene—someone who has power loses it, or someone who had no power gains it, and then we see what happens. What matters is what's going on between the characters, not whether someone is competent or not. We don't want to watch you trying to learn something, stumbling through all the manufactured problems of 'not knowing' how to do your activity. If we are using our imaginations, why choose to be bad at something? Be an expert. Be the best. And, if we WERE actually bad at something, we wouldn't likely broadcast it to the world.

Similarly, in acting class we explore impediments—physical conditions that affect our behavior. Injuries. Mental capacity. Illness and disease. Drunkenness. Drugs. Mobility. One thing we come to understand is not to PLAY the impediment. (And certainly not the broad-stroke stereotype of the character.) In truth, if someone is drunk, they are most likely trying hard NOT to appear drunk. If someone has a physical disability, they are not likely trying to draw attention to it. They are focused on whatever they are DOING, and the difference in ability is simply part of their reality in getting their task done. The same way scenes are rarely about the activity itself, an impediment is not likely the defining characteristic of who you are in the scene.

Same for spacework: **I don't want you to PLAY at it. I want you to REALLY do it. Use your imagination to make it real for yourself and your partners. Don't protect yourself from being bad at spacework by 'pretending.'** We KNOW you're pretending—you're creating something from nothing. We know the objects aren't there. We know the environment does not really exist. We know you are not actually your character. So, we want to meet you where you are: improvising. We are willing to give you the benefit of the doubt if we see you really exploring the truth of the person, the place, and the thing. And, if we are in the scene with you, we are going to do everything we can to help your efforts.

Last thing I'll say about character here is about playing non-human animals. For the most part, our spacework can create and keep the reality of an animal alive throughout our scene, the same way we would for an inanimate object. But, live things also behave. They DO things. They move. So, unless you hold the animal the entire scene, or have a hand on it, or a leash, it can be difficult to track. And this may create a lot of hiccups that we need to justify in order to move on. W.C. Fields once said "Never work with children or animals" because they have a way of stealing the scene. That definitely applies to animals in improvisation. Probably because it can be fascinating to watch an actor's imagination at work. But be aware we may miss other offers, as a result.

If you do find an animal is a part of your scene, it is perfectly fine to play an animal as your character. (I have done this MANY times with joyful abandon—bird, cat, dog, horse, cow, frog, elephant, walrus, giraffe, snake…You name it.) It can be beneficial for your partners to have a real, living thing helping create the reality of any animal in the scene. And, if this is a world in which all animals walk upright and communicate with words, we can establish that as the reality of our scene and move forward. If this is a world which more closely mirrors our own, however, it is probably better if the animals only mew or snort or bark, as they would. Having talking animals AND talking humans requires a bit more work to set up or justify, depending on when we realize both are true.

As with anything in improvisation, your behavior and your partners' agreement will lead you forward. If we accept the reality of the scene, whatever it may be, then it truly can be ANYthing and we will be able to believe it. Simply because YOU do. If you make it true, it is.

MISSED CONNECTIONS

In my acting class several years ago, I was working on a scripted scene. I learned the scene. I practiced my lines. I did my homework. I prepared. But there was a line I just couldn't get right. Each time I came to it, I stumbled. What I came to understand was that there was a disconnect. Although I knew what I was SAYing, I didn't know what I was DOing—what my action was when I said what I am supposed to say in that moment. And without a clear action, the line just didn't come to me. It needed to spring from the behavior, but I was trying to REMEMBER the line (and worried about forgetting it), and THINKING about what I was supposed to say, instead.

Then, I drew a parallel with the Pockets scenes. If what I am saying doesn't make sense to me, or it isn't clear what my intention is when saying it, I need to do the work of justification. Whatever my activity or action is in that moment, I need to find the reason why I speak those words—why they belong together. Once I create that specificity, that connection with my behavior, it is more likely the words will come to me. And there is a better chance my partners will receive my offer clearly, and be able to respond with clarity, as well.

Which makes me think of another instance from acting class. Once, after presenting a scene I had rehearsed with my partner, I was receiving some feedback from my teacher. Bill asked me what I was doing in a particular moment of the scene. I replied (naively, as it turns out) that it was just 'small talk'—a throwaway. Ooops! He put me straight right away: There is no such thing as small talk. Words matter. And behavior matters more. Often, what we are saying and what we are doing do not seem to align. But that does not diminish the moment—in fact, it likely expands and deepens it.

This goes to the idea of subtext. Sometimes our words do not appear to reflect our actions. If my line in a script is "I love you," the words themselves do not dictate the action, nor the intention. There is an infinite array of behavior that could accompany such a line. I say "I love you" yet my action is to deceive. Or to placate. Or to surprise.

Furthermore, if we were to believe that 'small talk' existed in a script, it would be akin to saying that 'small offers' exist in improvisation. We know, from our work, that this is not the case. The only thing that renders an offer 'small' is when we treat it as such—when we dismiss it. And that usually happens because we don't immediately understand the offer—we are not clear. But, instead of embracing it and looking deeper, we choose to abandon it, and in doing so we hope to abandon the insecurity and uncertainty we feel.

Sometimes what you're doing and what you're feeling won't match. Improv has given us the skills to find clarity and agreement. We never know where any particular offer is going to take us. And there is no way to pre-determine what's important and what's not. It's ALL important, unless we actively neglect it.

Improvised work applies to our scripted work in so many ways. It may seem paradoxical, since we KNOW what happens next in a script, to suggest that there is anything to be discovered. Yet, you hold the key to your actor's imagination. **We need to find a way to approach scripted work, work where we know the outcome, as though every moment is unplanned, just as it is in improvised scenes—unanticipated moment to unanticipated moment.**

THE SHORT AND THE LONG OF IT

Most of the work we've done so far would fall into the category of 'short-form' improvisation, in which the scenes are usually brief. We establish a foundation in a few beats so we can find the event, and then we spend the bulk of our probably 3- or 5-minute scene exploring the consequences, until we answer the question of the scene.

Short-form is well-suited to comedy, because it happens at what my master clowning teacher Christopher Bayes would call the "speed of fun." It often feels chaotic and hectic, like a roller coaster. Once it starts, it goes just a LITTLE faster than we are able to control. It seems at any moment the thing might fly off track. It feels dangerous and exciting, and it makes us giddy. And, as if the roller coaster wasn't enough, short-form scenes often layer a game or a gimmick on top, to increase the probability that something will go wrong and will make us all laugh.

Well, you are not performing in a comedy show, at the moment. In rehearsal and exploration, you should not feel any pressure to hurry. Or to be funny. Or to get to the joke. We want to find the 'speed of fun', in the sense that we want to give up control, be playful, and go on the ride. But there is no urgency to get a laugh and get out. I will often let scenes go on for 10 or 15 minutes or more if I see that players are making discoveries, or need additional time to break through. We simply use short-form to give our exploration structure, not to rush it along.

Long-form improvisation, by comparison, is not necessarily longer scenes. Rather, it's a longer story arc. Like short-form, long-form improvisation can follow many different structures—usually, several shorter scenes strung together into one longer narrative. If you look at the progression of classes for an improv comedy school, the path usually starts with short-form games, and by Level 3 or 4, delves into long-form structures, like the Harold. Or the Maude. At those levels, students join teams and create long-form structures with their own stamp. What most long-forms have in common is that they are likely 30 minutes (maybe up to an hour) of scenes and palette cleansers strung together to tell one thematic, if not narrative, story.

If we were to think of our story structure in long-form terms, we would likely have a few short establishing (platform) scenes at the beginning. We would be getting to know the world and the people who inhabit it. Or, if we are improvising around a theme, our characters may not all live in the same world or time, but their connection is similar. They are all on a journey. Or they are all searching for love. Or meaning. Universal themes can tie seemingly unrelated characters and worlds together, much like justification does. There is some 'mirroring' happening between characters and worlds that helps us tie them together contextually.

Then, we likely have a few short scenes where the shakeup happens—where we learn what the story is really about. What the question of the 'play' is. And then we'll have a series of short scenes that show us the exploration of consequences. 'If THAT happens, what happens as a result?' And by the final few short beats of the long-form, we'll be looking for a sort of moral. What did we learn? We answer our question of the play. Hopefully, there are no more offers left to pick up.

The primary thing you'll probably notice about doing long-form versus short-form is simply the pace. Short-form can FEEL very quick. And for actors in search of 'truth' who are used to having time to do their homework and craft their performance, it can even feel abrupt. But, I think this is one of the things that makes this improv work so powerful. In short-form, we have to get to it—we don't have time to let things formulate. We need to observe and react without delay. And fully commit to those spontaneous impulses. Perhaps the reason we usually take so long to craft is not that we need more time, but simply because we don't trust that our first impulse was good enough to follow.

Conversely, in long-form it can sometimes be too easy to lose the thread. Or to be too esoteric. We expect our audience to piece everything together, to 'understand' and make sense of our scenes. It is definitely harder to follow a narrative over 30 minutes than for 3. But, it's good to know how to do both.

A show I performed Off Broadway and on tour for many years called "Broadway's Next Hit Musical" cleverly combined short-form and long-form improvisation into a two-act musical comedy. The first act was a series of unique improvised short-form scenes (and songs!), each one inspired by a made-up song title written by audience members before the show began. And then, based on which short-form scene the audience wanted to see more of, the full story of the musical was told in the second act of the show—i.e. a long-form improvisation. To add to the fun (it was a comedy show, after all), the full musical included a recreation of the original short-form scene from the first act. So, the audience would now see it in context of the larger story.

Movies and full-length plays are long-form—shorter scenes strung together to tell a longer story arc. The big difference being that those stories are scripted, not improvised. It is easier to track a story that you have already read and rehearsed than one you are creating on-the-spot. But, if you think of your long-form work in terms of a series of shorter scenes, it may help you to feel where you are in the story.

There's nothing wrong in improvisation with using a familiar narrative structure to help guide you, either. Use a story you know, as if it is the suggestion for your scene—your jumping off point. ("Give me a well-know fairy tale." "Cinderella!", for example) The caveat, as always: don't ever assume you know what's coming next. If your story diverges from the familiar one you THOUGHT you were telling, you have to adapt and go with it. You cannot expect that events will go a certain way, no matter how obvious you think the path appears.

YOU'VE GOT GAME

Many improv comedy schools teach students the concept of the 'game' as a way to find structure in scenes—like a hook in a pop song. In our work throughout this book, we have layered some literal games on top of our scene-work to give us challenges in order to illuminate specific skills—we restrict one aspect like words, for example, so that we can discover some different aspect, like expansion. We build our ability to use what we HAVE instead of struggling with what we don't. We force ourselves to come back to the basics of behavior.

When these schools refer to the 'game' of the scene, they usually mean more of an emergent pattern—an offer gets 'called back' and explored. A 'callback' in improv is different than something you may receive from a casting director after a stellar audition. In improv, a callback literally recalls an idea or an offer from earlier in the scene. Often, just like our slow-motion and silence work, when the offer returns, it has expanded or changed, yet we still recognize it from when it happened previously. Repetition feels familiar. And each time we revisit something, the more we understand its relevance to the story and to the characters. Its meaning expands organically, just like our movement work did.

I think callbacks create a lot of the magic in improvisation. People are amazed, with all that's going on, with all the uncertainty of creating something out of nothing, that an improviser remembers some specific detail—something we likely forgot about. And when the improviser not only remembers it, but remembers it well enough to present it to us again with renewed context, we call that a "reincorporation". It creates those 'aha!' moments where, same as a justification, all-of-a-sudden something that seemed unimportant has become KEY to this moment and to the scene—seemingly insignificant things that an improviser did NOT dismiss, and is now able to re-apply in the exact right moment.

You actually see reincorporation in scripted work all the time. (Foreshadowing, anyone?) Little nuggets that seem too ordinary to even notice return later in the story to reveal their importance. It can be thrilling in scripted work. I contend it's MAGIC when it happens in improv.

And all we are doing is PAYING ATTENTION. Let yourself be a sponge that absorbs everything you observe. KNOW that nothing is irrelevant, and continue to build your skills to be able to balance and work through several offers at once. It's not easy. Offers DO get dropped. Just do your best to keep it simple. And to make what you HAVE be enough.

So, if you are on the lookout for patterns, you can have some fun making magic by exploring them. Maybe you mistakenly dropped an object in a scene. Instead of seeing it as something you (or your character) did wrong, you ACCEPT the endowment that you are clumsy or that you drop things. At various other moments as the scene progresses, you embrace the discovery of that endowment and drop something else. It doesn't have to derail the scene, or even pull focus. You are simply playing the 'game' and threading the offer through the scene at the right moments. And, MAYBE at a pivotal moment of the resolution of your scene, your habit of dropping things is the one offer that saves the day. Just like our Word-at-a-Time stories led to tragedy or triumph, one simple offer or object, when fully explored and expanded, can be the catalyst for change.

Playing the pattern of the 'game' is no different than the expansion work we did before. You are letting one offer organically evolve into what it needs to become. This requires staying focused and not letting things disappear from your scenes simply because you feel like you already have too much to focus on. We tend, as we've seen, to throw away offers that we don't immediately understand—instead of engaging and exploring until we find out what they mean, and why they're important. I tell you… It's magic when it happens.

As I begin work with each new group of actors, I tell them upfront that I am not likely going to teach them anything they don't already know. So, if you have gotten this far in the book and feel like you knew all of this already... Good! Because that's not what the work of this book is.

Improvisation is learning to give yourself permission to follow your own instincts—to unabashedly be your true self, and trust that you have everything you need, if you will simply ALLOW it to come forward.

You have all the tools you need to be able to create improvised scenes and stories—and the same skills apply to scripted work.

Listen.

Respond truthfully.

Mirror energy and behavior.

Focus on the DOING.

Let the words come organically.

Don't work for any result.

Go from unanticipated moment to unanticipated moment.

And let your actor's imagination be your guide.

10
Improv in the 'Real World'

I can't count the number of times my acting teacher would disparage the 'real world'—the world we leave outside the studio door when we come to work on our acting craft. The world filled with daily obligations and rules and restrictions that limit our behavior, yet form so much of our frame of reference. The 'truth' as we know it is based in what we have experienced in 'real life', and we inevitably bring that truth to our acting work.

Bill's point, of course, in encouraging us to reject the 'real world' was not to abandon the truth. Rather, his very improvisational approach was asking us to expand our imagined possibilities beyond 'reality'. He was saying, just as we do in our improv work: "What if...?" Let your actor's imagination take you someplace where responsible, ordered society would say is off limits. 'You can't do that!' Remember what I said about how to interpret your partner's command telling you NOT to do something? Right! I say the forbidden thing is the EXACT thing that you do next. We have to live in the world of "What if...?" in order to make any discoveries, and to reveal any and all possible outcomes—moment by moment.

Honestly, I don't see any real purpose to improvise if not to do the thing you think you probably shouldn't do, or say the thing that you probably shouldn't say. And in DOING it, in shaking things up and moving into the exploration of consequences, we no longer have to speculate about what WOULD happen. We SEE what IS happening—and it could happen differently every single time. Even if it was scripted. A play could happen differently every single night, based on some new perspective—perhaps a more detailed and curious inspection, or the slightest shift in behavior. With an expanded openness to receive, the subtlest of changes can give something a whole new color you never would have planned, even if you could have.

Bill would also point out to us, in no uncertain terms, that we needed to have a life OUTSIDE of our work as actors—that the 'real world' IS a place to live fully. He reminded us that in order to have a full imagination and to be able to explore and inhabit characters and behavior, we need to live rich lives. Have experiences. Fall in love. Feel loss. Succeed. Fail. It cannot be ALL about acting.

Yes…And…**I believe we can bring the skills of improvisation with us into the real world to improve our quality of life OUTSIDE of the realm of acting.** This is why I reference Bill's words so often—because they applied to my humanity, not just my work as an actor. In fact, some of you may not be actors yourselves, and chose to explore this work because you also see the potential benefits it holds for you personally and professionally. Who doesn't want to live in a world of 'yes'?

I think it's fairly easy to see the applications of improvisation to other creative efforts beyond acting—writing, design, filmmaking, dance and others. The ability to be receptive and to respond through expression lives in all creative people (even the ones who don't think of themselves as 'creative'), regardless of their chosen medium.

Painters and sculptors and designers of all stripes find ways to take static objects and surfaces and materials and set them in motion—into action. They create dimension and space and color and depth and movement simply in the way they use the offers they have, letting their art reveal itself, moment by moment. I think it may be nearly impossible for an artist to find their "Until finally…" moment. Is art ever 'finished'? Bill would invoke legendary dancer and artist Martha Graham who summed up this condition as "a queer divine dissatisfaction, a blessed unrest". It is not for us to judge what unfolds, but to remain open and forever marching forward. Because we HAVE to. In Bill's words, again, "There is no compelling reason to be an actor, except that you can't NOT do it."

I experienced firsthand how improvisation can work for screenwriters. I acted in two feature-length film projects which were developed and performed using improvisation, with writer/director Christina Kallas and the Writers' Improv Studio. I collaborated with writers and filmmakers to understand how the 'kernels of truth' in the scenes are uncovered. We would 'rehearse' improvised scenes using the circumstances of the scenes from the written screenplay—given to us much the same as we would get suggestions for any improvised scene, really. We would NOT read the written scene beforehand. We would do the improvised exploration and THEN read the scene.

I have used the word 'magic' many times in this book and continuously in my work. But, I tell you, the times when we would read the written scenes after our improvisations and EXACT bits of dialogue or action would appear on the page just as they had happened…I was amazed. THOSE, my colleague would say, are the kernels of truth. Those are the elements of the scene that are essential and significant, and they may not have been brought to light without the improvised work.

Writers I know also speak of the benefit of 'hearing it out loud'. But, for them to hear dialogue coming organically from an improviser, based only on a setup of character and circumstance for a written scene, it can be very revealing to be able to hear how people really speak. As a writer myself, I know how clearly my imagination sees and hears the scene, and yet what makes it to the page often sounds odd when spoken by a living, breathing, behaving human being. 'That's not how people talk' can be a difficult criticism to hear. Luckily, we have improv to set us right.

Employing improvisation is all well and good for people who are more accustomed to creative expression. But, what about improvisation for those who exist outside creative roles? Don't they deserve a little magic, too? YES! At your job, with your family, out with friends, you can apply the skills of improvisation in your own circumstance.

Listen more intently.

Don't assume you know where a conversation is going. Let others' ideas be considered, same as your own. Try agreeing with someone else and building on their idea rather than our usual m.o. which is to completely reject whatever someone else brought to the table so that there is plenty of room for our own idea. The key to listening is usually found in NOT speaking—or at least speaking less.

It can be difficult to be honest with ourselves about how little space we leave for others to express themselves, and how hard we push our own ideas. A lifetime of living in a world of 'no' can be debilitating. Fear not! Improvisation breeds reciprocity. If you allow space for others, it is very likely space will be made for you.

Look for the greater win in adapting to what the moment needs, rather than holding onto a pre-planned path.

Be open to the possibility that where you end up may be different than you thought. Not better or worse, just different. But, at whatever outcome you arrive, there WILL be something different: agreement—because it will be something that comes from the whole, not just one person.

Mirror in 'real life.'

Not as a way to annoy your friends or as some sort of party trick. Mirror to demonstrate how open and receptive you are. Be ABLE to hear other opinions and points of view and ideas, and repeat them back. Try them on as a way to better understand them. You've heard the expression "walk a mile in someone else's shoes." I am convinced that advice comes from an improviser. Just like any scene we've done, you may ultimately return to where you started, but you will have had a shared experience, and our 'new normal' will surely have evolved.

Don't anticipate. Wait.

Until the offer is on the table, there is nothing to respond to. Or, maybe there is SOMEthing, but you want to make sure you have as much clarity as possible before you act. So, leave room for others. Let them fully share their idea before you jump ahead.

Observe. Take it all in.

Notice little things. I'm not talking about pet peeves and petty judgments about idiosyncrasies. Don't take things personally as a way to provoke some fight you planned to have the next time you saw this person. Don't look for clues to prove your case against them. Use your curiosity to understand, and to find agreement.

Find your pace.

We can miss a lot when we are racing toward the finish. Take the opportunity to slow down to create a richer experience for yourself. Make discoveries about your connection to the activities and the people in your life—especially those that we take for granted, because we have done the same task a million times before, or known someone forever. There's always more to notice.

Focus. Be present.

Stay off your smartphone and have a full interaction. Be generous. Give your time and energy in service of others and the moment at hand. Reward someone with your attention. Give it freely without keeping score. Multi-tasking is ALWAYS a last resort. Be here now.

(As an aside, in a moment of serendipity as I am editing this book, I only recently learned about a book with the title "Be Here Now" by Ram Dass—a book about meditation, spirituality and yoga. Although I have not read it yet, I imagine that it mirrors our improv-meets-life goal to focus and be present. I could write another entire book about the parallels I find between improvisation and meditation. So, if you are looking for another way to apply improvisation to your life, perhaps meditation is worth a look. For now, I'll write one book at a time.)

Now, we have a few ideas how we can apply improv in our non-actor lives. Of course, in the 'real world', a lot of people don't know what you now know. They don't possess the same superpowers you have cultivated. No matter. Energy has a way of reflecting back. When you approach the world in pursuit of agreement, it has a way of being returned in kind. When you understand that adaptation and compromise (what we called 'losing' in our Kiss or Kill improv shorthand) actually moves EVERYONE forward, including you, who cares if someone claims they 'won'? They only get there because YOU make it possible—the 'loser' is in control.

It's hard. We don't want to 'lose.' And we don't want to always be the one to make room and compromise for the greater good. Often, it doesn't feel very rewarding. But what is the alternative? Resistance? I say it takes way more energy to battle against something than to look for the agreement. It may APPEAR that there is no common ground, no overlapping Venn Diagram circles, to guide us. But it ALWAYS comes down to basic human behavior. Each response leads to the next response. Resistance pulls your energy away. It slows the 'scene.' It negates, when we want to agree. 'You don't have to like it, but you must agree it is the truth of the moment in order to move forward.' Otherwise, you're not in the same 'scene.'

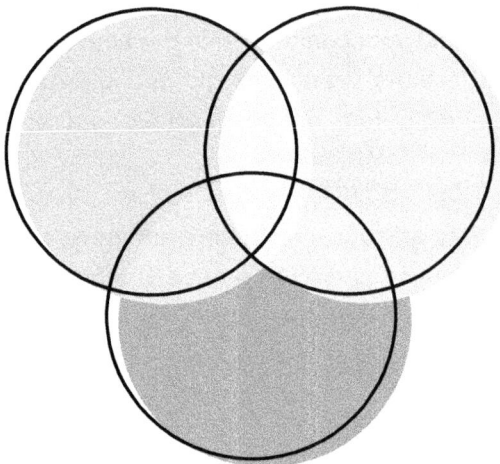

An entire cottage industry has been built around the application of improvisation skills to work teams—countless seminars and sales meetings with breakout sessions to give teams a chance to think creatively, play, be spontaneous, and above all: find the "Yes!" Salespeople, by trade, are constantly overcoming objections. And any 'justification' is only possible if salespeople are able to be good observers and to look for agreement—often, on BEHALF of their customer, to show their customer where there is common ground, even when the customer doesn't see it.

The objection to exploring improvisation is usually: 'well, I'm not an actor.' Or the thought of 'performing' improv for your coworkers may fill you with anxiety. These skills are not just about performing—not just about public speaking or presentations or pitches. They are about being present in the moment, REALLY listening, and BUILDing on what came before—all of this so that EVERYONE can move forward.

Within a shared improv experience, team members are often emboldened by having their peers support them and take on the same challenges. Most refer to it as 'stepping out of your comfort zone.' I say it is merely giving yourself permission to try (knowing that the disastrously embarrassing outcome you foresee is just your own cooked-up drama), and then to get yourself a 'win' when you get through it. Not just get through it, but conquer the challenge. Make your partners look good. It's the surest way to have that same principle returned to you. Improv creates the ultimate 'team player'.

And, lastly, family dynamics. It shouldn't seem like much of a leap to see how listening and an increased focus on agreement could aid families. Or partners. Or spouses. Or siblings. It is very easy, within families, to take one another for granted. We ASSUME we know how the argument's going to go, and how our family member is going to respond. We feel like we have to fight for what's ours because there isn't enough (money, time, food, love, support, whatever) to go around. We often feel like we are the ONLY family member who ever has to compromise. 'You always get your way!' 'I never get what I want!'

If we are open to things changing, if we are looking for agreement, if we are making room for others' needs and ideas, and fully hearing them, there is a lot better chance we will find the overlap—see the areas of commonality. Every 'scene' is different. So **approach even the most familiar people in your life with openness and acceptance. Listen.** Simply by giving one another our full attention from time to time, and listening before we jump to our response, we may open a dialogue and a path to resolution that previously felt impossible.

It doesn't require any more time or effort. It is merely an application of some basic human behavioral skills that we have explored, to help us be more adaptable and ready to find the 'yes' in any circumstance or relationship. **Observe and respond. You can't choose the outcome, but you can ABSOLUTELY choose the approach. And it unfolds one moment at a time.**

11
More Fun Things to Try

I never said improv shouldn't be fun. And much of our exposure to improvisation is actually 'improv comedy', which is to say it's INTENDED to be fun and playful and loose. And quick. And did I mention funny? I don't teach improv 'comedy'—I think comedy is a style, like soap opera or western or Shakespeare. I have performed improv comedy (and musical improv comedy) for many years, all across the U.S. and internationally, and my goal, when I do, is always to avoid relying on the gimmicks. The games. I feel like a hack when I trot out some trick I KNOW will get a laugh. (Getting laughs seems like the whole point of a comedy show, I know... Welcome to my world.)

This is why I take the comedy requirement out of it for my students: the games can distract from the fundamental skills. We begin to crave the reward of the laugh at the expense of truthful storytelling, detailed spacework and clear offers. You've heard the expression: 'It's funny because it's true.' If we recognize ourselves and truthful human behavior in what we are seeing, we laugh from familiarity. And we laugh at good improv because we delight in watching actors solve the 'problems' of the scene, especially in ways we ourselves would not have imagined or done. Cheap tricks are just that: cheap.

All that said, the purpose of this book is not to disparage improv comedy and the many people who perform it, teach it, and enjoy it. I come from the same place. My roots in improv, as for most, are with short-form games. And it was the lessons I took from these games that helped me create my own approach to improvisation—recognizing the value in the foundational skills that supported my acting craft. Games CAN give us a fun challenge and a chance to make a discovery through play.

Your solid spacework and scenework should be a given for any scene, at this point. Don't throw your skills out the window in search of a laugh, or fall into the 'wacky improv comedy' traps. Allow the game to lay on top of all that solid work, and to give your scene some shape.

There are seemingly endless variations of improv games to layer onto your scenes—or just to play with some friends at a party for a change of pace. Or at your school's variety show. Here are a few I've played over the years that I like:

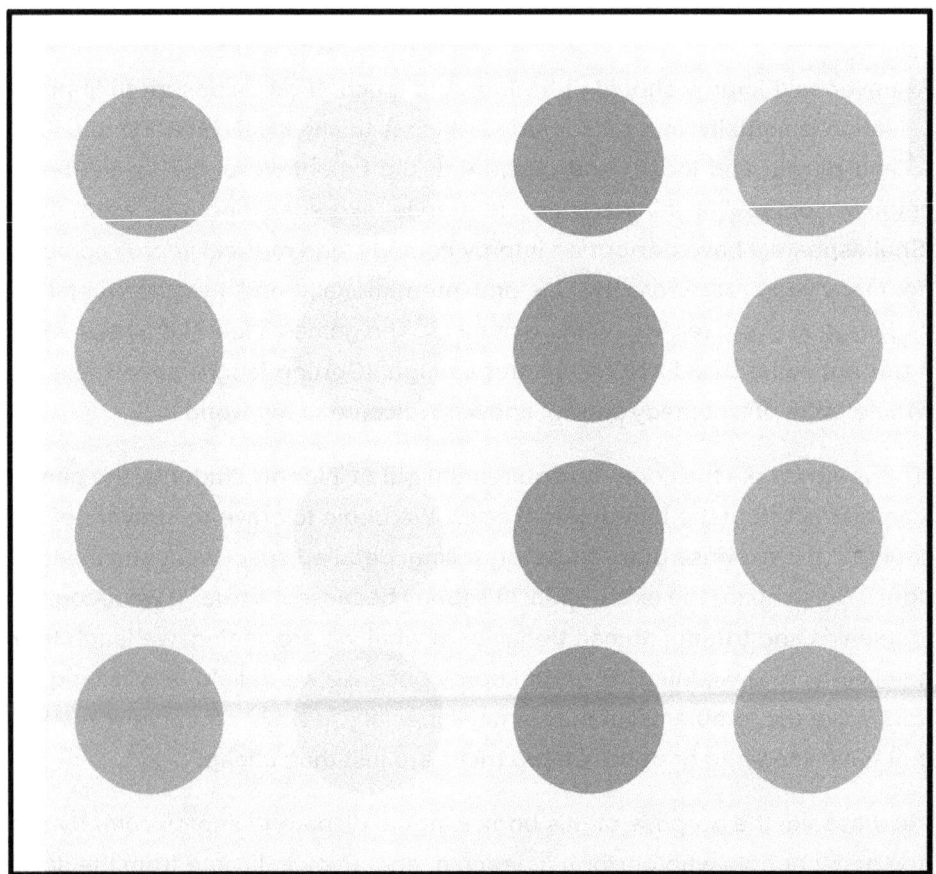

ZIP-ZAP-ZOP
WARM-UP

Using a repeated series of syllables ("Zip!", "Zap!" and "Zop!"), players make an offer by pointing to another player while saying a syllable. The first player points and "Zip!"s to another player. That second player then points and "Zap!"s to a different player. And that third player then points and "Zop!"s to another. The pattern continues, pointing at another player and either "Zip!"ing, "Zap!"ing or "Zop!"ing, always in that order. "Zip!" "Zap!" "Zop!" "Zip!" "Zap!" "Zop!" "Zip!" "Zap!" "Zop!"

WHA
WARM-UP

This one requires collaboration, and is another sequence of three beats, like Zip-Zap-Zop. The first beat: a player presses his hands together over his head (like prayer hands) and, as though holding a knife between his hands, throws the space knife toward another player while shouting "WHA!" The next beat: The receiving player catches the space knife between her hands, similarly raising them over her head, and shouting "WHA!" The third beat: while the space knife is still overhead, the players to either side of the receiving players will use their prayer hands to simultaneously 'chop' toward the abdomen of the receiving player (no actual physical contact, please) while shouting "WHA!" Then the sequence repeats when the receiving player (her hands still over her head) throws the space knife to a different player with a "WHA!" That player catches it overhead with a "WHA!" And the two players on either side of the receiver chop toward the receiver's abdomen with a "WHA!"

CRAZY 8'S
WARM-UP

This is a good one to get the blood flowing. Everyone raise your right hand over your head, shake it eight times, each time counting down from 8. Then raise your left hand over your head, shake it eight times while counting down from 8. Right leg for 8. Left leg for 8. I like to add the booty for 8. Then, right hand for 7, left hand for 7, right leg for 7, left leg for 7, booty for 7. Then, right hand for 6... repeating the countdown until the last, which is right hand for 1, left hand for 1, right leg for 1, left leg for 1, booty for 1. As a final gesture, everyone puts a hand to the center of the circle and cheers, "Craaaaaaaazy 8's!!"

MANTRA
WARM-UP

This one uses our 'word-at-a-time' skills while also sharpening our group agreement. Using words (English or whichever language you improvise in), the first player will make an offer by snapping (or pointing, or throwing a space ball) toward another player while speaking one word. For example, maybe the word is "Happiness..." The receiving player then makes an offer by snapping toward another player while adding the next word of the phrase we're building, for instance "...is..." The player then makes an offer and adds a word, perhaps "...found..." The next player's offer is perhaps "...wherever..." And we continue this passing and adding of offers until we collectively reach what sounds like the end of the thought. How do we know when the thought has ended? We show that we ALL agree by taking a moment of reflection, nodding our heads, and saying "Aaaaaaaaahhhh." Then the last player to whom the offer was directed can begin a new phrase.

PASS THE CLAP
WARM-UP

This one has an unfortunate name, but is an incredibly useful game. The challenge is to turn to your partner and for both of you to clap your hands together at the same exact time. The receiver then turns to the next person and those two both clap their hands together at the same time. This continues around the circle, same as Whoosh Whoa. In order to reverse the direction of the clapping in this game, the receiver simply returns the offer. For example, I turn to you, we clap together. Then, instead of turning to the next person in the circle, you simply offer it back to me, and we clap together a second time. At which point, I turn to my previous partner and the offers are now going in the opposite direction.

3-LINE DRILL
PLATFORM-BUILDING EXERCISE

To get the rhythm of building a scene into our bones, line up in two parallel lines, facing downstage. The two players at the front of the lines will be in the first 'scene'. The player on line one begins an activity and makes a simple verbal offer that focuses on the WHERE. For example, setting up a picnic, player one says, "There's no better place to meet on a warm and sunny today than right here in Willoughby Park." The player on the second line, having already joined in the activity, then adds an offer that gives a detail about the WHO. In this case, perhaps "Yes, Daryl. When we were kids, every sunny day mom and dad would bring us to Willoughby Park to play on the swings. Too bad we're all grown up." Then the first player finishes the interaction with the 'What's new?' moment that breaks the pattern. In this example, maybe Daryl shows his sibling the swing he stole off the playground. "If WE can't swing, then no one can." Or perhaps he grabs his sibling by the arm and drags them toward the swings, saying "I'll show you who's too old!" Or takes off running, "Race you to the swings!" Then those two players go to the back of the lines, and the two players now at the front of the lines start a new 'scene.'

The challenge is to quickly establish a platform (who, what and where) and have a shakeup, all in three lines/beats. Move quickly so that you don't think too much about whether or not you're doing it right. And, be sure to start by engaging in the space to add offers and detail, so that you are not just standing there talking to one another—as always, DO something.

CONDUCTED STORY
STORYTELLING GAME

Players stand in a line, all facing another player who will 'conduct' the story, as though musicians in a symphony. Get a topic or title or style for the story. The conductor points to a player, who begins to tell the story. (I recommend following the story structure we practiced... "Once upon a time..." or a similar setup to establish the platform.) The player who is speaking will continue to speak until the conductor points to another player, who will pick up the story right where the previous player left off. The conductor continues to point at subsequent players until the story ends.

Like our Give-and-Take work, if you are speaking and the conductor points to someone else, you must stop speaking IMMEDIATELY—mid-thought, mid-sentence, mid-word. The new speaker must likewise pick up EXACTLY where the previous player left off—finish the thought, the sentence, the word. The story should be seamlessly shared, and told in one voice.

NARRATED STORY
STORYTELLING SCENE

One player will tell a story, describing characters, events and action, as usual. And from time-to-time, the narrator will pause to leave space for other players to create the next aspect of the story. The story is shared by the narrator and the players in the scenes. We don't want to see the players act out everything the narrator just told us. Rather, the narrator tells part of the story, then we see part of the story created in a scene, then back to the narrator, etc. The idea is to tell ONE story, partly narrated and partly acted out—both parts of the story building on what the others created.

EULOGY
STORYTELLING SCENE

This is a similar set-up to the Narrated Story. One or more players will eulogize someone who has died, as though speaking at a funeral. Each speaker will tell a story of an important memory or moment from the life of the deceased. Once the speaker has set up the memory with the platform elements, other players will take over to create the rest of the memory in live action, like we are seeing the flashback. We don't want to see the players act out everything the speaker just told us—just pick up the story and finish playing it out. Probably good if actors play the same characters from flashback to flashback, so we don't get confused about who's who.

SIGN LANGUAGE INTERPRETER
TRANSLATED STORY

One player will tell a story which another player will translate for us using gibberish (i.e. made-up) sign language. As the story unfolds, the interpreter should translate everything that is said, in real time. Look for repeatable gestures. Every time the storyteller uses a repeated name, or repeated object, or place, we want the interpreter to use the same repeated gestures which were created for those words when we heard them the first time. The interpreter does not need to act out the story—rather, create gestures to represent the words being spoken. Make the translation as literal as possible.

Try this game solo. Interpret for a TV show you're watching, or a podcast.

SUBCONSCIOUS
TRANSLATED SCENE

This is a bit like Film Dub—the difference being that instead of translating the dialogue, players will be speaking their partners' inner thoughts. Two players create a scene. Intermittently, 'subconscious' thoughts will be interjected. Sometimes these inner thoughts may be the subtext or alternate truth of what was just said. Other times, the inner thoughts may be spoken during times of silence, as though we can HEAR what someone's thinking. (Obviously the players IN the scene would not be able to hear the other's thoughts, but the offer may still be used to inform your response.)

This theatrical device of speaking someone's thoughts could also be applied to animals or other objects that are unable to speak. A sort of Dr. Doolittle variation. We can maintain a reality to the world (which doesn't have to be magic or a cast spell) and also allow interspecies players to communicate.

SLOW-MOTION OLYMPICS
EXPANSION SCENE

Two players are in a competition, and two other players are providing the sports commentary of the action. First, get an activity (which uses objects) that is not considered a competitive sport (brushing your teeth, or building a canoe, or folding towels, for example). The two competitors will not speak in the scene, only make behavioral offers. They can begin the scene by 'warming up' for the competition—prepare your objects, do your warm-up routine, size up the competition, etc. While the players are warming up, the commentators can help set the scene. Name the players. Name the competition. Give us some history. Be experts. After a bit of setup, let the games begin. TWEEEEEEET!

Once the actual competition begins, ALL action by the competitors will be done in SLOW MOTION. Commentators should describe what they see. Competition is exciting, so really invest. Remember our Kiss-or-Kill work. And allow the slow motion to EXPAND your experience of the events—let us see every detail of what you're doing and what you're experiencing until someone wins and someone loses. Once the competition is done, competitors can return to regular speed as the commentators quickly wrap up the broadcast.

REMOTE CONTROL
CONDUCTED SCENE

Players create a scene. From time to time, another player will give commands, as though pressing buttons on a remote controller. The commands could be "Pause." "Stop." "Play." "Fast forward." "Rewind." "Slow motion." "Skip." Etc. The goal of the players in the scene is to maintain the integrity of the scene, despite the timeline being manipulated by the controller.

STYLES REPLAY
STYLES SCENE

Players create a short 'neutral' scene, with a platform, event and resolution. Once the short scene has been created. We pause and get a suggestion for a different style in which to replay the scene—maybe the suggestion is "Children's TV show" or "Western" or any number of possible genres. The players then recreate the same scene using elements of the new style suggestion. The original scene can be replayed several times using different styles. An alternate version is to play one continuous scene (instead of replaying the same scene), pausing from time to time to get suggestions to change the style. The scene then continues where it left off, only in the new style.

MAKE UP YOUR MIND
EXPANSION SCENE

Two players begin a scene, and another player will be calling the scene by ringing a bell. From time-to-time, after an offer is made in the scene (verbally or physically), the third player will ring a bell. Before moving on with the scene, the player who made the last offer prior to the bell needs to make a different offer. That new offer may also get a bell ring, or the scene may be allowed to continue. The idea is to allow yourself to make vastly different offers, and to surprise yourself with the directions the scene could go. For example, if your physical offer is making pasta, and you hear the bell, you don't want to get stuck in a loop of just changing the type of food you are preparing, like a hamburger, or a salad. Try offering a completely different activity, or vastly different emotion, and see where that takes you—and then justify the offer that is allowed to move forward. Why, if you were making pasta, did you choose to now go hang gliding? Perhaps that is the fastest way to get to Italy? Justify why you made the new choice.

"HAND ME THE SOAP"
JUSTIFICATION SCENE

Players engage in an activity and begin a scene. At some point, one of the players will ask another for an object that is needed for the task—something you would ACTUALLY need. However, a player will hand you an unrelated object instead. For example, your activity is washing dishes, and at some point you request for your partner to 'hand you the soap.' Your partner gladly obliges by replying "Sure. Here's a diamond ring." and handing you the object. Your challenge then, like our Birthday Party scenes, is to make that object make sense for the task at hand, to identify why it is the perfect choice, and to use it accordingly. In this example: "Great! Nothing is going to get this caked-on mess off these plates better than a diamond! And the ring is like a little handle." Then set about scrubbing the plates with the diamond ring.

Each player can do this a few times—ask for something you need for the task and then justify the object you are actually given.

ALPHABET
LANGUAGE RESTRICTION SCENE

Players engage in an activity and begin a scene. The scene will follow the English alphabet, so will only contain 26 lines total. Each subsequent line of dialogue must begin with the next letter of the alphabet, from A through Z. Let the letter inspire your offer, rather than put you in your head trying to think of the order of the alphabet, or scrolling through a dictionary. Don't forget that you can, and should, still make offers through behavior and spacework. And don't depend too heavily on your words, because you will run out of them quickly!

1-10
LANGUAGE RESTRICTION SCENE

Same basic idea as Alphabet, except this time it is a total of only 19 lines in the scene, AND we are limiting the number of words you can say each time you speak. Unlike 1-3-5, though, the number of words you can speak will change from line to line—from 1 word up to 10 words, and then back down to 1 word. Once you finish your allotment, you must wait for someone else to finish theirs before you can speak again. For instance, if you spoke the first line and had only one word to say, you may not speak again until another player has spoken two words, at which point you could speak a total of three words, and on it goes up to ten, and back down to one. Even more than in Alphabet, don't rely on your words to get you through—there must be action and behavior to move the short scene forward.

It can be helpful to have a third player to count the words so that you can stay engaged in the scene and not have to worry so much about counting. And if you forget how many words you have used or how many you have remaining, they can confirm for you.

STAGE DIRECTIONS
JUSTIFICATION SCENE

This scenic game is very similar to Pockets, except instead of getting suggestions for lines of dialogue, the suggestions will be actions or activities. They can be actual stage directions ("Exit right." "To the audience." "Cross downstage left." Etc.), or physical or emotional directions ("Cry." "Jump up and down." "Sing." "Laugh." "Run in a circle." "Glare." Etc.) Get lots of suggestions ahead of the scene, write each one down on a piece of paper, and let each player choose a few randomly to put in their pockets. At some point in the scene, reach into your own pocket and do whatever is written on the piece of paper. JUSTIFY why you did what you did in that moment. No one is 'crazy'—make the behavior make sense, to propel the scene.

ACTOR'S NIGHTMARE
JUSTIFICATION SCENE

There are a couple of variations to this scenic game. The basic idea is that several players are playing a scene and ONE of them is not prepared—that player must read their lines from a script, while the other players are 'off book'. Using an actual, written play, flip to a random page, decide which role you are going to read, and then stick with that throughout the entire scene. When it is your turn to speak, simply respond with whatever the next line is for the character you've chosen in the script. The 'off book' players can say and do whatever they want to make the scene work, doing their best to justify the lines spoken from the script and to move the scene forward.

In some versions of this game, the 'unrehearsed' player will step outside while the other players 'rehearse' the scene by discussing the basic who, what where, and arc of the scene, so that we know what play we are attempting to put on.

UNDERSTUDY variation: Instead of using a written script, three players create an entire improvised scene while the 'unrehearsed' player is outside, unable to see or hear anything happening inside. Once the scene is done, one of the players suddenly takes ill and cannot do the next performance. So, the 'unrehearsed' player comes in, and the entire scene is recreated as closely to the original as possible with the understudy filling in for the missing actor.

FIRST LINE, LAST LINE
JUSTIFICATION SCENE

Along the lines of Pockets, we will get dialogue suggestions. However, we are only going to use two of them: one that will be the first line of the scene, and one that will be the last line of the scene. It is up to the players, then, to bridge the offers and dialogue between those two lines. To start, get several suggestions for lines of dialogue, write them down on pieces of paper, and put them in a hat. Before selecting the lines, get some additional suggestions to set up the scene: a who, where, and/or an activity.

Then choose the lines randomly from the hat. The LAST line should be known—everyone should agree which suggestion will end the scene—so, that can be pulled from the hat and read aloud. The FIRST line should be a surprise, so one of the players can put a random suggestion from the hat into their pocket to pull out and speak once the scene has begun. Since we don't know who will speak first in the scene, you could also have every player put a random suggestion in their pocket for the first line, just in case.

As another variation, each player could have their OWN first and last line. It works pretty much the same, except we now know the last thing EACH person will say in the scene. (Whether or not it is also their exit line, we won't know until it happens.) We also know that the first thing EACH person says will be random and need to be justified.

12
For Starters

If you were creating an improvised scene, you may start by gathering a suggestion or two. These are commonly known in improv as "ask-for"s—literally, the thing you ask for at the top of the scene. It's a good habit to get suggestions from those who are not in the scene, or to jot down a collection of suggestions from which to pull randomly, much like we did in Pockets.

In keeping with our approach throughout this book, my advice is to work with starting suggestions that are simple and clear, and to avoid suggestions that are solely meant to shock or embarrass players, or to invent problems for the players to solve. There is already plenty of justification to do, so let the character and storytelling and spacework be the focus, not the 'wacky' improv nonsense.

On the pages that follow, I have created a grid to get you started with suggestions for the who, what, and where, along with some potential ask-fors. (Many additional suggestions and scene set-ups can be found in the "Whole Deck of Trouble" playing cards available at **improvforactors.org/bookstore**.) I am also including some examples of potential shifts that may lead to a change in your scene—your "One day..." moment. In many cases, the shift is a simple reversal, although an event is not often so black-and-white. As a place to begin, I am purposely keeping it simple so you get a feel of what to look out for.

For Starters

ASK-FOR	SAMPLE SUGGESTIONS
WHO	
Give me an occupation **HINT:** Keep it simple, and be specific where you can. Avoid suggestions that are designed to embarrass or shock players: While 'proctologist' is a perfectly respectable specialty, that suggestion is commonly given with the sole intent to make the players uncomfortable, and get a laugh.	**Medical:** Doctor, Nurse, EMT, Pharmacist, Dentist **Law:** Attorney, Judge, Baliff, Stenographer **Arts:** Painter, Sculptor, Actor, Writer, Dancer, Designer, Musician, Filmmaker **Trades:** Plumber, Carpenter, Farmer, Electrician, Mason, Landscaper, Mechanic, Cobbler, Tailor, Milliner, Factory worker **Scientist:** Chemist, Physicist, Astronomer, Biologist, Botanist, Laboratory Technician **Retail:** Florist, Store manager, Cashier, Salesperson, Stockperson, Giftwrapper, Jeweler **Finance:** Banker, Trader, Teller, Accountant **City:** Police officer, Firefighter, Mayor, City Councilperson, Sanitation, Mail carrier **School:** Principal, Student, Teacher, PTA member, Librarian, Janitor, Student Council member **Hospitality:** Chef, Maitre d', Waiter, Hotel Clerk, Housekeeper, Tour Guide, Hairstylist, Manicurist, Bartender **Transportation:** Pilot, Flight attendant, Train conductor, Taxi driver, Ferry captain, Valet, Bus driver **Sports:** Player, Coach, Ref, Equipment Mgr. **Office:** Executive, Manager, Office Worker, Receptionist, Security

ASK-FOR	SAMPLE SUGGESTIONS
WHO	
Give me a relationship between two people / How do these two people know one another?	Siblings Parent/Grandparent and Child Best friends Couple/Dating Engaged or Married Boss and Employee Coworkers Roommates Teammates Doctor and Patient Teacher and Student Sorority/Fraternity members Schoolmates
HINT: Try not to stir up drama with the relationship. We don't need any judgments or qualifiers—No "Long lost twins!" or "Mortal enemies!" please. And, the relationship does not dictate the activity. A doctor and patient could be setting up the field for a Little League game, or carpooling to work, or skiing. They don't have to be in an office getting/giving an exam just because that's how they know one another. Lastly, and perhaps most importantly: NO STRANGERS. Have history. Know one another well, even if the scene puts you both in a new situation.	

For Starters

ASK-FOR	SAMPLE SUGGESTIONS
WHAT	
Give me a physical activity—one that involves objects **HINT:** Activities that use objects will keep players more engaged in the space. And a 'physical' activity is preferable because it is more active. Reading a book is technically an activity that uses an object, but it is too easy to ignore when we get distracted by another offer. And, as with the WHO, there is no necessity for a person to be doing an activity that directly relates to their occupation. A doctor giving an exam is perfectly fine, but a doctor could also be cleaning fallen leaves out of a gutter, or making coffee, or mending socks. How would someone with the skills of a doctor do those tasks?	Repotting a houseplant Painting a chair Preparing a meal Decorating for a party Raking fallen leaves Glueing a broken vase back together Playing a sport Building a canoe Packing/unpacking a suitcase Cleaning the house Making the bed Brewing coffee Washing the dishes Folding laundry Washing a car Restringing a guitar Replacing a broken pipe Cutting a pattern out of fabric Lifting weights Laying tile Chopping wood Building a campfire Shoveling dirt or snow Polishing silver Picking apples Carving a pumpkin Setting up a tent Rewiring a fan Throwing clay Stacking a house of cards Whittling a wooden figurine

IMPROV AND THE ACTOR'S IMAGINATION

ASK-FOR	SAMPLE SUGGESTIONS
WHAT	
Name an important life event **HINT:** Remember that this is a jumping off point—any aspect of the suggestion is fair game. The suggestion of a 'wedding' could take us to an actual wedding in progress, or one of the characters could be assembling a scrapbook for a future dream wedding. Or be at a cake tasting.	Wedding Funeral Bar/Bat Mitzvah Coming out Engagement First date First kiss Birth of a child Buying a house/apartment Buying a car Graduation Being hired Being fired Moving Travel
WHERE	
Where would this activity likely take place? **HINT:** Start with the obvious. Don't purposely set a scene in an unusual location just to create a problem to solve.	[If we already know your occupation or your activity, the suggestion for the WHERE should closely align. If we know you are a mechanic, then let your scene be set in a garage or on the side of the road, rather than at a base station on the moon, or at the top of a ferris wheel.]

For Starters

ASK-FOR	SAMPLE SUGGESTIONS
WHERE	
Give me a non-geographical location. **HINT:** 'Non-geographical' is meant to create localized specificity. Instead of wider options like "Brazil!" or "The Gobi Desert!" or "On a mountain!", we narrow to a particular spot, or room. "A seaside surf shop in Rio." or "a cave in the middle of the Gobi Desert" or "a tent at a basecamp on Mount Tinder". Naming places is always encouraged.	The patio at Captain Barrow's Crab Shack Cafe table at Mocha Mike's Sweetie's candy store Specific room in your home: Kitchen, Bathroom, Bedroom, Basement, Attic, Garage, etc. Tower dungeon of a palace School principal's office Executive boardroom ATM vestibule of Moneywell Bank Sidewalk outside Danz nightclub Pitcher's mound of a baseball field Green of the 18th hole, Verde Country Club Sandy Wheels beachside bicycle repair shop The end of a dock on Lake Fischer Upper deck of a yacht Aerobics studio at The Werk-Out gym Candlelit dinner table at So-posh Upper tier of an arena In an elevator of an office building A dressing room of a theater Parking lot outside the grocery store Picnic blanket in the park Public library Billiard room in O'Dooley's bar Subway car Food court at a mall Train station Hotel lobby Secluded beach on a tropical island Pantry of Lohfer's Bakery

ASK-FOR	SAMPLE SUGGESTIONS
WHERE	
Someplace you've gotten lost	Paris hotel casino in Las Vegas
Furthest place you've ever been from home	Cliff at the Cape of Good Hope A remote towel factory
Someplace you go to be alone	A bench in Marcus Garvey Park
Secret hiding place when you were a kid	Hallway broom closet Garden behind the garage
Favorite place to go for fun	Bowling alley Broadway theater
STYLE/GENRE	
Give me a style of story **HINT:** Look for familiar characters, places and activities within a style. Don't mix-and-match. When getting this type of suggestion, I usually ask a follow-up to clarify some common elements of the style, like: **What do we typically see in a _____ story?** (e.g. In a Western, we would expect cowboys, good guys and bad guys, shootouts, horses, saloons, etc. You don't have to include EVERYTHING, but having a shared idea of the style will set a stronger foundation.)	Detective/Noir Western Romantic Comedy Adventure Sci-Fi Spy Thriller Mystery Fable/Mythology Shakespeare Farce Fantasy Period Drama Sit-Com

OPPORTUNITIES FOR A SHAKE-UP

Opposing states are good examples of the shift that can happen in any scene. The shift is usually brought about by the event of the scene—something happens that causes us to change, even temporarily—the "One day..." moment.

A character can begin in either state, and one state is not better than the other, nor is one 'good' or 'bad'—just fully expand and commit to whichever state you're in. Practice in extremes so that you have maximum clarity.

LOVE or any Positive emotion	**HATE or any Negative emotion**
Attentive	**Aloof**
Present	**Gone**
High status/ Powerful	**Low status/ Powerless**
Rich	**Poor**
Employed	**Jobless**
Optimist/ Positive POV	**Pessimist/ Negative POV**
Together	**Alone**
Restless	**Contented**
Frightened	**Brave**

The event is the occurence that moves us in one direction or the other.

IMPROV AND THE ACTOR'S IMAGINATION

THE ARC OF THE SCENE

If we begin in one state, and the event moves us into an opposing state, we have no way of knowing how it will resolve until we experience the consequences—we can't know what's going to happen until it happens. We may remain changed, return to our original pattern, or somewhere inbetween.

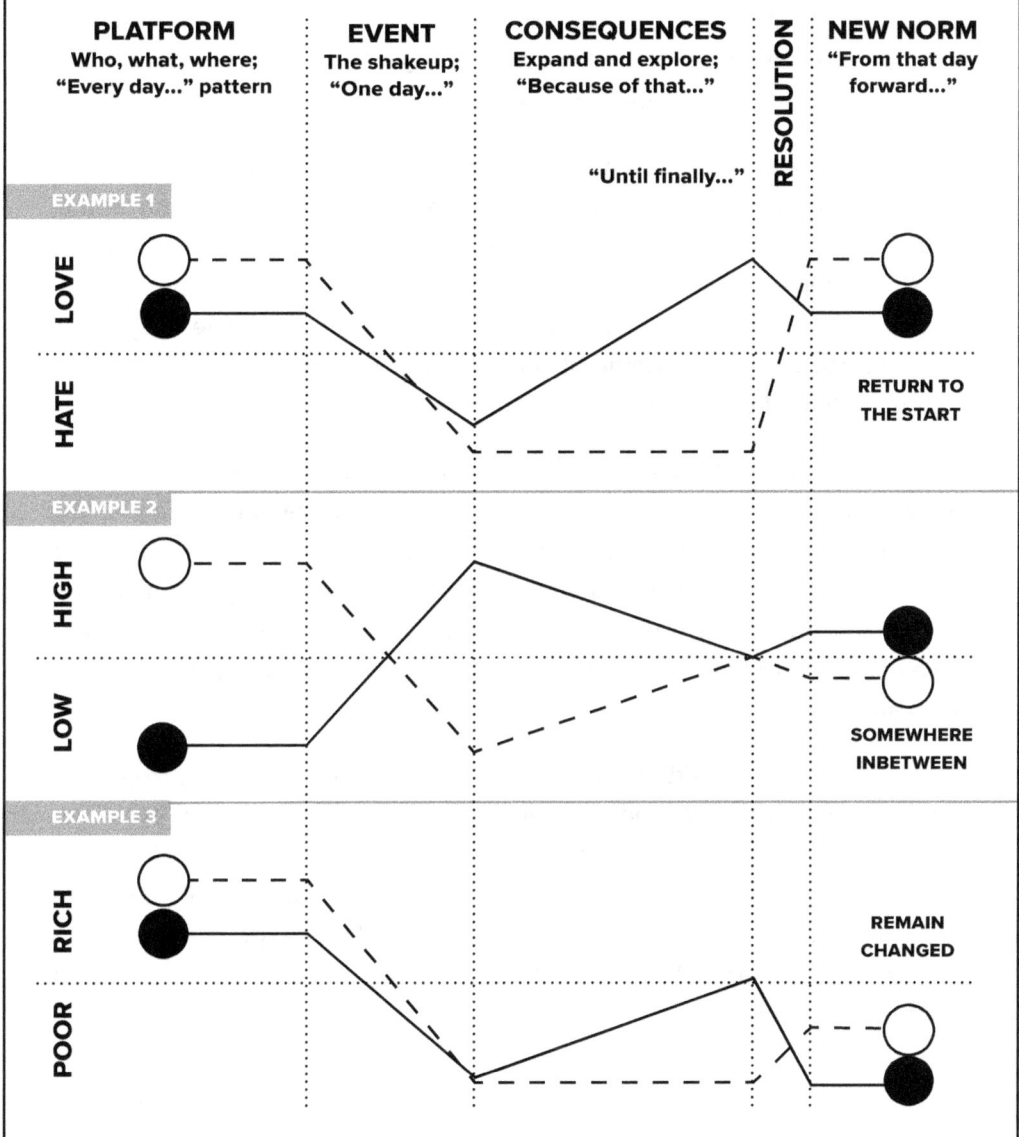

When we refer to a "return to the start" in our story arc, this is not to say that we are back at the beginning as though nothing happened at all. Even when a world returns to a familiar pattern, there is now a new, rich experience underneath it—which serves to make a character and a world MORE familiar and relatable.

I think every episode of "The Honeymooners" followed the first example. I don't think Ralph and Alice ever actually HATED one another, but the behavior was crystal clear that it was the opposite of love as they worked through Ralph's weekly shakeup. Thankfully, we could rely on the fact that, by the end of the episode, their deep love for one another would be restored.

You can also see that, although two characters may begin in the same state (deeply in love, for instance), they do not have to follow the same path. Sometimes only one person sees things differently. Perhaps one person represents the status quo—the way things OUGHT to be—and the other rebels. As we said above, if someone maintains or returns to their original state, they HAVE changed, regardless of whether it is apparent. They (and we) have a deeper understanding of their behavior—why they are the way they are.

A character may find themselves exhibiting more than one state simultaneously—both in love AND powerless AND hopeful, for example. I suggest you focus on whichever state is really bringing you to life—the dominant feeling or position. Our emotions and points of view are not easily separated or compartmentalized, so the goal is to be as focused as possible so that we can have agreement about what is happening. Too many offers at once can dilute them all.

Lastly, it SHOULD go without saying that the preceding are merely examples, and are in no way meant to be an exhaustive list of possible ask-fors, outcomes or story paths. The goal in presenting examples is not to be prescriptive—to say 'this is how it should go'—rather, to be sure that we are RECEPTIVE to the many opportunities for change, and realize that the change comes directly from what we already KNOW to be true in the scene—true of the characters, and true of the world.

Now, go get yourself into trouble!

ABOUT THE AUTHOR

Robert Z Grant is an actor, improviser, teacher, director and producer based in New York City. He teaches improvisation for actors at the prestigious William Esper Studio, where he first studied the Meisner technique and the craft of acting with Bill Esper. Robert has performed and taught improvisation across the U.S. and internationally, and continually strives to inspire students and audiences alike.

www.robertzgrant.com

REFERENCES (MOSTLY DATED)

"The Actor's Art and Craft", William Esper

"ACTIONS: The Actors' Thesaurus",
Marina Calderone and Maggie Lloyd-Williams

"The Artist's Way", Julia Cameron

"Café d'Automatique" from "The Collective:10 Play Anthology, Volume 2", Dave Hanson

"The Carol Burnett Show", created by Bob Banner and Joe Hamilton

"Creative Screenwriting: Understanding Emotional Structure", Christina Kallas

"The Electric Company", created by Paul Dooley

"The Girl with the Lower Back Tattoo", Amy Schumer

"Girls & Boys", Dennis Kelly

"The Honeymooners", created by Jackie Gleason and Harry Crane

"I Love Lucy", Harpo Marx, Season 4, Episode 28,
Jess Oppenheimer, Madelyn Davis (Pugh), Bob Carroll Jr.

"The Matrix",
written and directed by the Wachowskis

"Star Wars", created by George Lucas

"This Is Spinal Tap",
Christopher Guest, Michael McKean, Harry Shearer, Rob Reiner (director)

> There is a vitality, a life force, an energy, a quickening that is translated through you into action, and because there is only one of you in all of time, this expression is unique.
> And if you block it, it will never exist through any other medium and it will be lost. The world will not have it.
> It is not your business to determine how good it is nor how valuable nor how it compares with other expressions.
> It is your business to keep it yours clearly and directly, to keep the channel open. You do not even have to believe in yourself or your work. You have to keep yourself open and aware to the urges that motivate you. Keep the channel open.
>
> …
>
> No artist is pleased. [There is] no satisfaction whatever at any time. There is only a queer divine dissatisfaction, a blessed unrest that keeps us marching and makes us more alive than the others.

—Martha Graham

> For what it's worth: it's never too late or, in my case, too early to be whoever you want to be. There's no time limit, stop whenever you want. You can change or stay the same, there are no rules to this thing. We can make the best or the worst of it. I hope you make the best of it. And **I hope you see things that startle you. I hope you feel things you never felt before.**
> I hope you meet people with a different point of view.
> I hope you live a life you're proud of. If you find that you're not, I hope you have the courage to start all over again.

—F. Scott Fitzgerald

GET YOURSELF INTO A WHOLE DECK OF TROUBLE

Available exclusively at
IMPROVFORACTORS.ORG/BOOKSTORE

LOTS OF WAYS TO PLAY ALL IN ONE DECK!

CARD GAMES
You can use this deck as you would a standard deck of playing cards. Imagination cards are WILD and can replace Jokers.

CHARADES
Pick a card. In 1 minute, act out as many suggestions from the card as you can.
1 correct guess = 1 point
All 4 categories = 1 BONUS point

GIBBERISH
Draw several cards. Combine the sounds to make gibberish phrases. See if a partner can correctly translate what you're communicating to them.

SCENE SUGGESTIONS
Pick a card. Use 1 or more of the suggestions from the 4 possible categories to start your improv scene.

- activity
- object
- character
- location

STAGE DIRECTIONS
Pick 3-5 cards without looking and keep them in your pocket. Improvise a scene, pull a card at random intervals, and follow the directed action.

STATUS
Pick a card without looking at it. Place it on your forehead where your partners can see. Improvise a scene and see if you can each figure out your own status.

JUSTIFICATION
Pick a card. The first suggestion is your activity. Pick 3 more cards. These are the objects you must use to complete your activity. How do you do it?

WILD IMAGINATION CARDS
Mix these cards into the deck to shake up your games. Use your imagination for all the ways they can be used:
- extra point • free turn • freeze
- wild suggestion • card swap
- extra time • free hint • pass

DECK INCLUDES:
- 52 playing/game cards
- 2 WILD imagination cards
- 1 Guide card
- Improviser's guide

FREE* Limited Edition BOOKMARK

Available only at
improvforactors.org/bookstore
Use code: EXTRA
at checkout.

*$1.00 USD
shipping & handling
fee applies.
U.S. domestic standard
USPS shipping only.

IMPROV AND THE ACTOR'S IMAGINATION

copyright © 2021 Robert Z Grant. New York, New York.

Cover by Robert Z Designs LLC. All rights reserved. Published in the United States of America. No part of this book may be used or reproduced in any manner whatsoever without written permission.

www.robertzgrant.com

Cataloging-in-Publication Data is on file at the Library of Congress.

ISBN: 978-1-7366104-0-4

Printed in the United States of America

10 9 8 7 6 5 4 3 2 1

www.ingramcontent.com/pod-product-compliance
Lightning Source LLC
Chambersburg PA
CBHW072343100426
42738CB00049B/1530